Separate Roads to Feminism

Black, Chicana, and White Feminist Movements in America's Second Wave

Separate Roads to Feminism is the first book to examine the simultaneous emergence of feminist movements from the Civil Rights/Black Liberation movement, the Chicano movement, and the white Left in the 1960s and 1970s. Challenging the picture of "second-wave" feminism as monolithically middle class and white, Benita Roth argues that the second wave was instead comprised of *feminisms*: organizationally distinct movements that influenced each other, as well as other movements, in complex ways. In different communities that were situated in an overall framework of intersecting class and racial/ethnic inequalities, feminists overcame challenges to forming new organizations, not the least of which stemmed from their concerns for (male) activists "left behind." Finally, feminists made their new movements in a crowded and competitive intermovement milieu that shaped their political decisons and discourses. Roth's dynamic picture of Black, Chicana, and white feminists constructing distinct autonomous movements alters the picture of left social protest in the era and highlights the way that second-wave feminisms provided insights into the intersecting nature of oppressions – of gender, race/ethnicity, class, and sexuality – that still resonate today.

Benita Roth is Assistant Professor of Sociology and Women's Studies at the State University of New York, Binghamton. Her work has been published in the journals *Gender & Society, Work and Occupations,* and *Womanist Theory and Research.* This is her first book.

Separate Roads to Feminism

Black, Chicana, and White Feminist Movements in America's Second Wave

BENITA ROTH

State University of New York, Binghamton

PUBLISHED BY THE PRESS SYNDICATE OF THE UNIVERSITY OF CAMBRIDGE
The Pitt Building, Trumpington Street, Cambridge, United Kingdom

CAMBRIDGE UNIVERSITY PRESS
The Edinburgh Building, Cambridge CB2 2RU, UK
40 West 20th Street, New York, NY 10011-4211, USA
477 Williamstown Road, Port Melbourne, VIC 3207, Australia
Ruiz de Alarcón 13, 28014 Madrid, Spain
Dock House, The Waterfront, Cape Town 8001, South Africa

http://www.cambridge.org

First published 2004

Printed in the United States of America

Typeface Goudy 10.5/13 pt.   *System* LATEX 2_ε [TB]

A catalog record for this book is available from the British Library.

Library of Congress Cataloging in Publication Data

Roth, Benita.
Separate roads to feminism : Black, Chicana, and White feminist movements in
America's second wave / Benita Roth.
   p.   cm.
Includes bibliographical references and index.
ISBN 0-521-82260-2 – ISBN 0-521-52972-7 (pb.)
1. Feminism – United States – History – 20th century.   2. African American
women – History – 20th century.   3. Hispanic American women – History.   4. White
women – United States – History – 20th century.   5. Women – United States – History –
20th century.   I. Title.

HQ1421.R684   2003
305 42'0973'0904 – dc21

                                                                    2003046182

ISBN 0 521 82260 2 hardback
ISBN 0 521 52972 7 paperback

This book is dedicated to the life and memory of
Minia Luwiszes Roth
aleha hashalom

Contents

Tables

Preface/Acknowledgments

How and why feminist movements emerged in the "second wave" of American feminism is the subject of this book. My interest in this subject was prompted by lacunae in the literature on feminists of color in the second wave, but also by personal experiences. I started college in the Boston area at the end of the 1970s and was active in feminist circles there until I left Massachusetts in 1984. Throughout that period, racism within the (white) feminist movement was an inescapable issue, and racial division among feminists was the subject of many discussions and workshops. Over and over, in group after group, the failure of white feminism to attract women of color – often characterized as the failure of women of color to be attracted to feminism – was bemoaned. In my own experience, the activist women of color that I met in those years (and since) did not seem any less "feminist" in their politics, and they were not hostile to feminist issues. But they were reluctant to participate in all-white groups, fearing tokenism, and they maintained that educating white women about white racism was just too hard. Many then went on to argue that white feminist organizations were generally irrelevant to the kind of social change they envisioned. At the same time, the white feminists I knew were reading more and more work by feminists of color, and were thus more and more inspired by the vision of liberation from multiple oppressions of class, race, homophobia, and sexism that these writers offered.

Those are the roots, then, of the questions that lie at the center of this study: Why were there organizationally distinct feminisms in the late 1970s and early 1980s, largely organized along racial/ethnic lines? What led to the development of feminisms, when there was at least some agreement about feminist issues? Rather than assume that the divisions of the late 1970s were somehow "natural," in this work I argue for understanding the historical development of second-wave feminisms as shaped at its core by the dynamics of race/ethnicity and class among feminists. I argue that we need to understand that these dynamics were not solely about interpersonal interactions but also about the overall structure of the social movement sector, that is, the intermovement political field of the era, and about the overall structure of inequality in the United States.

Researching and writing this book have taken a number of years and been done in a number of places. Early on, I came to the conclusion that if it takes a village to raise a child, it takes several villages strewn across the country to aid one in writing a book. I would first like to thank the librarians at the following institutions: the University of Illinois, Circle Campus; Smith College; the Schlesinger Library at Radcliffe College, Harvard University; the State Historical Society of Wisconsin; Duke University; and the Southern California Library for Social Science and Research. The staff at Special Collections at Northwestern University (or, as I like to call the place, "The Mother Lode") were particularly helpful and accommodating.

Much of this research was conducted with funding from the following sources: the Woodrow Wilson Institute in Princeton, New Jersey; the Institute for American Cultures at UCLA; UCLA's Center for the Study of Women, and its Department of Sociology; the Department of Sociology and the Office of Sponsored Research and Programs at Binghamton University. A Dean's Leave from Harpur College at Binghamton University was also instrumental in the completion of the project. An Individual Development Award from United University Professions of New York paid for indexing, and Ari Ngaseo did a fine job of it. At Cambridge University Press, editor Mary Child was key to the process of getting the book started, and Alia Winters helped bring it home; in the middle, anonymous reviewers gave comments that fundamentally changed this work (and very much for the better).

This book is based on dissertation research, and my committee members, Ellen DuBois, Michael Mann, Vilma Ortiz, and Ralph Turner, contributed mightily and in myriad ways to the work. Special thanks are due my chair, Ruth Milkman, who provided me with insight and support throughout this project. Julia Wrigley read and contributed to the master's paper that formed the nucleus of the dissertation. Raphael Allen, Wendy Dishman, Kerry Ferris, Duchess Harris, Leland Saito, Kimberly Springer, Jill Stein, Eleanor Townsley, and Dolores Trevizo read early and late bits, and were gracious in their critiques. At SUNY Binghamton, a number of colleagues read and commented on sections of this work, including Nancy Appelbaum, Deborah Cahalen, Michael Hames-García, and Carlos Riobó. Sid Tarrow made succinct but cogent comments on elements of the introduction and conclusion. I would also like to thank discussants and attenders at various conferences and meetings for comments, including the Workshop on Contentious Politics at the Lazarsfeld Center of Columbia University; the American Sociological Association meetings; the Eastern Sociological Society meetings; the Society for the Study of Social Problems meetings; the American Studies Association meetings; the "Alternative Futures and Popular Protest" conferences in Manchester, UK; the "Feminism and Power" Conference in Albuquerque in 1993; the Feminist Graduate Student Conference in 1997 in Chicago; and the Women's Studies Workshop Symposia at SUNY Binghamton.

Among others who must be thanked by name for providing lodging, sustenance, and support are Ron Ben-Ari and Jeannie Chang, Miriam Berman and Michael Morrow, Sharon Fagen, Eva Fodor, Craig Hayes and Brigitte Daloin, Judith Hecker, Alice Julier and Zachary Rubenstein, Susan Markens, Karen O'Neill and Alex Ridgway (for especially excellent accommodations and board in the greater New York City area), Julie Press, Peter and Susan Sheridan, and Mark Sterling and Kathy Stanton-Sterling. Going back a bit, Gordie Fellman and Karen Klein, my mentors at Brandeis University, are owed special thanks for not being at all surprised that I decided to pursue an academic career. And my family, Gerald Roth, Dolly Roth, and those who have left us – Minia Roth, Israel and Manya Rotblit, *zichronam l'vracha* – were always there for me.

A great debt of gratitude for time and generosity is due the nine feminists whom I interviewed who were active in the Black and Chicana feminist movements during the 1960s and 1970s: Frances Beal, Irene Blea, Brenda Eichelberger, Jane Galvin-Lewis, Aileen C. Hernández, Dorothy King, Dorinda Moreno, Margo Okazawa-Rey, and Mirta Vidal. As discussed in the Appendix, they continue to lead activist and feminist lives. I also used two additional interviews, with Leticia Hernández and Ana Nieto-Gómez, conducted by Maylei Blackwell and archived by the Oral History Program of the California State University at Long Beach. I wish to thank that institution and Sherna Gluck, the program director, for that access.

To all the villagers, I owe a heartfelt thanks.

The Emergence and Development of Racial/Ethnic Feminisms in the 1960s and 1970s

I refuse to choose. And by that I mean I refuse to choose between being black and being a woman. Men don't have to choose. I don't know why women have to choose. I am both equally, and I'm proud to be both. I wake up, and I don't like what they're doing to Black people, and I'm mad; I wake up, and I don't like what they're doing to women, and I'm mad.

> Dorothy King
> Harrisburg, Pennsylvania
> February 2000

I was at a NOW meeting and being told by women in Denver, you have to choose between being a Chicana and being female . . . and what I'm saying is "I cannot separate the fact that I'm brown and I'm female, I cannot do it physically to this body, I cannot do it emotionally, I cannot do it spiritually. . . . "

> Irene Blea
> Albuquerque, New Mexico
> March 2000

Second-Wave Feminism(s)

Feminist mobilizations in the United States during the 1960s and 1970s – commonly known as the "second wave" of U.S. feminist protest – challenged and changed the political and cultural landscape. Having read the first sentence of this work, the reader should be alerted to my use of a plural noun to describe feminist protest in the second wave, and this book is about feminist mobilizations, feminist movements, and *feminisms*. In their words at the beginning of the chapter, both Dorothy King and Irene Blea take the stance that their life experiences as women of color in a structurally unequal society informed their decisions about organizing as feminists of color in organizations that were distinct from so-called mainstream white feminist groups. What I wish to do is develop a picture of second-wave feminisms, feminisms that were plural and characterized by racial/ethnic organizational distinctiveness. This distinctiveness based on racial/ethnic (and class) difference was not "natural" but a result of the way that feminists understood their choices given a particular set of circumstances within which they were activists. In this book, I explore the ways in which feminists in different racial/ethnic communities stratified by class made decisions about organizing in particular nested contexts, including the overall structure of economic inequality among groups of women, relationships with activist men in their communities, and the exigencies created by organizing in a vibrant, complex, and competitive social movement milieu.

From the beginning of their mobilizations, resurgent feminisms were the subject of study; as the years of mass, highly mobilized protest have passed, feminist movements have become the focus of scholarly work aimed at understanding the nature of the movements and the nature of the changes they wrought. But previous pictures of second-wave feminism have erased the early and substantial activism of feminists of color embedded in these movements, for reasons that I will come back to, and scholarship has generally failed to capture the genuine complexity of feminist mobilizations in this era. In much of the literature on the second wave, one finds a standard conceptualization of what the feminist movement was: white, primarily middle class, although arising out of two distinct social bases (Buechler 1990; Carden 1974; Freeman 1973, 1975; Hole and Levine 1971; Marx Ferree and Hess 1985, 1994). Various labels were used to distinguish the kind of organizing that grew out of each social base, or the social base itself. One branch was, to use Freeman's terms, "older" and one was "younger"; Marx Ferree and Hess referred to one strand, characterized by groups like the National Organization for Women (NOW), as "bureaucratic" and the other strand, which came out of the Civil Rights and New Left movements, as "collectivist"; still another characterization, by Buechler, had one branch of feminism as the liberal wing of the movement and another as "liberationists" who folded socialist and radical feminist ideological components together. All of these ways of talking about the two social bases of second-wave feminism have in common the implicit recognition of the multiple and plural nature of the era's feminist resurgence, although the full implications of this recognition were bounded by a "whitewashed" vision of movement, singular.[1]

---

[1] In one area – that of the links between institutionalized and mass feminist protest – the picture of the second wave has been made more complex. The idea of a discrete "wave" of feminist organizing, that is, the appearance of wide-scale feminist mobilizations sui generis has been made problematic by work on the importance of preceding "abeyance" structures for feminist mobilizations (Rupp and Taylor 1987; V. Taylor 1989). Related scholarship has argued against an overemphasis

(In this book, I argue that the second wave has to be understood as a group of feminisms, movements made by activist women that were largely organizationally distinct from one another, and from the beginning, largely organized along racial/ethnic lines. In other words, there were more than two twinned social bases of feminism in the 1960s and 1970s; feminisms were articulated in diverse political communities. Feminists of color argued that their activism was written out of the histories of second-wave feminist protest; they argued that racial/ethnic and class biases that were part of white feminist ideology and practice have shown up in subsequent scholarship about that ideology and practice (García 1990, 1997; Giddings 1984; hooks 1981, 1984; Hull, Scott, and Smith 1982; Mohanty, Russo, and Torres 1991; Moraga and Anzaldúa 1979; B. Smith 1979, 1983; Smith and Smith 1981). In light of their critiques, a different picture of feminist protest in the U.S. second wave has begun to emerge, one that argues that feminist protest in the 1960s and 1970s was shaped into feminist movements, plural (Gluck et al. 1998).

I trace the emergence and early development of Black, Chicana, and white feminist movements on the left during the second wave. I do not suggest that these three movements exhaust the list of feminisms, or that there is no room for the adding of other feminisms, racial/ethnic or otherwise. Working-class white women certainly felt distance from an organized (white) feminist movement that was perceived to be middle class (see Naples 1998a, especially Chapter 6) and feminist groups were organized in other communities of color, although as Gluck et al. (1998) have noted, feminist organizing in some other communities of color, for example, the Native American community, was delayed and made relatively difficult by competing loyalties and overall political circumstance. I selected Black, Chicana, and white feminisms for study because of the timing of their emergences, the multistate scale of their organizing, and the kinds of connections and cleavages that existed on the ground between feminists from these communities. Nor do I wish to suggest that the only women's movements worth addressing are feminist ones, or that feminism is not manifest in other kinds of women's organizing, for example, community organizing.[2]

---

on extra-institutional protest as distinct from important institutional feminist efforts, which in some cases predated feminist movement emergence (Hartmann 1998; Katzenstein 1998).

[2] The literature on women's protests in and for communities is large and growing; among others see Ali (1987), Aulette and Mills (1988), Bookman and

Overall, I have two main concerns in this work. First, and following the critiques of the feminists of color noted, I document the articulation of feminisms in diverse communities. Recognition of feminist organizing in different communities allows us to ask questions about who came to feminism, how they came to feminism, and how feminism was done in different social spaces. Charting the organizing of feminists of color also requires that we acknowledge that self-identified feminist activism is a political choice among other choices for empowering action that women can take for their communities. Second, I look at feminist emergences explored here as stories about the connections and cleavages between feminist movements, of the relationships between differently situated feminists, and the complicated movement dynamics that militated against those relationships. In choosing to refer to Black, Chicana, and white feminisms on the left as "organizationally distinct" movements, I acknowledge that defining the boundaries of social movements is always an exercise in some degree of abstraction – and therefore some degree of frustration. I am mindful that positing the existence of organizationally distinct racial/ethnic feminisms may not capture some of the contact that occurred between feminists of different racial/ethnic and class backgrounds during the era, especially those feminists committed to bridging racial/ethnic divides (see Thompson 2001). But my characterization of racial/ethnic feminisms as organizationally distinct is not only accurate in the main but is, in fact, useful in exploring what linked feminists in different communities and what separated them.[3]

In the following, I look at the development of feminisms from the African American Civil Rights/Black Liberation movement, the

Morgen (1988), Cameron (1985), Dowd Hall (1990), Kaplan (1982), Kingsolver (1996 [1983]), Milkman (1985), Naples (1991, 1998a, 1998b), Omolade (1994), Piven and Cloward (1977), Ruiz (1990), and Townsend Gilkes (1980) on the activities of working-class women in workplace strikes, in protest and community work within neighborhood settings, and as "auxiliaries" to striking men.

[3] My view on the necessity of conceptualizing second-wave feminist protest as *feminisms* is different from the one taken by Marx Feree and Hess in the latest edition of their key work, *Controversy and Coalition* (2000). While they acknowledge that it is difficult to think of second-wave feminism as a truly unified movement, they state that "the fiction of unity within a single movement is . . . necessary as a political tool" (2000:vii). However, feminists of color have argued that it is precisely "the fiction of unity" in feminism that is harmful to the full participation of women of color (see Sandoval 1990). The question of the roots of the "fiction of unity" within white feminism will be further explored in Chapter Five.

Chicano movement, and the white Left as a set of linked cases, and draw out the key factors that led to the emergence of organizationally distinct racial/ethnic feminisms. Feminists in each racial/ethnic group were affected by their race and class status, by their own experiences within their movements of origin, and by the structure of political choices for activism available at the time. At the macro level, Black, white, and Chicana women were situated within an unequal racial/ethnic hierarchy at a time of general postwar prosperity. The emergence of a postwar middle class in the Black and Chicano communities was an incomplete process that did not put feminists of color on an equal footing with white middle-class feminists when it came time to organize. Although women in all three racial/ethnic communities were gaining some greater economic independence, and were entering higher education in growing numbers, these improvements in women's access to the resources necessary for social protest were unequal across racial/ethnic communities, putting emergent feminists in different places from the start. These starting places mattered to feminists in making their movements.

On the level of micropolitics, African American, white, and Chicana feminists were, for the most part, members of oppositional protest movements that provided them with organizing skills and social networks. These protest movements were communities of activists that both gave to and demanded from their members. As members of these communities, emergent feminists shared ideologies of general liberation from oppression with men (and with nonfeminist women), ideologies which they extended to address the specifics of gender oppression. But as feminism developed in these women activists, it did not obliterate their other concerns, or set them immediately loose from the oppositional communities within which they lived. Over the course of a number of years, when it became clear that existing left movements could not easily accommodate a feminist agenda, feminists activated their networks, argued for a particular kind of feminist organizing, and created the new communities they would need to form their own more fully autonomous movements. Forming these movements was a complicated process in all three racial/ethnic communities, but issues of loyalties to movements of origin were particularly acute for feminists of color, and difficulties in resolving those issues were compounded by the successful and visible organizing of white feminists on the left.

Following directly from this last point, intermovement politics in a competitive social movement sector influenced the choices that Black, white, and Chicana feminists made to remain organizationally distinct from one another. Women ran the day-to-day activities of oppositional movements in the 1960s and 1970s, and feminist challenges were a threat to the economy of social movement activism; we can see that threat marked by the different ideological arguments that men in each parent movement made about why feminism threatened movement unity. Feminists in each racial/ethnic community developed counter-claims, specific political arguments meant to allay fears of feminism's divisive and destructive nature. And, in a crowded and competitive so-cial movement sector, increasingly (but not inevitably) structured along lines of race and ethnicity, feminists encountered what I have called an ethos of "organizing one's own" as being the only authentic form of activism. Feminists in different racial/ethnic communities adopted the ethos, which led to the structuring of feminist movements along the lines of race/ethnicity. In summary, the exigencies of political organizing in a crowded field and the ideas about the best way to organize informed decisions feminists made about how to be feminists and at the same time stay true to their prior political investments. These exigencies and these decisions led to the emergence of organizationally distinct feminisms.

As should be clear from this summary of the book's arguments, I challenge the idea that these racial/ethnic feminist movements emerged "naturally," as a result of race/ethnicity being a natural division for women. Even if racial/ethnic identities were particularly salient in the United States during this wave of protest, they were not "naturally" chosen ones; identities, as links put forward by "social actors with certain historical experiences" to particular socially salient groups, are constructed contingently (della Porta and Diani 1999:86). And as will become clear in the narrative to come, I also challenge the idea that feminism among women of color emerged solely as a result of (demon-strably present) racism in the white movement; this is an inaccurate conception that negates the agency of feminists of color. Different contexts for doing politics influenced how feminists situated in Black, Chicano/a, and white oppositional communities were able to relate to their movements of origin, and to one another; it is precisely with these different contexts and their impacts that I concern myself in this work.

The Whitewashing of the Second Wave

Above, I stated that one of my chief concerns in this work was actu-ally documenting activism by feminists of color in the second wave, so as to counter "whitewashed" versions of a singular feminist movement. Case studies about second wave (white) feminism began to be written almost from that movement's inception; they continue to be written, and memoirs and documentary histories have been added (see Brownmiller 1999; Buechler 1990; Carden 1974; Chancer 1998; Echols 1989; Evans 1979; Freeman 1975; Hole and Levine 1971; Marx Ferree and Hess 1985, 1994, 2000; R. Rosen 2000; Ryan 1992; and Ware 1970; note the dates of publication for Carden, Hole and Levine, and Ware). But the literature on second-wave feminism – singular – has not, to date, considered in a full and dynamic fashion the reality of the existence of second-wave feminisms. African American feminist organizing has generally been given a nod in the form of a mention of the National Black Feminist Organization and a query as to why Black women did not join feminist groups in greater numbers, a view that ignores their instrumental role in forming liberal feminist organizations such as NOW (see Buechler 1990; Echols 1989; Freeman 1975; Marx Ferree and Hess 1985, 1994). Chicana feminism is given only the barest of mentions, and no analysis whatsoever as a distinct and wide-scale social movement.

It is important to note that most feminists in the 1960s and 1970s were white because most people in the United States were white. Certainly mass media further whitewashed the movement by focusing on the activities of a relatively few selected spokeswomen for the movement, drawn most consistently from the "older," bureaucratic, and liberal branch of feminism (e.g., Gloria Steinem and Betty Friedan). But within feminist scholarship itself there have been several analytic tendencies that add (unintentionally, I think) to the whitewashing of the second wave. After considering these, I next explore how feminist theory on the intersectionality of oppressions – theory that itself came out of theorizing by second-wave feminists of color – can help recast a vision of 1960s and 1970s feminist protest as composed of multiple feminisms, and understand how those multiple feminisms came to be.

First, on the question of the whitewashing of the second wave, scholars of postwar feminist protest have, to some extent, conceptualized second-wave feminism as white by focusing on the number of feminists of color actually in the second wave, that is, on the number of feminists of color in white feminist organizations. The supposed absence of women of color from the development of second-wave feminism became, for some, a problem to be explained, primarily by resorting to arguments that women of color – in the racially dichotomous vision of the time, chiefly Black women – were less relatively deprived vis-à-vis the men in their communities than were white women, a problematic argument that I further address in Chapter One (Freeman 1975; Lewis 1977). In any case, as will be argued, looking for feminists of color in white feminist organizations, not finding them, and then explaining their absence makes feminists of color invisible: Not only were they not in white feminist organizations; there is no sense in these explanations that they could have possibly been organizing on their own.

Second, scholars have misunderstood the timing of feminist emergences. White feminism has been seen as first on the block, with Black feminism and Chicana feminism coming later to add the factor of race/ethnicity to the feminist project. This picture of the later emergence of feminism among women of color is not correct. There was roughly simultaneous emergence by 1968 of white and Black feminist groups, although certainly more white feminist groups emerged from the New Left and the remnants of civil rights organizing by whites. And while it is true that the first national Chicana feminist conference was held in 1971, Chicana feminists organized as early as 1969, with this negligibly later start a product of the timing of the Chicano movement itself, and possibly of the onset of recruitment programs that brought Chicanas into universities in greater numbers. The failure to see the early emergences of Black and Chicana feminisms also obscures the mutual influence that feminist activists had on one another across racial/ethnic lines. Authors of case studies of second-wave white feminism have noted the impact that Black women civil rights activists had on emergent white feminists as role models (Evans 1979), but Black women were not solely proto-feminist examples for white feminists. Early Black feminists were involved in political relationships with early white feminists, and influenced each other's thinking, as there were real and personal connections between them. White feminists remained, however fitfully, in dialogue with women of color as they mobilized, and Black and Chicana feminists knew and debated ideology and strategy with radical white women, directly and indirectly. Black and Chicana feminists' political stances should also be understood as in dialogue with white feminists, and not merely in a reactive way. Rather, feminists of color confronted white feminism's blinders on matters of race and class, just as they confronted the neglect of gender inequality on the part of the movements from which they emerged.

Third, as a result of the failure to think in an intersectional fashion about second-wave feminist mobilizations, feminist scholars waded into a problem of where to draw the line in calling a movement "feminist." There is a sometimes explicit definition of feminism as being about organizing around gender unencumbered by thinking about other oppressions. The feminist organizing of white middle-class women in the United States has been seen as a kind of model for feminist activism, such that a real feminist movement must be one that makes claims solely on the basis of gender. Model making by scholars can be quite explicit, as in Chafetz and Dworkin's (1986) typology of women's protest; other times, model making takes place as scholars devote little or token attention to the organized feminism of women of color, presumably because that feminism has been mixed with claims based on racial/ethnic status, or with nationalist demands. Implicit model making can be seen in some later case studies of second-wave feminist protest, where the organizing efforts of feminists of color were included in case studies, but bracketed, such that they appear in chapters about different varieties of feminism.[4]

Clearly, even equating feminism with making claims solely on the basis of gender does not really illuminate the variety present in the feminism of white women in the second wave; socialist feminism fits uncomfortably into this construction, as do women's movements that make claims on the basis of gender difference and complementarity, rather than gender equality (on the latter point, see Cott 1989; DuBois 1989; and Offen 1988). One can, as I do, define a feminist movement as one that calls itself "feminist," and yet not require that the political label be held to the exclusion of all others. Following West and Blumberg (1990:19), a feminist movement is one in which women make claims based "on the rights of women **as** women and citizens of society." When feminists aim to change "gender relations" (Marx Ferree and Hess 2000:x), they are not precluded from also asking for the rights due them as members of racial/ethnic groups or classes. Feminists of color in the second wave made just such claims on the basis of their being women who were members of racially oppressed, economically disadvantaged communities; selecting the label "feminist" was not a simple or automatic act but a political choice among other political choices. Accounting for that choice and understanding the circumstances under which the choice was made is the subject of much of this work.

---

[4] See Marx Ferree and Hess (2000) or Ryan (1992). A recent collection of primary documents from the second wave, *Dear Sisters: Dispatches from the Women's Liberation Movement* (Baxandall and Gordon 2000) does a better job of representing the writings of feminists of color as part and parcel of feminist protest.

Related to the question of the whitewashed vision of second-wave feminist protest is the question of class. Case studies of second-wave feminism have noted the middle-class backgrounds of most (white) feminists, as middle-class women were the ones with the resources necessary to act on women's grievances. As will be further discussed in Chapter One, gender-specific changes in women's labor force participation and attendance at institutions of higher education were seen as indicators of an increased level of resources available to potential women activists, an increase crucial for feminist mobilization. In the "younger" branch of feminism especially, African American, white, and Chicana feminists were largely college educated – indeed much of the organizing they did was campus based – and by virtue of their college education, upwardly mobile in comparison with others in their communities. Hence, it has seemed legitimate to label feminism – that undifferentiated feminism in the singular – as middle class.

But the question of class differences among racial/ethnic communities has been glossed over, and as I will argue, awareness of these class differences mattered greatly in constructing distinct racial/ethnic feminist movements. Arguing that middle-class status was common to feminists in each community because they were well-off compared to others in their communities is not the same as arguing that being middle class had the same meaning for feminists across communities. Because the general rise in resources postwar was not a uniform one for African American, white, and Chicana communities, the differences in the class status of the feminists embedded in those communities were important for feminists constructing collective activist identities. Women in the African American and Chicano communities faced racial and economic barriers to participation in the public sphere that white women did not, and the expansion of the middle class in communities of color did not mean that these communities were suddenly on an equal footing with the white majority.

In any case, early characterizations of feminism as white and middle class by the media, and, as will be seen, by activists hostile to feminist organizing, have not been effectively countered by scholarship; the whitewashing of second-wave feminism has enabled the rise of a myth about all women of color being hostile to feminism, a myth that fails to explain the actual organizing done by feminists of color. As will become clear, I argue that a more fruitful approach for understanding the emergence of racial/ethnic feminisms lies in understanding that some women of color who were activists began organizing as feminists when some white women who were activists did, in the late 1960s, during a time of heightened popular protest, and that as organizationally distinct movements, these feminisms proliferated, related to each other, cooperated, and competed. Feminists of color saw themselves as belonging to a different movement than white feminists did, a self-perception that should be taken seriously; understanding why they saw themselves as different requires taking a feminist intersectional approach to the matter of oppressions.

Feminist Movements and Intersectionality: Recasting the Second Wave

Many African American women activists and many Chicana activists became *feminists*, choosing a political label and a political path that was not encouraged by male (and many female) activists in their communities (Blackwell 2000b; Cortera 1977; García 1990, 1997; Gray White 1999; Harris 1999; hooks 1981, 1984; Moraga and Anzaldúa 1979; Saldívar-Hull 1991; B. Smith 1983; Springer 2001). In the groups and organizations they formed, they espoused a feminism that incorporated analyses of the consequences of mutually reinforcing oppressions of gender, race/ethnicity, and class (and, less frequently, sexual orientation), analyses which in turn influenced white feminists, such that feminists today acknowledge as axiomatic the necessity of recognizing multiple sources of domination in women's (and men's) lives. In short, in Black and Chicana feminisms of the second wave we find the roots of feminist insights about the *intersectionality* of inequalities in people's lives. I wish to take seriously what this feminist scholarship has to say about exploring the social world in the very examination of the movements that gave rise to that scholarship.

Theory on the intersectionality of oppressions was part of Black and Chicana feminist thinking from the start of their organizing. In her 1970 piece "Double Jeopardy," Frances Beal argued that Black women occupied a social space constituted by their gender, race, and class (and subsequently, the Third World Women's Alliance named its newspaper *Triple Jeopardy* in order to incorporate the insight that class oppression intersected with race and gender). Later in the 1970s, the Combahee River Collective explicitly took an intersectional stance; they added heterosexism as a key component of Black women's oppression, ending the relative silence in Black feminist theory over lesbianism. The need to do their "politics in the cracks," what Springer (2001:155) has characterized as "interstitial politics," with Black feminists caught between the blind spots of most of white feminism and most of Black liberationism – all this meant that Black feminists early on saw the shortcomings of a "monist" (D. H. King 1988) politics that focused on only one axis of oppression. Although Black feminism varied in its organizational form and ideology, in its theory it was nonetheless characterized by a consistent examination of interlocking oppressions and oriented toward action agendas that linked solutions for gender oppression with solutions to other forms of oppression.

Although differently situated in the racial/ethnic hierarchy and left political milieu, Chicana feminists initially organized an interstitial politics as well, in and around the Chicano movement. Feminists in the Chicano movement challenged that movement's shortcomings regarding the liberation of the Chicana in her community, arguing from the inception of their movement that it was only with Chicanas' liberation as women that the entire community could move forward (Cortera 1976a, 1976b; Flores 1971a, 1971b; *La Raza* 1971a; Longauex y Vasquez 1970; Nieto-Gómez 1976; Rincon 1971; Sosa Riddell 1974). Chicana feminist organizing was therefore interstitial in its formation, but not in its aims; feminists strove to stay linked to streams in the Chicano liberation movement, and sought to distinguish themselves from what was seen as a very different "Anglo" form of feminist praxis. In an intersectional way, Chicana feminists analyzed their situation as women as the result not just of gender but of racial/ethnic, national, linguistic, and class dynamics. Later critiques by Chicana lesbian feminists deepened this analytical intersectionality by filling in earlier lacunae around issues of heteronormativity.[5]

Thus, theories of intersecting oppressions as mutually constitutive were rooted in feminist politics, born of experience and created to guide

---

[5] On a more general note, the later "addition" of heterosexism to intersectional analyses in feminisms of color does not reflect total silence about sexuality, as will become clear in the narrative of this work. Rather, early in the emergence of second-wave feminisms, and particularly in communities of color, questions of lesbianism and homosexuality were broached in an inconsistent way. Clearly, criticisms of lesbian feminists of color as to their movements' failure to incorporate a struggle against heterosexism as an element of their political agenda were accepted and influential (see Alarcón, Castillo, and Moraga 1993; Anzaldúa 1999 [1987]; Castillo 1994; Clarke 1983; Combahee River Collective 1981; Lorde 1982, 1984; Moraga 1983; Moraga and Anzaldúa 1979; Pérez 1991; B. Smith 1979, 1983; Trujillo 1991a, 1991b).

activism (see Anzaldúa 1999 [1987]; Beal 1970; Cortera 1977; Crenshaw 1989, 1995; Hill Collins 1990; D. H. King 1988; Naples 1998a, 1998b; Sacks 1989; Sandoval 1990, 1991; Spelman 1982; Thorton Dill 1983). As Kimberlé Crenshaw (1995:358) wrote, for women of color, there was (and is) a "need to account for multiple grounds of identity when considering how the social world is constructed." The need to account for one's disadvantaged position as part of a disadvantaged community was based on experience, but it promoted a particular kind of knowledge; as Paula Moya has written, a kind of "epistemic privilege" comes from being at the intersecting point of oppressions, such that women of color actually have "a special advantage with respect to possessing or acquiring knowledge about how fundamental aspects of our society (such as race, class, gender, and sexuality) operate to sustain matrices of power" (2001:479). And knowledge of the intersectionality of oppressions at the core of women's lives then further facilitated a particular kind of awareness when it came to political activism, one that relied on "new subjectivity," constant political revision, and the "capacity to recenter [one's politics] depending on the kinds of oppression to be confronted" (Sandoval 1991:14).

Thus, feminists of color constructed intersectional theory on the basis of their lived experiences and embodied knowledge. Their theories were oriented toward guiding their activism; in a continuing process, theory and activism constructed further definitions of what constituted a feminist agenda. There were, however, some silences in the earlier constructions of intersectional feminist theory around questions of heteronormativity and sexuality. Early feminists on the left broke silences about the effects of gender domination, racial/ethnic domination, and class domination in their lives; they did so in order to argue for a politics of liberation that would address these dominations simultaneously. But while the archival record of political discussion reflects feminists' displeasure with sexual double standards, there was initially little *written* discussion of homophobia and little *written* theorizing about the oppressiveness of heterosexism. These lacunae in intersectional feminist theory were, of course, filled by feminists who reacted to initial silences with very loud shouts. For example, as will be further discussed in Chapter Three, Black feminists in the Third World Women's Alliance would stress the jeopardy that Black women faced as a result of gender, race, and class oppression; later Black feminists in the Combahee River Collective would include critiques of heterosexism and homophobia in their analyses of what needed to change in order to liberate women. By the

1990s, the intersectional political agenda of feminists of color – the need to simultaneously analyze and battle dominations of gender, class, race/ethnicity, *and* sexuality – migrated to the "mainstream" of feminist scholarship and activism, moving beyond the starting point of their own feminist movements. If the reader wonders where there were feminists discussing the constraints of heterosexuality and whether I am leaving them out, rest assured of my certainty that the discussions were taking place; the reader can draw her own conclusions as to why it took many feminists a little while to circulate their discussions about heternorma-tivity in written form.

Feminist Emergences, Intersectionality, and Social Movement Theory

I start from the position that the emergence of feminist movements in any time and place is an interesting problem for those who care about the way that women choose to protest, because self-conscious feminist protest is a relative rarity in women's social protest. The emergence of a feminist social movement is infrequent, analogous in its rarity as a response to gender oppression to that of revolutionary movements as working-class responses to class domination; both feminism's rarity and its potential for large-scale social change make it of enormous interest – to scholars, to the public at large, and even, if grudgingly, to the main-stream press. In this work about the making of racial/ethnic feminisms in the second wave, I combine a feminist intersectional approach with a compatible "multilevel" constructionist perspective that takes seriously questions of structure, opportunity, perception, and interaction (Taylor and Whittier 1998). I believe these approaches are compatible because while both acknowledge structural inequalities in social locations, and the role that such inequalities have in determining consciousness, nei-ther approach is deterministic when it comes to assessing the effects of structure on consciousness. In other words, in explaining activism, both feminist intersectional theory and social constructionism mandate an exploration of the way that structure, social locations, and activists' awareness interact in political decision making, and thus in movements' emergence and development.

The social constructionist turn in movement scholarship (see espe-cially Morris and Mueller 1992) was a result of scholars trying, since the early 1990s, to redress what came to be seen as a neglect of inter-action in studies of social movements. Interaction in movements came to be neglected with the rise of "resource mobilization" in the study of social movements in the 1970s.[6] The turn in movement scholarship in the United States toward social constructionism was coupled with another related turn in European scholarship toward theorizing "new social movements," that is, toward the study of movements built on newly formed, nonclass collective identities (J. Cohen 1985; Kitschelt 1985; Melucci 1980, 1989). Social constructionist movement scholars have attempted to take into account the interplay between structural factors, such as the context of political opportunity and access to resources, and social psychological factors, such as identity and group interaction, in explanations of movement emergence and development. Social constructionism in studying movements therefore calls for consideration of how activists' perceptions shape access to resources, and vice versa; how those perceptions shape action; and how perceptions and structure constrain as well as enable protest.

Most social constructionist studies of social movements do not have feminist intersectional theory per se at the center of their analyses (more probably should), but a feminist intersectional approach to considering the emergence and development of movements mandates social constructionism. In considering the linked emergences of Black, Chicana, and white feminist movements in the second wave, both approaches require that we understand the impact of feminists' different and unequal social locations, their consequently unequal access to resources, *and* how structural inequality mattered to activists making political decisions on the ground. African American, Chicana, and white women occupied different social locations in a race- and class-stratified society and had

---

[6] In reaction to an earlier literature of movement studies in the collective behavior tradition, which emphasized social psychological factors in movement development, resource mobilizationists were influenced by organizational and economic studies, and charted the tangible resources – money, leadership, space, numbers of activists, access to elites – that allowed groups to challenge authority. Other somewhat less structurally focused approaches – collective action and political opportunity – also seemed well suited to explaining social protest by the relatively well-off (i.e., middle class), such as that which occurred in the United States in the 1960s and 1970s. In any case, social constructionists in the 1990s argued that studies gave matters of consciousness, perceptions, and group interaction analytical short shrift, and that what was needed was an approach that required scholars to look at both structure and interaction in explaining social movement developments (Fireman and Gamson 1979; Gurr 1970; Klandermans and Tarrow 1988; McAdam 1982; McCarthy and Zald 1977; Morris 1984; Smelser 1963; Tarrow 1994; Tilly 1978; Turner and Killian 1987; Zald and Ash 1970).

varying degrees of access to resources for their social movement activity, and this mattered for how they organized and with whom. Because of being in different social locations, feminists in different racial/ethnic communities were differently situated vis-à-vis the political landscape that confronted them, and therefore had different issues about ascribed and activist identities and about loyalties toward and commitments made to fellow activists. Only an approach that combines intersectional and interactional analyses can account for the different situations of feminists in the second wave.

Feminists' choices in organizing cannot be derived by looking at unequal structural background factors or the availability of one or another set of resources, because feminists' decisions were made within nested sets of relationships to power, to money, and to others. Historically, feminist movements in the United States have emerged from prior movements (Buechler 1990; DuBois 1978; Evans 1979; Freeman 1975), and Black, Chicana, and white feminism developed from three "parent" movements: the Civil Rights/Black Liberation movement, the New Left, and the Chicano movement. An intersectional/social constructionist approach suggests that it is important to understand how these parent movements trained feminists in the basics of organizing, and why (and how far) feminists moved away from the men with whom they initally worked. These parent movements took women – a dispersed potential pool of activists – and put them in face-to-face contact with one another; they gave incipient feminists access to communication organs – journals, newsletters, and conferences – an important "precondition" (Freeman 1975) for feminist emergence.

Although the public quality of women's lives varied by race and class, women in these social movements were able to challenge some parts of women's traditional roles in a still uncomfortable public sphere (see Buechler 1990; DuBois 1978; Echols 1989; Evans 1979; Freeman 1975; Marx Ferree and Hess 1985, 1994; McAdam 1988). In interaction, by means of increased public participation through movements for social change, contradictions were generated for emerging feminists, since participation in movements did not automatically change "traditional" notions about gender roles. Thus, even while emergent feminists in their parent movements had the opportunity to shape and be shaped by liberationist ideology, they extended the idea of liberation to their own oppression within male-dominated movements and a male-dominated society. The challenge that this extension of movement principles presented was not welcomed in the parent movements, and feminists were faced with decisions about how – and really, whether – to use acquired skills and resources for feminist organizing.

As I will argue throughout this book, the kinds of choices confronting feminists in different racial/ethnic communities were not identical, and in using a social constructionist/intersectional approach to look at feminisms in the second wave, I highlight the complexities of the movement contexts for feminist emergence. I therefore take into account the different access to resources that feminists in different racial/ethnic communities had, the special challenges of interaction that feminists faced in forming a specifically feminist identity in each of the parent movements/communities from which they emerged, and the ways in which feminists in different racial/ethnic communities were shaped by organizing within a larger left multimovement sector, particularly at the role played by ideological developments that reverberated between movements. My theoretical goal, then, is to use social movement theory and feminist theory together in explaining the development of organizationally distinct racial/ethnic feminisms on the left during the second wave.

Methodological Considerations/The Plan of the Book

I consider African American, white, and Chicana feminist emergences as a linked set of cases, and I used comparative historical method to look at their similarities and, especially, at their differences. For some, these would constitute a contradictory agenda, insofar as comparisons are generally made between cases considered to be distinct. I solve this problem by conceptualizing feminist movements in this era as organizationally distinct – as indeed they were – but situated in a social movement milieu that created awareness and connections among them. To date, this is the first time that these three cases have been compared in this manner, and I argue that the three feminist movements that emerged out of grassroots and student activism in the 1960s and 1970s can only be understood in relation to one another.[7] For one thing, emerging feminists in all three racial/ethnic movements were already situated within activist networks; that is, they had made the choice to be involved

[7] The comparative historical approach has been used by Marx Ferree and Hess (1985, 1994) and Freeman (1975) to look at the two branches of white second-wave feminism; by Buechler (1990) to look at white women's feminism in two different time periods; and by Banks (1981) and Bouchier (1983) to contrast white women's feminism in the United States and the United Kingdom.

in left oppositional politics, and in some cases, knew of one another's work. Since racial/ethnic feminist movements emerged at roughly the same time; since the three feminist movements studied here were characterized by a similar communications network that was informal and decentralized; since they emerged from "weblike" (Gerlach and Hine 1970) networks of like-minded individuals who participated in groups linked through "intersecting sets of personal relationships" (Turner and Killian 1987:373); since there were personal relationships and communications networks that sometimes crossed racial/ethnic lines; and since feminists in all three communities did share some common ideas about "liberation," racial/ethnic feminist emergences need to be understood as developing to some degree in interaction with one another.

In telling the story of feminist emergences of the second wave, I have used a variety of sources. I used primary materials – internal and external movement documents – left by the movements themselves, and collections of "underground" or grassroots journals, newsletters, and magazines. Looking at grassroots journals and underground publications is essential for understanding how feminists viewed things on the ground.[8] Underground newspapers and magazines should be seen as organizations in themselves that both disseminated information and articulated discontent (Blackwell forthcoming; G. Rosen 1974). By 1971, more than 100 (white) women's liberation journals and newspapers were in circulation (Hole and Levine 1971; Marx Ferree and Hess 1985:72); Marta Cortera (1980) estimated that during the 1970s, there were at least ten newspapers and magazines dedicated to Chicana feminism (with other popular Chicano movement journals publishing feminist writings). Within the decentralized oppositional social movement sector of the 1960s and 1970s, feminist groups used their publications to communicate ideas through the reprinting of articles from one movement journal to the next. Additionally, two news services, the Liberation News Service and the Underground Press Service, circulated articles to left publications, and several small presses (for example, Pathfinder Press and The New England Free Press) distributed reprinted articles in pamphlet form at events and bookshops. Thus, underground publications, internally circulated pamphlets, and position papers were

---

[8] Taylor and Whittier (1992:105–106) defined primary materials as "books, periodicals and narratives by community members," as well as "newsletters, position papers and other documents from . . . organizations." Other primary materials might include flyers (and other such ephemera) and personal correspondence.

accessible to feminists and used to discuss the meaning of their brand of feminism.

My exploration of these materials has not been strictly representative of the movements, but I have taken pains to look at materials from different parts of the country and from different organizations. Given the informality of membership (Baxandall 2001) in the reticulate, decentralized, and fluid left social movement sector in the 1960s and 1970s, constructing a "universe" to randomly sample from would itself be suspect. The movement journals in particular have been used to explore the debates that went on within the emerging feminist communities. As published, disseminated documents (perhaps "mimeographed and mailed out" is a more accurate phrase), they were relatively accessible to both direct and indirect input by feminist activists. Lastly, where appropriate, I also made use of mainstream newspaper and magazine accounts of the feminist movements, and of scholarly secondary literature, to document the emergence and development of these movements.[9]

In addition to exploring the archival record left by second-wave feminisms, I conducted nine interviews and used material from two oral histories with African American and Chicana/Latina feminists who were active in feminist politics during the second wave. I do not consider the interviews to be oral histories as such, nor is this book based primarily on them; furthermore, the reader will note that Chapter Two, in which I consider the separation of white women's liberation from the Civil Rights movement and the New Left, is based entirely on archival data. Instead, the interviews were conducted in order to explore questions raised by the archival record, and to give voice to Black and Chicana feminists who have not, until recently and in contrast to white feminists, been asked about their experiences as activists. The interviews ranged from an hour to three hours, and although I asked the interviewees some questions about their social background and the life choices that led to their feminist activism, conversations chiefly focused

---

[9] The *Herstory* microfilm collection was a chief source of women's movement publications, particularly for the white women's movement. Archival collections I visited included Northwestern University's Special Collections (their Women's Ephemera Files were especially useful); the National Black Feminist Organization papers at the University of Illinois, Circle Campus; the Sophia Smith Collection at Smith College; the Schlesinger Library at Harvard University; the Social Action Collection at the State Historical Society of Wisconsin; Duke University's collection of papers from the Atlanta Lesbian Feminist Alliance (ALFA); and the Southern California Library for Social Studies and Research in Los Angeles.

on their second-wave feminist activism. The interview process and the interviewees themselves are further discussed in the Appendix, "The Interviews/Living After the Second Wave."

I begin by directly addressing the repercussions of a macrostructure of inequality among groups of emergent feminists in Chapter One, "To Whom Do You Refer? Structure and the Situated Feminist." In this chapter, I look at how African American, Chicana, and white feminists were situated in different locations in a race/class hierarchy that mattered to them as they constructed movements. Structure was apprehended on the ground by feminists of color as they compared themselves to white feminists and framed the issue concerning those with whom they had common cause as being one of shared gender, racial/ethnic, and class inequality. I challenge relative deprivation arguments, which posit that women's disadvantages in public life vis-à-vis men explain the activism of white women coming out of left movements, and that relative equality within communities of color explain the reluctance of women of color to organize as feminists. Instead, I argue that an intersectional approach shifts our attention to the way that feminists of color who were recruited to oppositional politics for reasons other than gender liberation (just as white feminists were) perceived inequalities *between* groups of women, and organized accordingly.

In Chapter Two, "The 'Fourth World' is Born: Intramovement Experience, Oppositional Political Communities, and the Emergence of the White Women's Liberation Movement," I begin a three-chapter discussion about intramovement relationships within different racial/ethnic movement communities. In this chapter, I examine the role that activism within the Civil Rights movement and the New Left had for white women's liberation, with special attention paid to the question of whether prior movement experience is merely facilitative of feminist movement emergence. In contrast to the case of the emergence of NOW from a network of professional women already committed to working on issues involving women's equality, white women's liberationists were attracted first to activism around other issues of oppression, most notably race. These experiences within oppositional communities gave emerging white feminists skills and contacts for constructing a feminist movement, but a commitment to being leftists required that emerging white feminists debate how best to organize for liberation, that is, whether to organize separately from or work in concert with men. Their debate continued for a number of years, as women were increasingly stymied by New Left hostility to their organizing within the ranks. White women's liberationists came in large part to reject the male Left, but only after years of trying to organize within it. By trying to "co-opt" New Left resources, they simultaneously built independent feminist organizations, making later efforts to reconcile with the New Left superfluous. But the protracted nature of white feminist emergence on the left should lead us to an understanding about the contradictory legacy of prior movement experiences for feminist emergence: Prior movements gift feminists with skills and contacts, while burdening them with loyalties to an existing community and potential constraints on feminist activity.

This contradictory legacy of constraint and facilitation was much more acutely felt by emerging feminists of color, as I argue in Chapters Three and Four. In Chapter Three, "The Vanguard Center: Intramovement Experience and the Emergence of Black Feminism," I consider the process of emergence of Black feminism, showing that Black feminist organizations arose at roughly the same time as white women's liberation (although on a smaller scale) as a consequence of Black women's experiences in a changing Civil Rights/Black Liberation movement. Black feminists began their organizing in the mid-1960s, as the Civil Rights movement shifted to a northern, younger social base, as resurgent masculinist Black nationalist ideology forced Black women activists into constricted, merely supportive roles, and as the white women's liberation movement was growing. Black feminists were critical of both the Black Liberation and the white women's liberation movements, and their critiques focused on the middle-class biases of both movements; they developed an intersectional analysis of the interlocking dimensions of race, class, and gender oppressions, as they formed influential Black feminist organizations from 1968 through the mid-1970s.

In Chapter Four, "'We Called Ourselves "Feministas"': Intramovement Experience and the Emergence of Chicana Feminism," I consider how a different social location and different movement dynamics impacted the formation of Chicana feminism. I argue that Chicana feminism needs to be understood not as a mere variation on white or Black feminism but as a consequence of Chicanas' participation in the Chicano movement of the 1960s and 1970s. Like Black feminists, Chicana feminists organized an interstitial politics, in opposition both to antifeminist forces in their parent movement – particularly the student branches within that movement – and to middle-class biases they perceived in "Anglo" feminism. As in the case of Black feminists, Chicana feminists faced internal pressure to limit their roles within their movement, in the supposed interest of preserving their culture. But because they were differently positioned in the race/ethnicity hierarchy, and in the left political milieu, Chicana feminists used different arguments for the importance of feminist organizing, making different claims about Chicanas' history and their role in the family than Black feminists did. These claims were strategic and oriented toward solving practical political problems of mobilization, and to a large degree, they worked; despite a backlash, Chicana feminists created a distinct set of feminist organizations beginning in the late 1960s, and were able throughout the 1970s to maintain close links to the general Chicano movement even as they did so.

A multilevel social constructionist approach dictates that the question of intermovement politics of the Left in the 1960s and 1970s should not be bracketed from the question of the micropolitics of feminist emergence. Therefore, intermovement politics are the focus of Chapter Five, "Organizing One's Own: The Competitive Social Movement Sector and the Rise of Organizationally Distinct Feminist Movements." In it, I argue that the competitive intermovement politics of the 1960s and 1970s need to be considered in order to understand what kept three emerging feminist movements organizationally distinct in a crowded movement field. Social movement organizations proliferated in this era, and women activists formed the backbone of these groups; as such, women's energy was a much-fought-over resource, and feminist emergence was seen as a threat to the economy of social movement activism. Male activists competed for the loyalties of feminist women, loyalties that were particularly acute for African American and Chicana feminists. Competition among social movement organizations resulted in a set of "either/or" demands on feminist activists, who felt forced to choose between organizations oriented toward one or another form of oppression. In this "either/or" context, emerging feminists made different kinds of arguments for feminism as good politics; white feminists constructed a universalist picture of gender oppression that obscured differences among women, and that was then held up as a negative example of the dangers of feminism by those wishing to prevent Black and Chicana feminists from organizing. Underpinning feminists' decisions about how to organize on the left was a consensual ethos of "organizing one's own" as the only authentic style of activism, and keeping feminist movements distinct along racial/ethnic lines came to be seen as part of a truly radical feminist praxis.

In the conclusion, "Feminists on Their Own and for Their Own: Revisiting and 'Re-visioning' Second-Wave Feminisms," I consider what this different picture of the making of racial/ethnic feminisms in the second wave means for our understanding of dynamics of race/ethnicity, class, and gender in movement politics. Looking at second-wave feminisms in the plural carries lessons about centering questions of gender, race, and class in the study of social movements generally; it also speaks to the power of a *feminist* conceptualization of the intersectionality of oppressions for articulating and fighting inequalities. I also address the question that underlies the stories of division among feminists: What are the possibilities for coalition making across racial/ethnic, class, and other divides?

CHAPTER ONE

To Whom Do You Refer?

Structure and the Situated Feminist

It's very understandable why you would want to start someplace where you resonate more with the people who you are involved with from a lot of different levels, and who you aren't always educating in the process.

Aileen C. Hernández
San Francisco, California
July 2000

Structure in Accounts of Feminist Emergence

Structural changes in opportunities for women in American society facilitated feminist activism in the 1960s and 1970s. Changes in women's participation in public life – indicated by higher rates of women's participation in the labor force and growing numbers of women in higher education – gave women the resources necessary to organize for gender equality (Buechler 1990; Carden 1974; Freeman 1975; Marx Ferree and Hess 1994).[1] There is, however, a logical problem with positing that rising resources facilitated feminist mobilization in the 1960s and 1970s: If women's circumstances were improving during this period, why did they mobilize? If things were getting better, from where did women's discontent emerge?

This is a good question but not the only one to ask. Movement experiences also mattered for feminist mobilizations, since in the United States, feminist movements have historically come from movements organized to fight forms of oppression other than gender oppression

---

[1] Buechler, Freeman, and Marx Ferree and Hess all also argued that demographic changes, specifically a rising divorce rate and long-term drop in birth rates, led to women's increasing control over the use of resources. However, the evidence for demographics being at the root of availability of resources for feminist resurgence is mixed. Marx Ferree and Hess acknowledge that the effects of higher divorce rates would lead to more freedom for women, but also to a reduced standard of living and an increased responsibility for minor children. Additionally, at points in the 1950s – e.g., in 1958, when the divorce rate was 8.9 per 1,000 married females – the divorce rate was only slightly higher than the 1937 rate of 8.7, and the 1970

(Buechler 1990). Movements for racial/ethnic liberation have been crucial to the emergence of both first- and second-wave white feminism and the feminist movements of women of color, both in the United States and in other countries (see Ray 1999, for example, on Indian women's movements). It is in movements that structural changes are contemplated and constructed as opportunities or, alternatively, as causes for discontent.

In this chapter, I argue for a respecification of the role that structural changes had in the making of organizationally distinct racial/ethnic feminisms by thinking about what changes meant to feminists situated in different racial/ethnic communities. I first consider past answers to the question of the impact of structural changes on feminist mobilization. Focusing on relative deprivation arguments made by previous scholars, which see feminist mobilization as a result of inequality between women and men, I take a more intersectional and constructionist approach, arguing that it was differences among women, and among feminists, that mattered in structuring distinct racial/ethnic movements. Decisions about how to organize as feminists were indeed structured by existing inequalities among women, but these were mediated by movement contexts that generated awareness of the contours of inequalities. In this chapter, then, I put forward a different picture of what structural barriers that did indeed exist *meant* for cross-racial/ethnic feminist organizing, a picture that requires us to think about what structure looks like from the ground up.

How Much Is Enough? The Relatively Deprived as Challengers

Within social movement studies, relative deprivation theory has been used to account for (white) women's social protest in the relatively

---

rate of 14.9 was roughly comparable to the 1945 rate of 14.4 (U.S. Bureau of the Census 1975, p. 64, Table B 216-220). Regarding birth rates, Marx Ferree and Hess (1994:12) reported a reversal in a "long-term trend ... toward lower birth rates (number of children per 1,000 population) and fertility (average number of children to women in the childbearing years)" in the United States during the years 1947 to 1963. Of course, higher fertility rates would not be consistent with women's increased control over resources, but at the same time, the labor force participation of married women with children continued to increase. As Marx Ferree and Hess note, this meant that women entering college in the 1960s were more likely to have working mothers as role models, and this would have been especially true for Black women, who historically participated in the labor force in higher numbers than did white women.

prosperous postwar period and, as will be discussed shortly, the supposed failure of women of color to protest in a like manner. Such theory posited that structural changes in opportunities for women were accompanied by raised expectations regarding the power of work and school to change their lives, that these expectations were not met, and that protest ensued, because of women's dissatisfaction with the gap between the expected level of change and the actual circumstances of their lives.

Generally, theorists argue that collective action stems from individuals' psychological reactions to the gap between expected circumstances (or expected statuses) and actual ones, such as the one that women may have experienced postwar (see Davies 1971; de Tocqueville 1978; Geschwender 1968; Gurr 1970). A group of such aggregated individuals mobilizes when there is a gap between their "value expectations and value capabilities" (Gurr 1970:37); the gap itself becomes apparent to the challenging group when they perceive themselves to be in a relatively unjust position vis-à-vis another group to which they might reasonably compare themselves. Thus, relatively deprived potential challengers have a specific reference group in mind when they act (Gurr 1970:37). The key issue then becomes who compares whom to whom.

However, relative deprivation theory takes a profoundly individualistic view toward the causes that generate collective action. How does this aggregated group of discontented individuals come together to form a challenging group? But even with this central problem at its core, it is easy to see why scholars of second-wave white feminism have been attracted to relative deprivation arguments, especially when attempting to make sense of the role that structural changes had in facilitating feminist mobilization. It is true that women as a group needed some resources to rebel, absolute deprivation being conducive to inertia rather than action, and it is reasonable to assume that women who had experienced improvements in their circumstances would be likely to rebel, as long as they had in mind the goal of being as well-off as a reference group, assumed to be their male counterparts. It would make sense for them to organize as feminists to allay gender disadvantage. Feminist organizing would alleviate the "structural strain" (Buechler 1990:9, following Smelser 1962) that women felt as a result of growing public participation juxtaposed with continued obligations in the domestic sphere, and address the continually experienced "psychological sense of marginality as a result of their secondary status in employment, education and other institutions" (Marx Ferree and Hess 1985:8). Since women were better off and since (some) women did rebel, relative deprivation theory seemed to make some sense, at least in explaining the feminism of middle-class white women.

But relative deprivation arguments about the role of structural changes in feminist mobilizations are class and race delimited. They don't fit the situation of Black women, who had traditionally higher levels of labor force participation than white women (rates that were continuing to increase postwar), and they don't quite fit the experiences of Chicanas, who only had the doors to higher education pried open for them in the latter half of the 1960s through equal opportunity programs (EOP). It was the gender ideology of white middle-class America that was giving white, middle-class women an increasingly conflicted sense of identity postwar (Freeman 1975). It was these white middle-class women who felt "a deepening sense of bewilderment about how to define their identity," and they were the ones who felt guilty about their public participation in the light of society's expectations that they draw their sense of themselves from domestic roles (Freeman 1975:25–26). These feelings purportedly formed a large part of the impetus toward second-wave feminism, as white middle-class women's bewilderment regarding the unresolvable tensions in their lives gave way to a sense of being relatively deprived and unfairly burdened when compared to white men.

But reliance on relative deprivation theory to explain even white middle-class feminism needs to be tempered with consideration of the actual trajectory of feminist organizing in the second wave, because structural tensions, or individuals' perceptions of those structural tensions, do not lead automatically to collective action (della Porta and Diani 1999:57). In the case of second-wave feminisms, only in the liberal branch of the second wave did women begin protest activity by forming a group specifically dedicated to alleviating gender oppression. Liberal feminists came out of activist networks and strongly identified with institutions for social justice, where questions of how to improve women's collective status were a part of political agendas (Hartmann 1999; A. C. Hernández interview 2000; Horowitz 1996).

And it is unclear if the founding of liberal feminist organizations was some sort of reaction to "strain." The creation of the National Organization for Women (NOW) – the central "liberal" feminist organization – is difficult to read as a collective moment of solving problems of role strain. NOW was founded in 1966 by professional women who served on state commissions on the status of women, and who had been appointed

to these commissions because of their roles in political interest groups,
trade unions, and other institutions (Freeman 1975:54–55). Conference
attenders at a June 1966 national meeting of these commissions were
thwarted in passing a resolution that would have asked the new federal
Equal Employment Opportunity Commission to take sex discrimination
as seriously as race discrimination. After this rejection, the women who
had proposed the resolution joined together and formed NOW, and by
the end of the conference, twenty-eight women had each paid five dollars to join the group. But discussion in liberal activist networks about
the need for an "NAACP" for women predated the formation of NOW,
with the actual idea of such an organization attributed by some to Pauli
Murray, a Black civil rights activist and feminist who had been active
with the National Council of Churches around issues of poverty and the
status of women of color (Hartmann 1999; A. C. Hernández interview
2000).

Therefore, even in the case of NOW, the assumptions on which relative deprivation explanations of feminist emergence depend – that a
group of women became aware of disadvantages vis-à-vis men and took
action *as women* to remedy those disadvantages – were met only because
these women were already to a large extent organized into a network
devoted to improving the lives of women; that is, they had some idea
that women's roles needed to change and were institutionally situated
in a manner that allowed them to do something about the problem.
NOW's speedy mobilization probably had much to do with the character of the social network from which it emerged, since Betty Friedan,
Aileen C. Hernández, and other early participants in NOW had activist
backgrounds, particularly in the labor movement and the "Old Left"
(A. C. Hernández interview 2000; Horowitz 1996). The professional
women who formed NOW were, as institutional activists, less likely to
be suffering from role strain; they were *already* activists, and many of
them were paid for their work. Liberal feminism could mobilize quickly
because by 1966, firmly established and semi-institutionalized networks
of women concerned with women's issues, and not aggregations of ag-
grieved individuals, were constituted on the ground.

When we look at feminists from the "younger," left-wing branches of
second-wave feminisms, where experiences inside social movements organized around issues *other than* gender oppression eventually produced
feminist responses, we should note that structural changes in women's
positions facilitated women's activism first around those other issues.
White women who later formed the women's liberation movement

became activists, and some took very great risks in order to participate in struggles for racial equality. Black women and Chicana activists of course risked much in working with men to liberate their communities; some of these women later formed feminist groups and organizations. The struggles themselves may have helped some women escape role strain, since social movement participation generally expands women's public roles and intermittently suspends domestic ideology and practice. But emerging white women's liberationists were initially drawn to activism within movements combating racial oppression because of the structure of opportunities for movement participation on the ground, and not their personal deprivation. And clearly, Black women and Chicanas who came to the Civil Rights movements in their communities came because of their desire to eradicate racial/ethnic oppression, and not because they felt less well-off than their men.

As I will address in the chapters to follow, feminist organizing on the left was precipitated by encounters within movements; white, Black, and Chicana feminists who emerged from movements for racial/ethnic liberation extended ideologies about liberation to include the liberation of women. Rather than acting on feelings of being relatively deprived vis-à-vis men in general, emerging feminists on the left acted on the basis of concrete complaints about being stymied in the fulfillment of their activist potential. Initially, they wished to perfect their movements, not leave them. They faced a problem different from the psychological strain created by conflicting roles; their roles were problematic, but their constricted roles were problematic *politics*.

Once again, a racial/ethnic specification of how relative deprivation theory might be applied to the mobilizations of Black and Chicana feminists reveals the theory's limits. African American and Chicana women joined protest movement in the 1960s due to racial/ethnic oppression, despite the fact that women of color were, by most measures, not as well-off as men within their communities. Structural inequality would have (should have) allowed them to feel relatively deprived vis-à-vis the men in their communities, if the structure of inequality between genders within the community were all that mattered to them. Since relative deprivation theory posits that inequality between the genders *should have* mattered to them, two scholars have made explicit arguments about why at least Black women did not become feminists in greater numbers in the second wave because of relative equality between Black women and men. Freeman (1975:37–43) argued that Black women did not embrace white feminist organizations because they were less likely to feel relatively deprived when they compared their situation with that of either Black or white men. She argued both that postwar gains left Black women less deprived vis-à-vis Black men than white women felt vis-à-vis white men, and (somewhat confusingly) that Black women's objective status as "most deprived" would eventually lead them to feminist organizing.

Lewis (1977), in a somewhat more nuanced approach, argued that what mattered most for Black women's organizing was the perception of the relative importance of different kinds of oppression in their lives (an insight that recurs in other writings by African American feminist scholars, and that comes closer to an intersectional perspective). Since formal racial inequality hampered life for both Black women and men, feminist activism took a back seat for most Black women. Lewis concluded that with the lifting of formal racial restrictions, Black women would encounter more discrimination based on their gender, and that they would become more sensitive to sexism as the distance between them and Black men grew. Thus, both Lewis and Freeman account for Black women's supposed lack of attraction to feminist organizing by asserting their relative equality with Black men. But some Black women, not to mention Chicanas, were attracted to feminism, and that was because they were already activists in movements.

Relative deprivation theory may have one insight left for us regarding the way that structural changes in opportunities for women mattered for second-wave feminist organizing. We should rethink the question of reference groups in the making of organizationally distinct feminist movements. For activists on the ground, structural changes are apprehended as activists make judgments about who is well off, and who is not. These assessments of relative status may not prompt mobilization as such, but they certainly matter when it comes to thinking about with whom one should organize. Assessments of relative status make a difference in constructing collective identity, in determining who is part of – and who is not part of – the challenging group.

As Black and Chicana feminists organized, the structure that mattered in terms of *feminist* organizing was the inequality that existed *between* groups of women. By the late 1960s, both the older and younger branches of the white feminist movement were growing quickly; Black and Chicana feminists alike had to grapple with white feminism when making the case for feminism to others in their movements. White feminism's vibrancy heightened the visibility of preexisting differences in racial and class status between white feminists and feminist women

of color. Given this political situation, we must ask about the reference group for feminists of color in this period: Was it white feminists, white men, or men within their own communities? To whom
were they comparing themselves? With whom did they feel common
cause?

The standard answer derived from reading the case studies of second-
wave feminism, and articulated in the arguments of both Freeman and
Lewis, is that each group of feminists compared themselves to the men in
their community. This standard answer is related to the practice of holding class and race constant when talking about 1960s social movements;
that is, since feminist activists in each community were middle class and
of the same race as the men in their communities, their problems with
equality consisted of gender oppression, and it is along that axis that
they suffered subordination. But if one thinks about inequality existing not just between women and men within communities but between
women situated in different communities, one sees that white women
and white feminists were a key reference group for African American and
Chicana feminist mobilization. Being middle class and of color was not
something that could be held constant for feminists of color; class status
did not mean the same thing in each community and across communities, and could not simply be bracketed from concerns with gender and
racial/ethnic status. The awareness of feminists of color of the structural
differences between women in different social locations helped to deter-
mine how feminists mobilized into organizationally distinct movements
in the second wave.

Inequality and the Positing of a Postwar Transracial/Ethnic Middle Class

The existence of inequalities among groups of women has long been acknowledged, but their effects on feminist protest have been underexam-
ined. The kinds of questions that scholars asked about the lack of feminist
organizing by women of color shows a reluctance to assess the interactive
effects of race, class, and gender oppression.[2] If we reject the implication

---

[2] Implicit in this approach is the assumption that white feminists established a
universally applicable working model for feminist protest (Cortera 1977; Freeman
1975; Giddings 1984; Joseph and Lewis 1981; M. King 1975; Lewis 1977). The
development and impact of white women's liberationists' universalist picture of
sexist oppression as primary in origin and importance will be explored in greater
detail in Chapter Five.

of relative deprivation arguments that African American women and Chicanas were somehow not structurally ready to protest, we must nonetheless acknowledge that class differences between racial/ethnic communities impacted the resources available for feminist protest and thus whether or not feminists in communities of color would want to organize with white feminists.

Beyond the commonly accepted view that 1960s and 1970s protesters were largely middle class in origin and character, and therefore had access to resources, explanations of feminist emergence to date have not systematically treated the question of class.[3] Indeed, middle-class women were the ones with the resources necessary to protest collectively; gender-specific changes in women's labor force participation and attendance at institutions of higher education indicated an increased level of resources available to potential women activists. In the "younger" branch of feminism especially, African American, white, and Chicana feminists were largely college educated, and by virtue of their college education, upwardly mobile in comparison with others in their communities. But to posit that emerging Black and Chicana feminists had some measure of class privilege when compared to others in their communities is to make the case only for resources being necessary to challenge oppression. Such an argument does not speak to the question of class inequality between racial/ethnic communities, and how that might have mattered for cross-racial/ethnic organizing.

Being middle class within an economically and racially disadvantaged community did not obliterate the concerns of feminists of color about those disadvantages, and being "middle class" had a different meaning within each racial/ethnic community. Because the general rise in resources postwar was not a uniform one for African American, white and Chicana women, the differences that existed among women were important and apparent. Women in the African American and Chicano communities faced racial and economic barriers that white women did not, since the expansion of the middle class in communities of color did not mean that these communities were suddenly on an equal footing with the white majority. Looking at Table 1.1, we can see that despite growing

---

[3] On the overall character of 1960s protest movements, see Zald and McCarthy (1979). The rise in Black insurgency and the formation of Mexican American political organizations postwar have been linked to the expansion of the middle class in those communities, and most activists came out of the newly expanded middle class (Gómez-Quiñones 1990; McAdam 1982; Morris 1984; Wilson 1978).

Table 1.1. *Median Money Income of Families and Households by Race and Spanish Origin of Householder (in constant 1979 dollars for families 1950–1970, constant 1981 dollars for households 1972–1979)*

Year	White	Black*	Hispanic[†]
1950	10,388	5,636	NA
1955	12,505	6,896	NA
1960	14,301	7,917	NA
1965	16,681	9,186	NA
1970	19,134	12,180	NA
1972	22,116	12,909	16,690
1975	20,852	12,518	14,980
1979	21,718	12,801	16,819

* "Other races" are grouped under "Black" before 1972.

[†] Median income statistics from "Hispanic" families/households prior to 1972 are unavailable.

Sources: U.S. Bureau of the Census, 1980, *Statistical Abstract of the United States (101st Edition)*, Table 745, p. 451; U.S. Bureau of the Census, 1982–3, *Statistical Abstract of the United States (103rd Edition)*, Table 709, p. 429.

median incomes for all three racial/ethnic groups, African American and Chicano/Hispanic households/families still lagged behind their white counterparts throughout the process of feminist movement emergences.

Looking more closely at women's participation in making the middle class in each community, and in gaining access to resources necessary for activism, Table 1.2 shows the labor force participation rates for Black, white, and Chicana women. We can see that the labor force participation rates of African American women – historically higher than white women's – and Chicana women – lower than white women's – increased in the postwar period, dramatically in the case of white women and Chicanas. The higher participation rates for "nonwhite" women extended as well to mothers; in 1965, 34 percent of white women with children under eighteen were in the labor force, while the corresponding number for nonwhite women was 46 percent (U.S. Department of Labor 1966).[4]

---

[4] The U.S. Department of Labor, Women's Bureau (1966) reported that by 1965, there were 3.5 million "nonwhite" women in the labor force (93 percent of whom

Table 1.2. *Labor Force Participation Rates for Women by Race/Ethnicity, 1954–1980*

Year	White	Black	Chicana
1954	33.3	46.1*	21.9 (1950)[†]
1960	36.5	48.2*	28.8[†]
1965	38.1	48.6*	NA
1970	42.6	49.5*	36.4[†]
1972	60.4	48.7	NA
1975	61.5	48.8	NA
1980	64.1	53.1	49.0[†]

* Includes "other races."

[†] Estimates taken from Almott and Matthaei (1991), Table C-1, p. 403. It is difficult to find statistics solely on Chicanas/os prior to the 1980s; before then, the U.S. Census did not have a separate enumeration for Hispanics; postcensus estimates were done for the 1970 census. The estimates for the years 1950 and 1960 are based on "whites" with Spanish surnames in the five southwestern states (Arizona, California, Colorado, New Mexico, and Texas).

Sources: For the years 1954–1970: U.S. Bureau of the Census, 1975, *Historical Statistics of the United States: Colonial Times to 1970, Part 1*, Table D 42–48, p. 133; for the years 1972–1980: U.S. Department of Labor, 1989 (August), *Handbook of Labor Statistics*, Table 5, pp. 25–30.

There was, in fact, a considerable narrowing of the gap between Black and white women's incomes during this period; in 1954, the median money income of all Black female workers was $914, as compared to white women's $2,046, and in 1970, the numbers were $3,285 and $3,870, respectively (U.S. Bureau of the Census 1975:304). Clearly, Black women contributed their incomes to the Black middle-class growth that Wilson (1978:127) characterized as "dramatic." And although Chicanas lagged behind Black and white women in labor force participation, they too contributed in the making of their community's middle class. World War II converted the Chicano community from a rural to an urban population (Barrera 1979; Gómez-Quiñones 1990; G. Rosen 1974), which enabled more Chicanas to find work, albeit in

were Black), and that they represented "13 percent of all women workers, and 11 percent of all women in the population" (1966:1).

the poorly paid service sector. Chicanas' labor force participation rate continued to increase for married as well as unmarried women; Cooney reported that in 1960, 24.4 percent of married Mexican American women ages 14 to 54 in the Southwest were in the labor force, a number that jumps to 34.6 percent by 1970, the largest relative increase (41.8 percent) among the three racial/ethnic groups (Cooney 1975:253).[5]

Increased labor force participation in all three groups of women supports arguments regarding the key role of resources for potential feminist mobilization, but is not the same thing as saying that all three groups of women had access to equal amounts of resources. Although Black women had higher rates of labor force participation during the postwar period, their earnings were not equal to those of white women or Black men (Milkman 1990), and the trend toward convergence of median incomes between Black and white women already noted nonetheless indicates that Black women had not "caught up" to white women in the second wave.[6] Black women had almost twice the unemployment rate of white women (9.3 percent versus 5 percent); more Black women worked part time, and more reported working part time involuntarily. Fully 48 percent of nonwhite women made less than $1,000 a year, in contrast to 39 percent of white women (U.S. Department of Labor 1966:1–2). Additionally, Black and white women did different kinds of work, with white women nearly twice as likely as Black women to be professionals, and close to a third of Black women employed as domestics through the mid-1960s (U.S. Department of Labor 1966:1).[7]

As was the case with Black women, Chicanas received much lower wages than white women and were segregated in low-skilled and low-prestige occupations. World War II enabled Chicanas to enter the labor market in greater numbers, but most often as domestics, or low-level service workers, as they replaced white and Black women who went to work in war industries (Cortera 1976a). Within a southwestern economy based on racial stratification, Chicanas were mostly unskilled and semiskilled workers overrepresented in such jobs as launderers, food

[5] Cooney's estimates of Chicanas' labor force participation vary slightly from those made by Almott and Matthaei (1991), but the increase in both cases is comparable.

[6] Nor have they yet; see the U.S. Department of Labor 2001 website document "20 Facts on Women Workers."

[7] More African American women did become professionals in the postwar years, but progress was relative, and the percentages of Black women in professional and managerial occupations continued to lag behind the corresponding percentages for white women (Higginbotham 1994).

Table 1.3. *Institutions of Higher Education/Degree-Credit Enrollment by Gender, 1946–1970*

Year	Total	% 18–24	Male	Female	% Female
1946	2,078,000	12.5	1,418,000	661,000	31.8
1950	2,281,000	14.2	1,560,000	721,000	31.6
1956	2,918,000	19.5	1,911,000	1,007,000	34.5
1960	3,583,000	22.2	2,257,000	1,326,000	37.0
1966	5,928,000	27.7	3,577,000	2,351,000	39.6
1970	7,920,000	32.1	4,637,000	3,284,000	41.5

Source: U.S. Bureau of the Census, 1975, *Historical Statistics of the United States: Colonial Times to 1970, Part 1*, Table H 700–715, p. 383.

processors, maids, and cooks; they also worked in seasonal agriculture, and in agriculturally related businesses, such as canneries and packing houses (Barrera 1979). Those Chicanas who participated in the labor force faced higher levels of unemployment, with nearly twice as many Chicanas unemployed as white women in 1960, a ratio that had changed little a decade later (Segura 1986:57). Overall, rising labor force participation by women in all three racial/ethnic communities did not result in equal rewards. The story of rising resources available postwar to African American, Chicana, and white women was thus also the story of continuing inequalities among communities and among the women working in those communities.

Opportunities for higher education also expanded postwar; having a college education was an important catalyst for upward mobility, and college campuses were crucial sites for organizing by Black, Chicana, and white feminists. Attendance at institutions of higher education did increase dramatically after World War II, as did the number of institutions themselves.[8] As shown in Table 1.3, women greatly increased their attendance in higher education in absolute numbers, but then so did men. Although almost five times as many women were attending institutions of higher education in 1970 as in 1946, women's relative

[8] In 1940, there were 1,708 institutions of higher education (junior colleges, four-year colleges and universities) in the United States; by 1970, the number had grown to 2,525 (U.S. Bureau of the Census 1975:382). Some of this surge in building was prompted by the return of close to eight million veterans – the vast majority of them men – who took advantage of the educational benefits in the G.I. Bill (Sacks 1994).

Table 1.4. *College Enrollment Rates of Women as a Percent of High School Graduates by Race/Ethnicity, 1960, 1970, 1975, 1980*

Year	White	Black	Hispanic	All (male/female)
1960	18.1	16.9	NA	23.8
1970	26.3	24.7	NA	33.3
1975	29.4	32.0	34.8	33.1
1980	30.9	29.2	29.4	32.3

Source: U.S. Bureau of the Census, 1994, *Statistical Abstract of the United States (114th Edition)*, Table 269, p. 177.

share of the total enrolled in higher education rose less precipitously, from 31.8 percent of the total in 1946 to 41.5 percent in 1970. Regarding racial/ethnic differences in college attendance, the Women's Bureau of the U.S. Department of Labor reported that the number of "nonwhite" women – largely Black in this period – who had "some college training" rose from 6 percent in 1952 to 10 percent by 1966; also significant was the fact that the percentage of "nonwhite" women going *beyond elementary school* rose from 31 percent in 1952 to 55 percent by 1966 (U.S. Department of Labor 1967). Chicanas lagged behind "Anglo" women and Black women in educational attainment levels and in attendance at institutions of higher education. Chicanas began attending secondary education in greater numbers only after World War II; whereas less than 15 percent of Chicanos ages 16 to 18 were enrolled in high school as late as 1955, by 1960, 60 percent to 80 percent were enrolled in secondary schools, schools which were sometimes officially and often unofficially segregated (San Miguel 1984).[9] However, in the 1960s and 1970s, African American women and Chicanas who graduated from high school attended college in greater numbers, as shown in Table 1.4.

We can see that by 1980 – well after the emergence of second-wave feminisms – African American women and Chicanas who graduated from high school were attending college roughly as often as white

---

[9] The U.S. Civil Rights Commission reported that as late as the end of the 1960s, 17 percent of school-age children with Spanish surnames that constituted school enrollments in California and Texas were isolated in specific regions, both by school district and by school within districts (San Miguel 1984:204).

women. But during the 1960s and 1970s, students of color were vastly outnumbered by white students on college campuses. The U.S. Department of Health, Education and Welfare/Office for Civil Rights data (1970, 1976) on racial/ethnic enrollments in higher education indicated that in 1968, white students of both sexes constituted almost 91 percent of enrollment in institutions of higher education, with Blacks at almost 6 percent and Latinos estimated at under 2 percent (Urban Ed., Inc. 1974). In 1976, HEW reported that white women on campus still formed just over 80 percent of women's total enrollment; Black women and Latinas both showed enrollment gains, constituting 11.5 and 4.8 percent of women's enrollment nationally. Chicanos and Chicanas in the 1960s remained particularly underrepresented in higher education, despite the institutionalization of educational opportunity (EOP) programs.[10] Given what we know about who was on college campuses in the 1960s and 1970s, we should ask if higher education was a comparable experience for African American, Chicana, and white feminists. The answer is "no."

Emerging feminists of color in higher education could not help but be aware of, and influenced by, their small numbers when compared to white women; this would have been especially true for Chicanas, since Black women had the option of attending Black-sponsored institutions.[11] Chicanas and Chicanos had no choice but to endure isolation on white college campuses. Leticia Hernández, one of the original Hijas de Cuauhtémoc, a Chicana feminist group started at California

[10] Of the more than 83,000 students enrolled at UCLA, University of Colorado at Boulder, University of Texas at Austin, University of Arizona, and University of New Mexico in 1968–1969, only 3,370, or less than half of 1 percent, were Spanish surnamed (Ortego 1971:168). On the role of EOP programs in enrolling Chicanos and Chicanas in higher education, see Lopez and Enos (1972: Appendix P-2); they reported that in California, 43 percent of Chicano students in the California State University and College system and 72 percent of Chicano students at the University of California were there through EOP.

[11] Giddings (1984:245) reported that in the early 1950s, Black women earned over 60 percent of all degrees from Black colleges, at nearly twice the rate of those earned by Black men. However, it was also true that college only prepared Black women for jobs with racial ceilings (Higginbotham 1994:118), and that Black women with "some college" in the 1950s and 1960s got a much smaller return on their educational investment than did Black men. The U.S. Department of Labor, Women's Bureau (1966) reported that "nonwhite" women with "some college earned less than nonwhite" men with some college: $4,047 versus $5,589 in median annual income, respectively.

State University, Long Beach, in 1969, reported feeling blatant discrimination for the first time on campus, given that she had grown up in a primarily Chicano neighborhood (Blackwell interview with L. Hernández 1992). One of the other Hijas, Ana Nieto-Gómez, recalled that she also felt intensely alone at Long Beach, and that in 1967, that feeling was broken when she saw a student carrying a sign that said "Chicano" on it. She recalled feeling "ecstatic because I felt so alone"; in her words, finding a fellow Chicano student was a feeling "like I had found someone from Mars" (Blackwell interview with Nieto-Gómez 1991). Attending her first meeting of United Mexican American Students (UMAS) – with all of eleven students there – was thus extremely important in communicating to Nieto-Gómez that her experience of alienation was not "unusual." Hernández and Nieto-Gómez thus both speak to the marginalization and social isolation that many other women of color felt in overwhelmingly white institutions of higher education.

Other than in social isolation, how did these structural differences manifest themselves to emerging feminists? When we consider how it was that feminists organized, we need to note not only that the white middle class was better off than the middle class communities of color, but also that these differences were discernable among groups of activists at the time. Two surveys of participants in the Black Civil Rights movement in the early to mid-1960s – Von Eschen et al. (1969) and Orum (1970) – showed that there were substantial differences between middle-class Black and middle-class white activists actually participating in the movement. Von Eschen et al. (1969:232) collected data from participants in a major Civil Rights demonstration in Maryland – the "Route 40 Freedom Ride" – in December of 1961, where members of CORE (Congress for Racial Equality) and others "drove along . . . the route requesting service at restaurants previously known to be segregated . . . sitting-in, picketing, or submitting to arrest if service was refused." Von Eschen and his colleagues were able to obtain data from 386 participants (an estimated 60 percent to 80 percent of the group).[12] They found that while both Black and white Freedom Riders overall had higher educational levels than their respective populations in Maryland, white participants were far better educated than their Black counterparts; fully 74 percent of white

[12] Von Eschen et al. reported that some participants did not fill out their questionnaires due to logistical problems, but that the researchers were "unable to discern any source of systematic non-response bias" (1969:233).

Freedom Riders were college graduates, compared to 47 percent of Black riders (see table, 1969: 218). All the white participants had at least a high school education; 13 percent of Black Freedom Riders did not. In this particular protest action, then, the Black participants did not interact with any white who had less than a high school education; conversely, only half of the Black activists were college graduates, and almost 20 percent had a high school education or less.

Orum's (1970) more comprehensive study of Black students in historically Black colleges – primary sites of Civil Rights activism – was based on a 1965 survey of college seniors by the National Opinion Research Center and provided a more general answer as to the class backgrounds of Black and white college student activists. He found that the families of Black college students – and the background of activist students did not differ significantly from the general Black college population – were well-off only "by comparison with the typical black family," and goes on to state that

> [t]he median income, for instance, of all families in the Negro population in 1963 was $3,465, compared with a median income of the students' families of approximately $4,119. *Yet on the average the family of the black college student was extremely poor in comparison to the family of the seniors attending other colleges*; one of every ten seniors from the black colleges came from a home in which the annual income was $7,500 or more, compared with a figure of six of every ten seniors who attended other schools. (1970:19–20; emphasis added)

In fact, the median income of Black college seniors' families was less than half that of those in the rest of the national sample: $4,119 versus $8,400, respectively (1970:19–20).[13]

Beyond income, class differences were apparent in the kinds of education obtained and jobs held in the homes from which Black students

---

[13] Orum had 3,243 responses; the sample of students from Black institutions was chosen so as to represent the universe of those who received bachelor's degrees in the spring of 1964 (77 schools). In 1965, there were 85 colleges and universities in the United States attended primarily by Black students, which enrolled the majority (70 percent) of Black college students. All but two of these schools were located in the South. Orum's (1970:15) sample of Black students had more women in it than the Black student population generally (35 percent male and 65 percent female, while enrollment at predominantly Black institutions was 54 percent female).

came. About one-third (36 percent) of Black seniors came from families in which the father had at least a high school diploma; the corresponding figure for white seniors was almost twice as high (70 percent). Furthermore,

the breadwinner of the typical senior's family at other [non-Black] colleges held a better job than his counterpart among the black college students. In particular, *three times as many of the other college seniors as black college seniors were from families in which the chief wage earner held a professional, managerial, sales or clerical position.* (1970:20–21; emphasis added)

Orum concluded that on "the three indices of socio-economic status – income, education, and occupation," the typical Black college senior was relatively privileged in comparison with others in the Black community, and very much disadvantaged in comparison to white students (1970:21).[14]

There is no reason to think that this gulf in class background between Black and white student activists was not clear to activists on the ground, and a sense of class difference from whites is a constant in the writings of feminists of color, as will be shown in Chapters Three, Four, and Five. But for the time being, we should need look no further than the so-called expulsion of whites from the Student Nonviolent Coordinating Committee (SNCC) in 1965 for evidence of this awareness (Carson 1981). The northern white student volunteers that had come south for 1964's "Freedom Summer" were seen as possessing racial *and* class advantages that led to increasing discomfort on the part of Black SNCC volunteers from both the university and the community. As Stoper (1989:97) wrote:

Virtually all of them [white student volunteers] had attended college and they tended to be highly capable and self-confident in

---

[14] Others found that this pattern of relative disadvantage on the part of Black college students continued through the 1960s and into the 1970s. Urban Ed., Inc., in a report for the Ford Foundation, reported that in 1971, Black families of college freshmen had incomes higher than the median for Blacks generally ($7,154 as compared to $6,714) but much lower than for all families of college freshmen ($12,162); almost one-quarter (23.1 percent) of Black freshmen in that year came from families with parental incomes of less than $4000 a year, as compared to less than 5 percent of all freshmen (Urban Ed., Inc. 1974: Table IV-6, p. 233, and Table IV-7, p. 234, respectively).

organizing skills such as typing, putting out newsletters, speaking at meetings, etc. They began to take over a number of these func- tions from black people, who had been doing them for the previous few years but were not as skilled or as self-assertive.

There was, of course, no analogous history of whites coming to the Southwest to aid Chicano students' freedom struggles. Instead, Chicano students on college campuses were most likely to organize within exclusively Chicano groups, which did not eliminate contacts on campus with more privileged whites. Chicanos were not only a numerical minority on campus but a new presence altogether; they were likely to be in integrated settings outside their communities for the first time; they were most often recruited through EOPs, with affirmative action programs then as now often negatively viewed by the majority of (white) college students (Lopez and Enos 1972). For these reasons, Chicano students were more likely than not to have felt a greater gulf between themselves and other college students than between them- selves and their community of origin (Nieto-Gómez 1970; Risco-Lozada 1970).

The readily apparent inequalities among different racial/ethnic groups in protest movements affected the way that feminist activists – who came out of other protest movements and networked on college campuses – saw one another. More generally, one could take issue with the idea that in an unequal society, getting a college education automatically makes one feel the same as all other students about one's future. To college students, the upward mobility that a college degree promises them is likely to be perceived as only a potentiality, a promise or connection to the future; in contrast, connections with communities and families of origin are and were ties to a lived past, and an actual, ongoing present. Belonging to racial/ethnic communities that were relatively disadvantaged vis-à-vis the white community clearly played a role in how feminist students of color saw themselves; the matter of those "other" disadvantages of race and class (in addition to gender) were part of their feminist thinking from the start.

To Whom Do You Compare? The Salience of Race/Ethnicity plus Class

I will deal more extensively with the linking of race and class concerns in the emergent feminisms of Black women and Chicanas in Chapters Three and Four. But for time being, I wish to emphasize that given these concerns, and given the existence of racial/ethnic *and* class disparities among communities, it was hard for feminists of color to accept an unproblematic sisterhood with white feminists from the very beginning. They rejected the idea that their relationships with the men in their communities were, or should be, equivalent to those that existed between white women and white men; they rejected the idea that possessing some upward mobility within their racial/ethnic communities translated to having the same class location as white feminists (Joseph 1981; D. H. King 1988; Lewis 1977; Smith and Smith 1981). Black women and Chicanas compared themselves to white women and concluded that women of color – indeed, people of color – as a group were unfairly disadvantaged. "Middle class" became firmly attached to the word "white" in their descriptions of the white feminist movement, indicating that race and class disadvantage was salient in the way they saw themselves in relation to white feminists; class differences as well as racial/ethnic differences mattered in discussions as to whether or not to organize with white women (Baca Zinn 1975; Beal 1970; Cantwell 1971; Cortera 1977; Ferguson 1970; Morrison 1971; Nieto-Gómez 1976).

In contrast to their vision of white feminism, feminists of color saw their movements as more strongly working class. Smith Reid (1972:21–24) and Lewis (1977:60) argued that Black feminists had more varied (i.e., poorer) class backgrounds than white feminists, despite being highly educated; Lewis claimed that the National Black Feminist Organization conference in 1973 attracted not only professional women, students, and housewives but also women who were on welfare and women who worked as domestics. Chicana feminists described their movement as working class in origin in their discourse (García 1990); given the recent urbanization of Chicanos, and the continuing immigration of Mexicans to the United States, Chicana feminism drew into it women who were "members of a different class and cultural group" than white feminists (del Castillo 1980:11).

Along with awareness of racial/ethnic differences in class, many feminists of color had a different understanding of what being middle class meant for people of color. In general, middle-class status was seen as a much more tenuous state of affairs for them than for white women, their thinking reflecting both the newness of the Black/Chicano middle classes and their relative lack of wealth. Some feminists of color, for example, saw middle-class white feminists as "arrogant" in their rejection of material comforts, unable to appreciate that those comforts had a very different meaning for those who had struggled for it (Smith and Smith 1981:113). And despite the emergence by the early 1970s of white socialist feminist groups, the image of white feminism as largely middle class in composition and as having middle-class biases in politics crystallized and contributed to how feminists of color made sense of the question of feminist organizing across racial/ethnic lines. Although Chicana feminists did make distinctions among different white feminist ideologies, and were more comfortable with socialist feminism's anticapitalist framework, there were few efforts toward coalition building with white feminists, as the general sense of white feminists as having little to lose prevailed (García 1990). Ana Nieto-Gómez (Blackwell interview with Nieto-Gómez 1991) did not want to join with white feminists because of her sense of their having class privilege that blinded them to the links between oppressions that she saw:

> I remember I went to a couple of NOW meetings, I went to women's studies meetings . . . I would talk to the women's studies teachers . . . and talking to them was like . . . well, the women's studies teachers on campus they were on their own onda [trip], they had their own issues . . . some made me feel like I was visiting people on an island, on an individual sanctuary, where they were doing their own self-exploration . . . without any threat to their security and I really resented that, I was jealous of that . . . because I was out on the battle lines . . . I didn't feel like I could trust people who had nothing . . . who didn't have anything to lose.

Therefore, whatever privilege accrued to African American and Chicana feminists as relatively middle class, or potentially middle class, in their communities, that privilege was coupled with racial/ethnic disadvantages suffered by everyone in those communities, and the fact that they were doing better than before did not mean doing as well as whites. Since (relative) privilege coexisted with disadvantage, "middle-class" status as such was not enough to generate much of a bond with middle-class white feminists. White women became the reference group for feminists of color, such that white feminists, as white women, were a group to be challenged for unfair advantages, just as white men were. The creation of white feminists as a reference group for feminists of color to challenge, based on an understanding of structural inequality, was one reason that the potential for cross-racial/ethnic feminist mobilization was dampened from the start.

Conclusion: Structure, Awareness, and the Background to the Making of Organizationally Distinct Racial/Ethnic Feminisms

The acknowledgment by Chicana and Black feminists of their lack of privilege vis-à-vis white feminists was not a simple "reaction" to white feminism, which therefore generated Black and Chicana feminist versions. In Black and Chicana feminist visions, the eradication of sexism could in no way be separated from projects to address the economics of racial/ethnic discrimination and to eliminate the former oppression together with the latter. This different vision occurred because structural inequalities mattered on the ground; inequalities created barriers between groups of feminists from the start of their movements.

Black and Chicana feminist critiques of white feminism were replete with references to the insensitivity of white feminists to, for example, the necessity of dealing with survival issues. Their views on how to do feminism and with whom was influenced by their views on class as well as racial/ethnic disparities. Feminists of color saw white middle-class women as insensitive to the kinds of lives that those without racial and/or class privilege had to endure. In the absence of concrete data about the race and class hierarchy, these self-perceptions by activists would not necessarily be compelling; however, class differences between groups of racial/ethnic feminists were both present, as demonstrated, and acutely felt. In short, structural inequality was the underpinning of choices feminists of color made to construct groups that emphasized the racial/ethnic *and* class differences rather than gender commonalities.

This chapter began with a critique of simplistic structural arguments that failed to take a ground's eye view of how feminists in the second wave constructed the issue of structural difference. Class inequality together with racial/ethnic inequality affected the potential for feminist solidarity across racial/ethnic lines because African American and Chicana feminists had white women in mind as their reference group, and thus did not see them as natural allies in the struggle for gender, racial/ethnic, and economic justice. Scholars have appropriately focused on greater labor force participation and college attendance postwar as factors that increased the resources necessary for feminist mobilization, but the increase in resources was unequal across communities. The growth of the middle class in African-American, Chicano, and white communities increased expectations for middle-class people in all three groups, but being middle class was not a status that could be compared across racial/ethnic lines. Middle-class (or potentially middle-class) feminists of color still

bore the burden of awareness of structural inequalities that existed between their communities and the white majority. Black and Chicana
women continued to lag behind white women in a race/class hierarchy,
and emerging feminists were conscious of these gaps.

For feminists of color, structural inequalities among women mattered
more than those between women and men within the racial/ethnic community. Social locations were not (and are not) simply places in a hierarchy, although they are that. Instead, social locations are constituted
by ties to one's community and to one's fellow activists. They are loci
where various relationships of race, ethnicity, class, sexuality, geography,
and family intersect, and as such, social locations generate knowledge
for activists about the world, that is, they generate particular "stand-
points" (Naples 1998b:8). Given the class differences among groups of
feminists across racial/ethnic lines, and the construction of gender discontent within movements, rather than in the general public at large,
it would have been difficult for feminists from different racial/ethnic
communities to mobilize together on the basis of women as disadvantaged vis-à-vis men. Scholarship based on the assumption that they
should have, or that Black women and Chicanas should have joined
white feminist organizations because of gender inequality, or that they
lagged in their feminist organizing because of relative equality within
their communities, misses the intersectional quality of oppressions, and
places too much emphasis on the ability of structure to directly compel
activism.

Feminists were largely situated within movements that were becoming increasingly separate along racial/ethnic lines, and increasingly separatist. As feminist emergence in these three linked cases was precipitated
by experiences in other movements for social change, in the next three
chapters I examine the intramovement experiences of white women's
liberationists, Black feminists, and Chicana feminists on the left. Feminists on the left formulated their struggles within oppositional political
communities, which complicated feminist emergence insofar as feminists had to work to overcome preexisting political loyalties and identities. How feminists wrestled with these loyalties and identities, and
how they emerged in autonomous feminist organizations, is crucial to
understanding how second-wave feminist emergence was the story of
feminisms, plural.

CHAPTER TWO

The "Fourth World" Is Born

Intramovement Experience, Oppositional Political Communities, and the Emergence of the White Women's Liberation Movement

[T]he movement has failed to create and even more to accept a radical analysis of the problems of women. It is for this purpose among others that radical women all over the country are forming groups for the discussion and implementation of women's liberation. Our discussions have led us to the beginning of both theory and perspectives for action.

Anne Bernstein et al. 1968[1]

Introduction: The Movement Level

In 1970, Caltha Mellor and Judy Miller took a tour of radical women's groups throughout the United States, and wrote that

[o]ne of the most impressive women's groups that we visited was in a city where many of the women had been in the movement before and already thought of radical politics as their priority. . . . [T]here appeared to be no other strong movement organization so it was relatively easy for these women to take the step of making the women's liberation movement their only movement activity. Usually, though, making one thing a priority means giving up other things[;] to make the women's movement a priority means giving up other movement activities. In many ways giving up their movement activities is a lot more complicated than giving up major amounts of time in the home, at school or on the job. Women radicals have gotten a lot of support from the movement and it means a lot to them. (1970:79)

In this chapter,[2] I examine the emergence of the radical women's movement of the late 1960s and early 1970s from the Civil Rights

---

[1] From an article reprinted from the *San Francisco Express Times*, "The Nitty Gritty on the Woman Question," which appeared in *Voice of the Women's Liberation Movement* in October of 1968.
[2] The chapter title is taken from Barbara Burris (1971), "The Fourth World Manifesto," in *Notes from the Third Year*.

47

movement and the New Left in order to address the same question that Mellor and Miller do: what it meant to organize as feminists in oppositional communities. Generally, it has been assumed that white feminists drew on the resources of the Civil Rights movement and, especially, the New Left in order to form their own movement. They certainly did, but Mellor and Miller point to the central place that radical politics had in the lives of white feminists on the left; they had choices, and not easy ones, to make about how to organize as feminists and radicals. Feminist emergence, the building of an ultimately autonomous white feminist movement among younger, white radical women, meant taking resources from the oppositional community that they lived in, and doing something different. In short, radical women's access to resources and political commitments were in tension with each other.[3]

Unlike their sisters in the National Organization for Women, who were brought together by the government and liberal institutions, and who organized quickly and bureaucratically beginning in 1966 (Freeman 1975), emerging feminists on the left debated questions about how to organize in order to redress gender oppression for a number of years. Their debate took place on the ground in small groups, found expression in left movement grassroots journals, and continued well past the point at which white feminists on the left were simply demanding space for their issues in existing left groups. Over the years 1964–1971, white women's liberation emerged as an organizationally distinct movement that in many senses left male leftists behind. This protracted process of debate and emergence – in a basic way, a debate about emergence – can only be understood by thinking about twin dynamics of facilitation and constraint caused by prior movement commitments.

To date, case studies of second-wave white women's liberation have not theorized the question of the constraining aspects of commitments to a political community for feminist emergence (even while accounts narrate the debate by white feminists about how and whether to organize autonomously). Therefore, I first consider the theoretical question that is raised in thinking about feminist emergence from prior movements, namely, how feminists' investments in existing groups required efforts to

[3] The term "radical women's movement" is not to be confused with the later phenomenon of "radical feminism" (see Echols 1989). The phrase radical women's movement was used in the emerging feminist movement's first national newsletter, *Voice of the Women's Liberation Movement*, in 1968. I use "radical white women's movement" and "white women's liberation movement" interchangeably in this chapter and in the chapters following.

remake their own identities as activists. I next consider the emergence process itself: how radical women redefined liberation to include the liberation of women; how they made critiques of the Left's failure to live up to its own standards by focusing on practical, personal politics; how left hostility to feminist organizing blurred the lines activists created between their oppositional communities and mainstream, so-called straight America; how this led to a reconsideration by emerging white feminists as to who their potential audience was; and how the process of organizing within the confines of the hostile environment of the Left led to the development of new feminist groups that differentiated themselves from the mixed-gender Left. I conclude that by looking at the case of white feminist movement emergence on the left, we can understand that reforming a political community is a very different enterprise than forming one from scratch (say, from an existing institutionally based network). Reforming one's activist identity is equally difficult.

Dynamics of Facilitation and Constraint

In case studies of white feminist emergence, scholars have focused on the facilitative aspect of prior movement experience, particularly the development of communications networks that allowed emerging feminists to talk to one another about their political lives and ideas (see Echols 1989; Evans 1979; and Freeman 1973, 1975, 1979). A communications network is one of the "microstructural preconditions" that was deemed necessary for feminist emergence (Freeman 1973:793). Feminists would co-opt communications when "galvanized" into action by a crisis (1973:795). In this resource-focused model, emergence from a prior movement was a "best-case" scenario for a new movement (Freeman 1979:170–171).

But in looking at white feminist emergence on the left in the second wave – and, as I will argue in Chapters Three and Four, the point needs to be made even more strongly for feminists of color – emergence from a prior movement may not be a best-case scenario. While it is true, from the standpoint of access to resources, that there is much to be said for already being an activist in an existing group, from the standpoint of fashioning a new feminist collective identity, there is much that is problematic in already being committed to an existing group. The crises that galvanize feminists into organizing should not be read as only about male hostility to feminist issues. An active social movement community can only be established through special efforts by activists who have abandoned, to various degrees, previous commitments and communities, and come together to form new ones. The younger white women's liberation movement was primarily a student movement, and although students are relatively unencumbered vis-à-vis prior commitments to work and family life, as members of oppositional communities, feminists had definite investments that obviated – or took the place of – work and family life. Prior social movement participation was therefore a complex legacy for radical white women, since their identification with specific groups on the left, and their social relationships within these groups, set up roadblocks to their emergence as a separate movement. These roadblocks had to be overcome through debate both among themselves and with other leftists.

There has been scant attention paid to this question of how other oppositional political movements might have generated obstacles for emerging feminists.[4] Case studies have made little use of interactional theory that posits that heavy personal investment in movements increases with participants' level of involvement. As Donatella della Porta and Mario Diani (1999:17) wrote, "social movements do not have members, but participants," and once mobilized, movement participants are enmeshed in new communities, with newly developed senses of self as partially or completely fused with group identity. Participants "cannot abandon the movement without undergoing a profound reorganization of their self-conceptions" (Turner and Killian 1987:340). Narratives in the case studies do indeed point us to this question of identity, as they show how much conflict there was among white feminists over how to fashion a new feminist collective identity.

---

[4] In one problematic exception, Chafetz and Dworkin (1986:77) argue that being part of a nonfeminist "movement in full swing is likely to so tap both material and nonmaterial resources, that it retards, at least temporarily, the emergence of subsequent [feminist] movements." This would seem to be congruent with the arguments I make in this chapter. But Chafetz and Dworkin entirely dispense with movement-level factors in accounting for feminist emergence. They argue that in spite of all that prior movements gave to feminists in terms of resources, feminist movement emergence is better explained by macrostructural changes, and not what they call movement "contagion" (1986:60–62). Contagion is essentially defined as feminists organizing as feminists because their participation in other movements gave them the idea to do so. Unfortunately for Chafetz and Dworkin, feminist movements in the United States have historically been formed by women who have been active in prior movements (Buechler 1990), through complex sets of dynamics that amount to much more than contagion, as I argue in this chapter and in the chapters to follow.

Adding to the weight of personal investment in existing movements is the way in which the New Left and the Civil Rights movements were "prefigurative" political communities, where the distance between the personal and the political was collapsed (Breines 1982; Stoper 1989; Taylor and Whittier 1992). In prefigurative political communities, the end goal of the political movement is enacted in the movement's day-to-day existence; the central feature of such a movement is the desire "to create and sustain with the live practice of the movement, relationships and political forms that 'prefigured' and embodied the desired society" (Breines 1982:6). Adherents of the social movements of the 1960s established community as a political goal and demanded the "politicization of self and everyday life" (Taylor and Whittier 1992:117). The ideology *and* practice of radical "community" in the Civil Rights movement and the New Left were seen as opposed to dominant American culture, with the left community understood to consist of "non-capitalist and communitarian ... counter-institutions" (Breines 1982:7). Emerging white feminists, therefore, were situated in a movement that made claims on their time and identity in almost all spheres of their lives, such that "[b]eing radical was not just part of their definition of themselves as feminists; it was a fundamental aspect of their self-identity" (Ryan 1992:63).

Thus, although the resources were there for radical women activists to set up a new movement, creating that feminist movement required a relatively extended period of activism internal to the mixed gender Left, through "internal conflict and competition" (Mueller 1997:168). Within the already oppositional communities of the Left in the 1960s, emergent feminists wrestled with the obligations and choices that confronted them as to how and with whom to organize. These conflicts were exacerbated by the central place that women's day-to-day labor within the community played in organizing, as will be discussed.

A few years can be a lifetime in a social movement, and activists' energy is a limited resource; advantages would accrue to a movement that could, relatively quickly and relatively unproblematically, establish a viable collective identity. Narratives of emerging white women's liberation show the energy that it took for white feminists to actually *separate* themselves from their parent movements, and that will be the focus of much of the narrative in this chapter. In theoretical terms, we can think of this separation process as being about the formation of a coherent collective identity as feminists with the license to organize women as women; this is a different form of identity than just *being* feminists or just *having* attained a feminist consciousness. As will be discussed in Chapters Three and Four, questions of autonomy and separation were even more acute for emerging feminists of color, given their lack of race and class privilege. Black and Chicana feminists faced situations where their energies were crucial, and where they were aware of the disadvantages their communities faced in doing oppositional politics. In all three cases, the matters of what women's energy meant for the success of the Left and where women's efforts should be directed were hotly engaged by emerging feminists.

Redefining Liberation

As early as 1964, radical white women had developed an emergent norm of sexism – the "collective redefinition of a condition once viewed as a *misfortune* into a state of *injustice*" – within the oppositional movements of Civil Rights and the New Left by extending the idea of liberation to address gender oppression (Turner and Killian 1987:287; emphasis in original). The phrase "women's liberation" was drawn directly from the struggle for racial equality – although used initially in an slightly ironic way to illustrate women's situation in comparison to Black and Third World peoples (Bouchier 1983:52).

The earliest challenges to male dominance in the social movements of the 1960s occurred in the Civil Rights movement. In 1964, Casey Hayden and Mary King, white members of the Student Nonviolent Coordinating Committee (SNCC), circulated an anonymous paper on the inferior status of women in SNCC that was attributed to Ruby Doris Smith Robinson, a Black founder of the organization (Carden 1974; Evans 1979). In 1965, Hayden and King went "public" with the memo "Sex and Caste," circulated to other Civil Rights organizations and to Students for a Democratic Society (SDS), as well as published in *Liberation*, a left-wing magazine, in April of 1966 (Baxandall 2001). Hayden and King's memo drew direct parallels between the position of women and the position of Blacks in society, thus applying SNCC's ideals of liberation to their own status as women within progressive groups. As will be discussed further in Chapter Five, the analogy of women's status to that of Blacks and other "colonized" peoples was used by Hayden and King to illustrate a contradiction within the Civil Rights movement – and, later, the New Left – that was interfering with the accomplishment of movement goals. The idea of liberation for women caught on, and by November of 1967, a group of women activists, self-described as mostly "of the movement," published a "Preliminary Statement of Principles" in *New Left Notes*. The women, who had been meeting for two months to "discuss our colonial status in this society," argued that "[t]he liberation of women cannot be divorced from the larger revolutionary struggle" (Evans 1979:240–241).[5]

Beginning in 1965, but especially after 1967, there was an outpouring of analysis of white women's positions within New Left organizations, and to a lesser degree within the Civil Rights movement, since there were fewer white women in that movement after 1965 (Seese 1969). These discussions led to the formation of the first left women's movement newsletter, the *Voice of the Women's Liberation Movement*, in 1968; in that same year, a conference was held in Sandy Springs, Maryland, to address the concerns of radical women activists working within the New Left (Echols 1989). As these women came together to talk, as they wrote to one another, as they published pieces in left journals, they focused on the practical problems of being women in oppositional communities. Specific themes emerged: 1) that radical women resented their relegation to tasks of movement "housewifery"; 2) that they were exploited as sexual objects; and 3) that they lacked access to public leadership roles (largely as a result of the problems caused by housewifery and sexual exploitation). The liberation of women would therefore redress the Left's failure to live up to its own ideals on the level of practical and personal politics.

Emerging white feminists felt that their potential as activists in the movement was blocked by their being assigned to a "housewife" role. This movement housewife role was often described (in less decorous

---

[5] Scholars have debated the extent to which white women activists, whose numbers in SNCC grew in the wake of 1964's Freedom Summer, were stymied by gender roles within that organization. Robnett (1997; see Chapter 7) noted that Hayden and King's paper was not so much an attack on SNCC's sexism as an attempt to bring up issues of hierarchy as the group wrestled with its overall structure and direction. Hayden and King both felt relatively well treated within the organization. However, it seems true that white women performed different roles in SNCC, and that Black women and Black men held more important positions in the organization (Evans 1979; Giddings 1984; Washington 1979). While this may have fueled white women's discontent, as Robnett argued, differences in roles for white women and Black women stemmed from the danger involved in using white women as activists at that time in the South. In Robnett's view, the mischaracterization of Hayden's and King's intentions was the result of the failure by subsequent scholars to understand what Black women were doing in SNCC, and their reduction of gender relations within the organization to those between white women and Black men.

terms) as being forced to do "shit work": cooking, cleaning, and typing for movement men (Davidica 1968: no page given; Piercy 1970). Marge Piercy (1970:423, 424) wrote that the New Left was an "economic microcosm" with movement women "concentrated at the bottom"; women in the movement formed a "largely unpaid . . . labor force that does the daily work." Piercy argued that in devaluing such daily work, the Left was simply reflecting the "values of the larger capitalist society, [where] there is no prestige attached to actually working." Jo Anne Robinson (c. 1970: no page given), a Freedom Summer volunteer, echoed Piercy's depiction of a movement based on women's devalued housekeeping, and wrote that during the summer of 1964, she and other women were expected to provide perennial "maid and steno service":

> My particular Freedom House sheltered and fed an ever varying number of civil rights workers, always an overwhelming majority of men. This meant not only dirty floors and toilets and bath tubs and stoves and refrigerators, but also never-ending stacks of dirty dishes and ubiquitous piles of soiled laundry. These always were the women's responsibility.

A second critique of male movement personal politics focused on the sexual exploitation of activist women. There was a strong sense among emerging white feminists that movement men exploited them as sexual objects. In the second issue of *Voice of the Women's Liberation Movement,* Fran Rominski (1968) wrote about a proposed antiwar movement program designed to influence the politics of Vietnam-bound soldiers by opening coffeehouses near army bases, to be staffed by attractive women. It was reasoned that women staffers would be seen as "warm and sympathetic listeners" by the GIs, and Rominski warned that the program made clear that activist women were considered a "commodity" to be offered to returning soldiers, and that in doing so, the movement "remained as chauvinist as any other part of society" (1968:1).

The countercultural ideal of free love was taken to task by emerging feminists. As Marilyn Webb (1968: no page given) wrote, "the male version of liberated sex means they fuck more women – that women should get over little hang-ups of monogamy. . . . There's no freedom in that kind of sex. It's just as exploitative as being a Hefner bunny." Such "macho" sexual attitudes were seen as hindering women's ability to function as activists at all, insofar as sexually "liberated" relationships – which men essentially controlled – were constructed as a kind of "revolutionary duty" (Evans 1979:178). Piercy (1970:430) called this kind of obligatory sexual freedom "fucking a staff into existence," and argued that it translated into a system of social control:

> Fucking a staff into existence is only the extreme form of what passes for common practice in many places. A man can bring a woman into an organization by sleeping with her and remove her by ceasing to do so. A man can purge a woman for no other reason than that he has tired of her, knocked her up, or is after someone else: and that purge is accepted without a ripple. There are cases of a woman excluded from a group for no other reason than that one of its leaders proved impotent with her.

Piercy further stated that a woman who was not sexually connected with a male "heavy" would not be respected and would often not even be heard in movement meetings.[6]

Lastly, emerging feminists argued that the Left did not let women take advantage of leadership positions, with movement housewifery and sexual exploitation directly playing into the creation of this obstacle. Radical women activists like Pam Allen (1968a), Marilyn Webb (1968), and Evelyn Goldfield, Sue Munaker, and Naomi Weisstein (c. 1968:10), all of whom went on to become key activists in the white women's liberation movement, questioned why so few women held public leadership roles, and why those women with leadership roles seemed to rubber-stamp men's projects and ideas. Beyond the issue of public leadership, emerging white feminists were concerned with women's ability to participate in internal decision-making processes. As noted, feminist radical women argued that women's opinions were often not even heard in meetings, and that a vocal woman would actually be stigmatized, seen as "the movement bitch" (J. Robinson, c. 1970, quoting activist Linda Seese: no page given).

The ideal movement woman was a silent one, according to Vanauken (1971:7–8):

> [W]hen a girl does speak, how often is she listened to inattentively – or even interrupted, actually shouted down by some guy with a bigger voice if not a better idea? Or how often does the

---

[6] Roxanne Dunbar (1969:55) recounted an anecdote that had Tom Hayden describing one such sexually liberated woman as "just a groupie"; Dunbar argued that a movement male who was sexually active but unattached would not have had his revolutionary credentials questioned in a similar way.

talk resume when she sits down exactly as though she hadn't spoken?... [H]ow often does a girl sit there silent for fear she'll seem to some guy, or guys in general, too aggressive... too intelligent, too "masculine"... too independent?

Emerging white feminists linked women's lack of access to power in internal decision-making processes and public leadership to the male left style of argumentation, which was built on a "competitive intellectual style" (Evans 1979:108). New Left political debate – in contrast to that in the Civil Rights community – was highly intellectualized, in a way that intimidated many women. Piercy (1970:428–429) accused the Left of being filled with "professional" revolutionaries who spouted "monstrosities of jargon"; she felt that women in the movement were disadvantaged because they had "trouble talking jargon," and claimed that if a woman activist "cannot talk their [men's] language, they cannot hear her."[7]

Thus, redefining liberation to include the liberation of women – a process that began in the Civil Rights movement – led some radical white women activists to examine the practical and personal drawbacks of their positions as women within the Left. Emerging white feminists critiqued the practical, personal politics of the Left, arguing that women were reined in by the obligations of movement housewifery, sexual exploitation, and the lack of leadership opportunities. Something had to change, and efforts to change the Left – and presumably the rest of the world from there – had begun in earnest, even while critiques of movement sexism were being made and circulated.

The Debate over Separation and Autonomy

The chronology of written discontent – from the Hayden/King memo in 1965 to arguments made about bad sexual politics in 1970 and 1971 – is

---

[7] The need to adapt to a male style of speech and comportment in order to gain legitimacy was not just an issue for emerging white feminists on the left. Ana Nieto-Gómez (Blackwell interview with Nieto-Gómez 1991) and Irene Blea (2000 interview with author) both reported having to adapt to male leadership styles in the Chicano movement, styles that emphasized a streetwise male persona and manner of speaking. Nieto-Gómez reported being heard in campus political meetings only after she decided to swear like men; Blea chose to participate in sexual teasing and banter, rather than shrink from it or take offense, in order to get along with the Chicano activists with whom she worked.

evidence of a largely internal critique of a movement that most emerging feminists did not want to abandon at first. As Pam Allen (1968a:9) wrote:

> [o]ne of the major disputes within the movement has been whether women's liberation groups should constitute themselves as an in-dependent movement. Reaction was very strong in 1967 and early 1968 against further segmenting an already divided movement.

Radical white women activists who critiqued the Left's treatment of women were in fact split between "politicos" and "feminists," that is, those who wanted to work within the New Left's existing organizations and those who wished to form separate feminist organizations (Echols 1989). The split indicated that choices about feminist organizing were complicated ones and that considerable sentiment existed for reforming the Left in mixed-gender groups. The question of what feminist orga-nizational autonomy would really mean to the Left was complicated because of the Left's structure. Both the Civil Rights movement and the New Left were organized in a weblike fashion, reticulate and de-centralized, made of loosely coordinated and localized groups (Gerlach and Hine 1970). Questions of what the formation of new groups meant and questions of group dissolution were already matters for discussion, as were relationships between movements that were seen as being differ-ent from each other; activists were not in agreement over what forming new groups meant, or how much "room" there was for new orga-nizing. This was, of course, especially true when it came to feminist organizing.

Because they were part of the movement, emerging white feminists, especially the "politicos," addressed themselves to challenging the New Left and attempting to play a larger role within it *as* feminists. These feminist radical women continued efforts to be included within the New Left proper well past the point at which the radical women's movement was a potentially autonomous force in left politics (Freeman 1975:106–107). The questions of whether and how to be tied to the Left were important to white women's liberationists because as members of opposi-tional communities, they saw a boundary between themselves and other women, and even other feminists: "We are not the gray-suited women of the twenties but colorful members of a turned on generation of women who are asserting themselves as females as well as intellectual-politicos" (Webb 1968: no page given). Movement men, for all their faults, were the very people with whom movement women worked and were involved romantically. How could radical women withdraw support from these men who were fighting the same battles against dominant American politics and culture that they were? How could they not, given their inferior position within the movement and the fact that the male Left would not even listen to them?

The debate between politicos and feminists centered precisely on issues involving the ability of radical women to be effective given movement shortcomings, the possibilities of organizing women as women, and the possible consequences of such organizing for the Left as a whole (Echols 1989). In 1968, a widely reprinted set of arguments for a separate woman's movement was written by Beverly Jones and Judith Brown from Gainesville: "Toward a Female Liberation Movement."[8] Jones criticized Students for a Democratic Society for a resolution that argued that SDS needed to become more responsible for women's position on the left; she charged SDS "politico" women with having failed to recognize the important links that women on the left had with other women beyond the movement.[9] Jones argued that women would have to organize on their own for the following reasons: Overcoming SDS complacency on the subject of women would require great effort and ultimately be unsuccessful; SDS women tended to fall into the trap of seeing other women as enemies; women needed liberation in general, and student women could not understand the oppression of family roles; and lastly, only an autonomous women's movement would be ready to work on real issues that affected women's lives, such as equal pay for equal work, abortion reform, the burdens of individual child rearing, and violence. In short, Jones stated that "people don't get radicalized fighting other people's battles," and men could not be expected to fight for women (1968:2–3).[10]

---

[8] Excerpts from "Toward . . ." appeared in a four-part series in the *Guardian* in January 1969, accompanied by drawings taken from a Seattle position paper, "Lilith's Manifesto," which depicted the woman's liberation movement incarnated as a female superhero (Seattle Women's Liberation 1969).

[9] Jones was referring to a 1967 SDS conference resolution. Addams (1968:10) argued in an article in *Voice of the Women's Liberation Movement* that Jones made a "straw horse" out of the resolution, because the authors of the resolution had acknowledged that the analysis in the resolution was weak and mostly a "gimmick" to start discussion about women's liberation in SDS.

[10] Jones's assertion that the only authentic and effective politics addressed one's own oppression, part of an ethos of "organizing one's own" present in the Left, will be further explored in Chapter Five.

In her part of the pamphlet, Judith Brown picked up the thread of Jones's argument and took it down to the practical level, citing insults made and actions taken against emerging feminists. She wrote that radical women, even if silenced at meetings, nonetheless retained intimate (mostly unflattering) knowledge of male movement leaders; this led movement women to have contempt for movement men that would be difficult to overcome. Beyond the "familiarity breeds contempt" thrust of this argument, Brown posited the need for a new women's movement as congruent with New Left philosophy and necessitated by New Left practice:

> A respectable canon of New Left philosophy . . . is that central theme that human beings, by combining in organizations, by seeking to participate in decision-making which affects their lives, can achieve a democratic society, and hence, a life-experience perhaps approximating their potentiality. . . . Most women are integrated with men in an on-going institutionalized set-up. . . . We are all separated from each other. (1968:28)

The "each other" Brown meant was the collectivity of women; a women's collective identity would therefore require a new structural setup that would involve overcoming separation from each other by becoming less integrated with men, however leftist those men might be.

The essays by Jones and Brown in "Toward a Female Liberation Movement" were only opening salvos about whether and how to organize within the New Left. Radical white women's efforts to be included within New Left events and politics extended past the point at which feminist radical women were a force on the Left, and it took a considerable amount of time before a consensus developed regarding the intractability of left sexism. Seen from a later perspective, the reluctance to give up the dream of a united Left was actually rather startling. To take a well-known example of egregious dismissal and humiliation of feminists and feminist politics, in January of 1969, two radical women activists attempted to speak about women's liberation at the Counter-Inauguration demonstration sponsored by the National Mobilization Committee (MOBE), an antiwar organization, outside Washington, D.C. (Carden 1974; Gitlin 1987).[11] The first speaker, SDS veteran Marilyn Salzman Webb (later

---

[11] The topic of women's liberation was in fact left off the list of issues listed in the *Guardian* advertisement for the Counter-Inauguration event. At the actual

editor of the still-published feminist journal *off our backs*), began to deliver "a mildly feminist, strongly pro-Left speech" (Carden 1974:61).
She was booed by the crowd, and heckled off the stage by such eventually legendary comments as "take her off the stage and fuck her." New
Left veteran Dave Dellinger, presiding over the rally, refused to quiet
the crowd so that Webb could continue.

Response to the Counter-Inauguration a month later in the February
1969 issue of *Voice of the Women's Liberation Movement* was not the one-
sided, wholesale condemnation of the male Left that might have been
expected from such a nasty incident. What emerged in articles by radical
women activists who had been critical of New Left sexism, including
one by Webb herself, was debate about loyalties to the Left as constituted,
and about whether organizational separation from the New Left made
sense politically. In essence, the meaning of the Counter-Inauguration
debacle for women's organizing was at issue. Writing from what might
be called middle ground, Webb (1969a:5) delineated three directions
feminist activism on the left could take:

> There seems to be three distinct views on organizing and ideology
> within our movement. The first is the view that by raising women's
> consciousness about their own oppression and by working only on
> women's liberation issues raised in this manner, women will be in
> the vanguard of a revolution. . . . The second view is that women
> are a constituency, like the working class, blacks, etc. [within the
> New Left]. . . . A third position is that women's liberation must
> be a separate part of a revolutionary movement. It must organize
> around its own consciousness and its own concerns.

Even in option number three, Webb described the radical women's
movement as constituting a separate "part" of the movement, and she
concluded that radical women must "do a better job on the local level
of explaining what we are about to both men and women" – this from
the woman who was booed off the stage.

Jane Addams's article in the same issue of *Voice of the Women's Liberation Movement*, entitled "Factionalism Lives," also reflected an ambivalent, "wait and see" attitude. For Addams, the Counter-Inauguration

---

demonstration, Dave Dellinger forgot to mention the issue of women's liberation,
and announced the presence of speakers on the subject only after being yelled at
by radical women sharing the stage (Willis 1970).

disaster could be chalked up to bad communications due to the charged atmosphere of the rally, and not bad faith. She implied that feelings of "intense anger and bitterness" on the part of feminist radical women were understandable, but not entirely justified (1969:10). But other radical women writing in the same issue took a more critical stance. In an article entitled "Declaration of Independence" (reprinted from the *Guardian*), Ellen Willis (1969a:14) exhorted feminist women to "shed our movement prejudices and help women's liberation go its own way." Shulamith Firestone's barely heard speech from the Counter-Inauguration was also reprinted in the newsletter. For Firestone, there was only one trajectory for left feminists, and the establishment of an autonomous radical women's movement was a foregone conclusion for her even before the Counter-Inauguration, because she took for granted that male left sexist hypocrisy would sooner or later cause the New Left to self-destruct.

Willis and Firestone may have been ready to pull away from the male New Left, but many other feminists were not. Sue Baker, interviewed in the March 1970 issue of *off our backs* by Webb, assumed continued feminist participation in the New Left; the women's movement would be a valuable organizing tool, "getting women into the *struggle* not just women's liberation" (emphasis in the original: no page given). And in the fall of 1970, writing in *Women: A Journal of Liberation*, Clara Fraser of Seattle Radical Women concluded her article "Which Road Towards Women's Liberation?" with a prediction that radical women would unite with the rest of the Left in the creation of a reinvigorated revolutionary movement. These white feminists favored a two-headed approach; women working within mixed organizations would be strengthened by the existence of an independent women's movement, and vice versa. The two-headed strategy was also accepted by the "Thursday Night Group" of Berkeley Women's Liberation, in their discussions in 1969 about women's liberation and autonomy. The Berkeley group recognized the ties and shared goals of the radical women's movement and the male Left, but continued to organize autonomously to guarantee the effectiveness of women still working with the male Left (Weinfeld 1970).

And another left group that managed the two-headed approach for a time was the Women's Caucus of the New University Conference, a group of radical academics founded in 1969. A women's caucus existing from the organization's founding convention was formed by "a small group of the women present at the time when the issues of women's liberation were new to most people" (New University Conference, Women's

Caucus c. 1970a:1). This caucus encountered a measure of hostility
from some NUC men, but it continued to organize women within the
organization, publishing a women's caucus newsletter over at least a two-
year period, from 1970 to 1971; before that, articles about the women's
caucus had appeared in the NUC newsletter. They also established local women's caucuses at some of NUC's local university and college
chapters. While acknowledging that "women in NUC fidget uncomfortably at their commitment to a male dominated organization," the
author(s) of "Whither the Women's Caucus?" (New University Conference, Women's Caucus c. 1970b:1) argued that both a strong presence
of women within the NUC and an expanding independent women's
movement strengthened the possibilities of moving toward socialist revolution. As NUC Women's Caucus member Beth Cagan (1971: no page
given) put it, "without an independent women's movement NUC would
not be in as good shape as it is today."

   Thus, white feminists on the left participated in a period of debate
over what course women's liberation should take. For a time, feminist
organizing continued within existing left organizations and groups. The
feminist critique of left movement practices was strong and growing
stronger, but at the same time, white feminists identified as leftists, and
they wanted to change the Left. Their efforts would eventually end, as
New Left hostility made the prospect of working with men increasingly
unappealing, and as separation and autonomy became more possible
through the building of new women's liberation groups and networks.

New Left Hostility to a New Feminist Movement

The New Left, and before it, the Civil Rights movement, were not
generally hospitable forums for raising the "woman question." Hayden
and King's signed memo sprang out of SNCC and went forth into the rest
of the Left after an SDS conference in the fall of 1965 failed to address
any women's issues at all (Carden 1974:60–61). Women's issues took
a back burner in SDS to what were considered more pressing issues –
"the war in Vietnam, black power, ghetto uprisings" (Evans 1979:164–
169). The efforts of women's liberationists generally received "rebukes
and scorn":

   at a SNCC staff meeting in the summer of 1964; at the SNCC
   Waveland Retreat in November 1964; at an SDS conference in
   December 1965; at a 1966 SDS convention; and finally . . . at the

first nationwide gathering of New Left groups in Chicago, the National Conference for a New Politics (NCNP) in September 1967. (Mueller 1997:165)

One might add to the list the unsuccessful attempts by women to get SDS to take real, concrete action on a women's liberation resolution first passed in 1967 (Echols 1989), the aforementioned 1969 incident at the Counter-Inauguration, and before it, the incident in 1968 recounted here in correspondence between Ros Baxandall and Pam Allen:

> It happened at the International Assembly of Revolutionary Student Movements at Columbia. Anne . . . got up to speak about women's liberation & after her first sentence she was booed and giggled. . . . It took a man to quiet the audience down & reiterate the importance of WL [women's liberation] to let her continue. . . . [S]everal guys wrote silly obscene statements on the board while she was speaking.

Although widespread, there was nothing inevitable about New Left hostility to women's liberation, and nothing inevitable in such hostility automatically producing a new women's movement. New Left organizations such as SDS could have tried to co-opt emerging feminists by adopting their agenda outright; they could have coexisted with new feminist groups by forming or encouraging women's caucuses within existing radical organizations, which did happen from time to time, as noted. But the pervasive response by male leftists was not one of co-optation or cooperation; it was denigration, as feminism was read as a basic threat to movement agendas and possibilities for success. Pam Allen (1968a:9) somewhat generously called this hostility "the repeated failures on the part of movement men to deal constructively with . . . elitism and male chauvinism."

The source of New Left hostility is difficult to pinpoint, but one can wonder about what the fear of the loss of women's day-to-day efforts within existing left organizations might have meant for male leftists, a point that I take up more extensively in Chapter Five. Beyond the practical concerns of male leftists, Echols argued that male New Leftists were unable to see middle-class white women as oppressed (1992:21) because "class and race were . . . enshrined as the privileged categories of radicalism," and thus may have reacted badly to activists who were more or less like them and claiming a label of oppression. Certainly the arguments that male leftists made against feminism centered on the inappropriateness of feminist struggle on the left, and the potentially diversionary character of feminism for the Left. When not actively ridiculing the women, movement men took ideological shelter in the idea that women would be liberated after the "revolution," a stand which assigned the liberation of women to the bottom of the list of movement priorities (Dunbar 1968; Koedt 1968). Until then, feminism would divert the movement from its focus on aiding "the working class against the ruling class" (*The Daily Gater* 1969b:4). Feminist organizing therefore represented selfishness on women's part, an argument that, as Carol McEldowney (1969a:2) has noted, "effectively [denied] the legitimacy of any woman's self-interest in fighting male chauvinism."

I stated above that male left hostility to feminist organizing could not on its own create a feminist movement. Even more to the point, that hostility did not preclude emerging white women's liberationists from using left-wing resources to communicate, and that ability to communicate was key for the new movement's formation. The informal quality and grassroots nature of left-wing organizations and journals made at least access to disseminating ideas possible for feminists (Echols 1989; Freeman 1975). Women's liberation was often trivialized in New Left media, but at the same time, grassroots newspapers and magazines were a forum for disseminating articles by feminists. These opportunities for discussion came to be seen by emerging feminists as more and more problematic – and more and more, emerging white feminists developed their own organs of communication – but they were clearly at least partially co-optable, and publishing in them was important for emerging white feminists.

In New Left press, attitudes of condescension toward feminist organizing on the left was present from the beginning of women's organizing. Attempts in 1967 to pass the SDS resolution on women's liberation – attempts stymied by men's parliamentary maneuvering (Gitlin 1987: 370) – were actually lampooned in *New Left Notes*, the SDS national journal, by a cartoon accompanying the actual text of the resolution of "a girl – with earrings, polkadot minidress, and matching visible panties – holding a sign; 'We Want Our Rights and We Want Them Now'" (Evans 1979:192). Emerging feminists Evelyn Goldfield, Sue Munaker, and Naomi Weisstein (c. 1968) wrote about the dismissive attitude taken by the widely read left magazine *Ramparts* toward women's liberation:

> The January, 1968 issue [of *Ramparts*] carried a story about
> "Woman Power" which was filled with more condescending

cuteness, more stylish photographs and chatter about clothing, more female stereotypes, more insulting metaphors . . . more political inaccuracies than any article in the establishment press. The article was announced on the *Ramparts* cover by a picture of a woman with two tits and no head. . . . After much criticism and pressure from radical women, *Ramparts* finally accepted what was, for that magazine, an unusually accurate, concise and well-written article entitled 'orgasms', which they promptly buried on page 59, under the erudite term, Sexology. (c. 1968:11)[12]

Goldfield, Munaker, and Weisstein (c. 1968:10) argued that, in general, the New Left's media were

full of 'revolutionary' cheese-cake[;] a recent issue of *Kaleidoscope*, a Chicago underground paper, contains a photograph of a nude woman sporting ammunition belt and rifle. (Will the 'hip chick' really fight naked at the barricades?) These papers contain articles praising hippy life because there are so many chicks around to screw and the chicks can help each other take care of the kids. They contain articles which clearly assume that men are the only people worth writing for – articles with phrases like "you and your chick" or "there will be lots of chicks around."

And hostility to attempts by women's liberationists to go around New Left media was also present; as Pat Galligan (Lund 1970:9) recalled when she tried to sell women's liberation literature on the street: "I was often confronted by people I knew from SDS. And they would attack me for joining the women's movement, tell me that I was deserting the revolutionary struggle, that the women's movement would divide the working class."

Emerging white feminists on the left reacted to New Left hostility publicly and began building their own grassroots journals. They also attempted takeovers of New Left journals; some takeovers succeeded to the point of permanence. Takeovers of existing media showed both the savvy use of existing resources by emerging feminists and their commitment to the Left as their community. In 1970, half the staff of

[12] In *Notes From the First Year*, Lynn Piartney (1968: no page given) also reprimanded *Ramparts*'s 1968 report on the women's liberation movement as amounting to little more than a "movement fashion report," especially the section on radical women entitled "The Miniskirt Caucus."

the *Guardian* struck, including twelve of the sixteen women working on the paper. Denouncing the paper's "bourgeois elitism and male chauvinism," the striking workers announced their intention to replace the paper with a new national paper, one where feminist radical women could sculpt the resources of the Left to their needs (*"Guardian," off our backs* 1970). Also in 1970, nine radical women activists were arrested for trying to take over Grove Press, where six women and two male workers had been fired for union organizing. The union was seen as especially crucial for the women, due to the fact that their wages at the press were lower and their health coverage less comprehensive than men's. Sixteen radical women "barricaded" themselves in the offices of the Grove Press with a list of demands that included a halt to the Press's publication of "high-class sex books," as well as reinstatement of the fired workers (Kearns 1970: no page given).

The most successful takeover of a left journal was that of the January/February 1970 issue of *RAT* magazine by an alliance of feminist radical women, some involved in the paper and some active in feminist groups. The initial takeover issue followed the Left's tradition, first started by *Motive* magazine's issue of March/April 1969, of having one special women's liberation issue. *RAT* was taken over permanently by women after male staffers, who put together an issue of the magazine immediately following the women's issue, "started fooling around with a pornographic cover" ("A Year Ago..." *RAT* 1971). Although the pornographic cover was ostensibly meant as a joke, *RAT* was simply not given back to the men after the special women's issue, and became a forum for that section of the radical women's movement most closely aligned with "revolutionary" and anti-imperialist politics.[13]

There were times when women were able to successfully co-opt movement resources and organize within a movement framework; by October of 1970, for example, the Liberation News Service was advertising for printers and editors, proudly reporting that "for the first time at LNS women form a majority of the staff" (Liberation News Service 1970:23). But successes like the coup at *RAT* and the change at the LNS were infrequent. More typically, attempts to use New Left journals to communicate resulted in frustration, as emerging feminists had to swallow the bitter pill of ridicule in order to have access.

[13] By its last issue in August 1971, *RAT* had actually decided to eschew reporting on the male Left to focus exclusively on "women-identified news articles," as reported in an unsigned editorial. However, it ceased publication with that issue.

Eventually, New Left communications organs were made superfluous by the existence of a radical women's communications network, a network developed partly because co-optation was so difficult in the first place.

Feminist Responses to Hostility: A New Audience for Organizing

In 1968, Robin Morgan, writing in *Liberation*, responded to the charge that women's concerns, and the women themselves, were "frivolous":

> [W]hat is "frivolous" about rapping for four hours across police barricades with hecklers, trying to get through to the women in the crowd...? What is frivolous...about a woman who isn't rich enough to fly to Puerto Rico for an abortion and so must lie on some kitchen table watching cockroaches on the ceiling?...What is frivolous about the welfare recipient who must smuggle her husband or boyfriend out of the house when the worker arrives...about the women in Fayerweather Hall at Columbia...ready to form a commune that would reflect alternative lifestyles to this whole sick culture, only to hear a male S.D.S. leader ask for "chicks to volunteer for cooking duty"? (1968:35)

As seen in this excerpt, emerging white feminists more and more called into question the boundary between their oppositional communities on the left and mainstream America when it came to women's struggles. The presumed existence of a barrier between the Left and the so-called straight world was present in the thinking of emerging white women's liberationists, and slowly erased by unrelenting New Left hostility to feminist efforts. The presumption of such a barrier by emerging white feminists caused their efforts at first to be centered within the oppositional community. Had they persisted in thinking that such a barrier existed – for example, as a result of some acceptance, nominal or otherwise, from the male Left – it is conceivable that emerging white feminists would have decided that the forming of a new movement was politically unwise.

But New Left hostility led women's liberationists increasingly to question the idea that leftist men were any different from men outside the movement. This idea – that as far as gender politics went, the movement was not different from society at large – was a crucial turning point for white feminist radical women, although it did not occur all at once. Rather, over time, emerging white feminists on the left shifted their focus of attention from reforming the Left to eliminating women's oppression everywhere it existed, and they shifted their target audience from movement men to all women in America (and indeed, the world). Radical women's ambivalence about how to organize, which came from sharing the ideals of the prefigurative, oppositional community, was remedied by a growing ideological consensus that the New Left's sexism was indeed irredeemable, that the goal of a feminist movement was the elimination of sexism, broadly and universally defined, and that, therefore, organizations extant on the Left could be rejected in favor of forming new groups that would make up an autonomous feminist movement.[14]

The question of what kind of, and whether, a barrier existed between the movement and the rest of America was directly linked to that of the potential audience of radical women's feminist efforts. A participant/analyst of the radical women's movement, Marlene Dixon (1970a:10), in fact used the term "audience" to explain why the emergence of the radical women's movement was such a struggle. A sociologist by training, Dixon wrote that during the first independently sponsored conference of feminist radical women in November of 1968, there were actually two significant audiences addressed by the women who participated: "other women or Movement men." She argued that the dual audience was a result of the fact that "the radical women had a prior history engraved upon their foreheads"; their involvement in the Left required that energy be diverted back into the Left, into "arguing-pleading-justifying their cause, i.e. to fight male chauvinism, male supremacy in the [male] movement."

Dixon's concept of a movement audience – that there were people and not just ideals that feminists needed to live up to – illustrated how intrinsically linked personal and political lives were for the radical women activists. As an oppositional community, the New Left demanded a certain amount of bridge burning with former social ties; this was especially true for active participants. Radical white women, for whom the movement had been a place of empowerment, had to fight their own self-identification as members of the very organizations that had built their sense of themselves as political people. Forging a new identity as feminist radical women required that these women reorient their political efforts toward a new audience: all women in male chauvinist society.

---

[14] The question of what the universalist conception of gender oppression meant for the organizing of white women's liberationists and that of feminists in other racial/ethnic communities will be further explored in Chapter Five.

This view developed only over time, and indeed, could only develop over time, as a result of interaction, dialogue, and frustration. Firestone's and Willis's prescient reaction to the MOBE disaster regarding irredeemable New Left sexism was not necessarily immediately or widely shared until other women amassed their own interactional evidence.

More and more, emerging women's liberationists came to the conclusion that the position of women within the New Left was "no less foul, no less repressive, no less unliberated, than it had ever been" (Goldfield, Munaker, and Weisstein c. 1968:3), despite feminists' best efforts. The view that "men and women were still brothers and sisters in one big movement" came to be seen by the radical women activists as a convenient lie; movement men were just as guilty of sexism as society outside the movement (Gitlin 1987:364). As Vanauken (1971:9) argued: "The radical guys of the Movement, whether freaks or not, with all their talk about the Revolution, begin to sound like establishment types when the Revolution arrives at their own doors. . . . [M]ost radicals aren't radical enough." If men in the movement were no different from men outside, their sexism was no more forgivable than anyone else's, and was even less so for being the result of not being "radical enough." In a letter to women's movement journals, Seattle's Anna Louise Strong Brigade (1970: no page given) condemned the male Seattle Liberation Front's overidentification with Hell's Angels bikers and the sexual bravado that came from the men's overidentification:

> Michael Lerner [lecturer at the University of Washington] could talk about the availability of a woman for his bed and joke, "Well, boys, I guess it'll take a gang rape for this one." (Hey, Mike, heard any good niggerlynching jokes lately?)

In short, emerging white feminists began to conceptualize leftist men as just "men," with access to privilege based on their gender (Densmore 1971). As Vivian Estellachild (1971:40) wrote, "the hip man like his straight counterpart is nothing more, nothing less, than a predator. . . . The source of our oppression is *all men*, no exceptions for bells and beads." Even New Left men who took the women's liberation movement seriously came in for critique, on the grounds that they were unable to stop acting like men; according to Goldfield, Munaker, and Weisstein (c. 1968:4), the sympathetic male movement attitude "begins with deep concern and understanding and quickly evolves into heavy political abstractions about why a woman's movement is useful and necessary and quickly degenerates into condescending advice about how we ought to run our movement."

In contrast to the audience shift experienced by many emerging white women's liberationists, Black and Chicana feminists did not seem to ever conceptualize their activist community as different from (or better than) their communities in general. Seen from a feminist intersectional perspective, emerging white feminists' reorientation of political effort and shift in audience resulted at least in part from their privileged position in the race/ethnicity and class hierarchy. Although, as I show in the following chapters, Black and Chicana feminists debated the ramifications of autonomous feminist organizing for their politics and their communities, community as such was conceptualized as the entire racial/ethnic community in battle against white America's domination. While also being situated on the left, Black and Chicana feminists did not make the same leap that some white feminists on the left made of ceasing to see themselves as *different* from other women. Instead, from the start of their organizing, Chicana and Black feminists insisted on how they were very much like other Chicanas and other Black women everywhere.

As emerging white women's liberationists increasingly saw the proper place for women's activism as being with other women, as they started to see that the "revolution is against sexism, wherever we find it" ("Ann" in "Women and Anti-war Work" 1970), as specific loyalties to the oppositional community of the New Left waned, white feminists asserted that all women were their community. The consensus grew that the position of women as women was fundamentally different from that of men. Organizing exclusively with women came to make much more sense politically, and moved women's liberationists further away from the organized male Left.

Organizing by Women's Liberationists: Creating an Autonomous Movement

Organizing by radical women increased dramatically in the years 1968 to 1971. The first national conference of radical women's liberationists in November of 1968 in Chicago (Echols 1989) was quickly followed by what Webb (1969b:3) called an "avalanche of regional meetings." In the South, Wells (1969) reported that by February of 1969, groups had formed not just at the University of Florida, Gainesville, but at the University of Arkansas at Fayetteville and in a variety of southern locales. In Atlanta, a women's conference was cosponsored by the Southern

Student Organizing Committee (SSOC), and SSOC hired a women's liberation coordinator to establish a southern newsletter and work with campus groups (Wells 1969). Feminist women were marching against the war under their own banner in demonstrations in San Francisco by November of 1969 ("Feminist Women March Against the War" 1969).

Such organizing certainly points to the growing excitement on the part of radical women about organizing as women, but it also indicates at least some potential for feminist organizing in the New Left and Civil Rights movements. But since feminist radical women faced continuous difficulties in their attempts to use the New Left's communications network, they built their own. They stopped battling for access to the New Left's resources when a separate women's movement communications network, whose creation was spurred by the battle, was in place. Once a certain level of women's liberation organizing had taken place – difficult to pinpoint as one moment – the question of just how intractable the male Left was grew moot, as the real dynamic of the organizational emergence of women's liberation was increasingly taking place away from it. Radical women had built their own movement, and when the male Left came belatedly knocking, white women's liberationists were not particularly interested in opening their door.

By 1971, feminist radical women for the most part had dropped efforts to communicate within mixed-gender left organizations, and established an autonomous communications network. Through an independent network of grassroots journals, and through friendship networks developed outside of the New Left, the radical women's movement completed the institutional separation of their movement from the New Left. Moreover, by 1971, most women's liberationists were regarding their movement as a distinct creation, a "fourth world" of white women's liberation (Burris 1971:102).[15] Women's liberationists saw themselves as separate from the male Left, and efforts by the New Left to reincorporate the proliferating feminist movement were largely rebuffed. The relative value of

[15] The reference Burris et al. make in the use of the phrase "Fourth World" is to the politically loaded conceptual division of nation-states into distinct "worlds." The "First World" of the United States and Europe was contrasted to the "Second World" of communist countries, with "Third World" referring chiefly to former colonial possessions in the process of struggling to liberate and develop themselves. Unlike the phrase "Third World," which became and remains to some extent popular today, "Fourth World" did not seem to catch on in other parts of the Left or, for that matter, among feminists.

the New Left's resources changed for white women's liberation activists; they had grown in strength, so working within the male movement was a waste of time.

The uselessness of feminists working within existing left organizations was sometimes articulated in just such terms. For example, Carol Hanisch (1970), who worked as part of the Southern Conference Educational Fund (SCEF), a Civil Rights organization, concluded that organizing for women's liberation within a mixed group of movement men and women was not possible, because the individual promoting women's issues within a mixed organization bore the entire burden of proof for the new movement on her shoulders. Also in 1970, a group of radical, primarily white lesbian-feminist women were promised by Huey Newton that they would be able to hold caucuses at the Revolutionary People's Constitutional Convention, sponsored by the Black Panthers. These women were then repeatedly denied the opportunity to meet once there. Attempts to place a "third world woman speaker" on the platform at an evening session were stopped when Panther security refused to even let the woman into the building. Throughout the convention, scheduled women's meetings were canceled, with the exception of one that was policed by someone the women felt was an unsympathetic "Panther woman" and male Panther security guards. Demands put together by the radical women were reduced in the convention's final platform to a one-sentence acknowledgment that women had a right to choose their sexuality, and that "technology relevant to women be made available to them, i.e., *child care*" (*Ain't I a Woman* 1970, emphasis in the original; see also Elkins 1970). The radical women involved in this political struggle not surprisingly concluded that Panthers were not a viable venue for feminist organizing, and urged others to learn from their experiences.

Grassroots journals from the radical women's movements report other examples of the "we tried, but it's not worth it" efforts on the part of radical white women's liberationists. The "Venceremos" brigades traveling to assist in the revolution in Cuba were condemned by one woman who was not allowed to join one brigade on the basis of her political naïveté, that is, her feminism (Tanner 1971). In *Notes From the Second Year*, an anonymous Redstockings member lamented the inability of women still involved in a male-dominated movement study group to even hear about the possibility that all was not rosy in the personal lives of other movement women ("Them and Me" 1970). An unsigned February 1971 critique of the New York City Alternate University in

RAT assailed its "attempt to manipulate women by rendering lip-service to Women's Liberation while fucking over women next to them in the name of the revolution" ("Alternate U" 1971:16).

In 1971, Barbara Burris and others had signed a declaration, "The Fourth World Manifesto," explicitly eschewing further efforts to work within the New Left. The manifesto was printed in the feminist anthology *Notes From the Third Year*, named so because it represented a collection of writings from the self-proclaimed third year of feminist organizing on the left. Burris, a self-described former member of SDS and veteran of the Civil Rights movement, wrote for a group who wanted to add an analysis of women's oppression to what they considered to be the narrow "anti-imperialist" focus of the male-dominated Left. Burris (1971:102) argued that working with the male Left was a danger to "the independent feminist movement." Responding partially to a concerted effort by the Socialist Workers Party–Young Socialist Alliance (SWP–YSA) to infiltrate the growing white radical women's movement, Burris argued that the male Left, despite its occasional lip service, would never develop an ideology or practice that would speak to the real issues of women's oppression because "the male Left has absolutely no interest in a female revolution. Rather, the male Left has a distinct interest in perpetuating the status quo, i.e. male privileges, and preventing any real threats to male supremacy from both within the Left and without it" (1971:105).[16]

Burris and her group concluded that separate organization was the only way for the women's movement to organize, that the male Left is "so hung-up on guilt and 'who's most oppressed' that they have lost an elemental sense of justice for all human beings" (1971:107). For these feminists, by 1971, whatever positive role the New Left had once played in fostering women's liberation was gone.

Conclusion: Reforming a Community Versus Forming One

White feminist radical women initially made use of the networks of the Civil Rights movement and the New Left to come together. These movements provided the initial spaces for feminist radical women's political education; feminist radical women extended Civil Rights and New Left ideology to include a redefinition of the notion of liberation.

---

[16] See Freeman (1975:129–134) for a further description of the crisis created in the radical women's movement by the SWP/YSA efforts at infiltration.

Redefining liberation led to critiques, from 1964 on, of the Left's pigeon-holing of women into movement housewifery, of its sexual exploitation of women, and of its failure to provide women with adequate leadership opportunities and decision-making power. As radicals, emerging white feminists tried to reform their brothers on the left, attempting for a number of years to work within left organizations. Living within the oppositional community compelled them to do this. They debated how to organize as feminists as they continued to encounter hostility to the feminist issues they raised with their male colleagues. Left hostility engendered a change in thinking among feminist radical women, so that their identification with left men was weakened. If movement men could not accept feminism, then they were as baldly sexist as the rest of American society, and movement women were no better off than other women for trying to change them. Feminist radical women shifted their audience from movement men to all women in society, a crucial step in defining their collective identity and their need to organize as an autonomous social movement. In doing so, they eventually abandoned efforts to continue to co-opt left resources; they created their own networks and rendered the resources of existing mixed-gender groups on the left superfluous.

Some have argued that white women's liberation was a result of more opportunistic efforts on the part of women activists, and that white women staying linked to the male Left might have saved it. Young (1977:372) saw radical women's growing activism around their own issues as being a result of the New Left's "degeneration" as a movement. Todd Gitlin (1987: 377) wondered, "Might women have salvaged the self-destroying Left had they stayed inside it, not organized autonomously? Would they have injected sanity and clarity into a movement by this time sorely lacking in a sense of the real?" While the answer to both questions might be "yes," there is almost no sense in feminists' debates over organizing that they wanted to disassociate themselves from a weakening Left (Echols 1992) because it was weakening, and thus the opportunism/abandonment argument is hard to sustain. We do much better in actually tying New Left disintegration, whether by "implosion" or "centrifugal forces" (Gitlin 1987:377) to what many of its members – women – were doing. Feminists knew that in organizing they risked the Left's further fragmentation (one need only remember Pam Allen's words as to how feminists in 1967 and 1968 worried about "further segmenting an already divided movement"). By their critiques and their efforts to organize within the New Left, emerging white feminists showed that they considered it to be a viable movement.[17] The reality is that both the New Left and emerging women's liberation depended on the energy of women, and New Left leaders' insistence that women continue to work on issues like the Vietnam war, racial problems, and working-class organizing was an admission of just how much women's work was needed (Davidica 1968). Concerns about how leaving the existing male-dominated groups might hurt the larger cause of changing society were simultaneously at play for feminists with their doubts that much could be accomplished by and for women within mixed-gender organizations.

The struggle that women's liberationists engaged in to separate from the male Left leads us to conclude that as much as participation in a prior social movement facilitated the emergence of women's liberation, it complicated and potentially delayed it. Competing loyalties and identities had to be reckoned with through political debate before women's liberation could come into its own, and the pull of competing loyalties was even more acute for women of color situated in oppositional communities. Black feminists and Chicana feminists emerging from movements for Civil Rights and national liberation faced both gender and racial oppression in American society, making their loyalties to their movements of origin even more acute than those of white feminists, and making their links to activist men, unlike those of white women's liberationists, inescapable. It is to the stories of Black and Chicana feminist emergences that I next turn.

[17] Shulamith Firestone and Ellen Willis would be the exceptions to understanding the New Left as a viable forum for feminist organizing, especially by 1969.

The Vanguard Center

*Intramovement Experience and the Emergence
of Black Feminism*

Many people don't believe that Black women were involved in the feminist movement
and many people don't believe Black women should have been involved in the feminist
movement, and I think it's important to tell the truth.

> Dorothy King
> Harrisburg, Pennsylvania
> February 2000

Introduction: Black Feminism as the "Vanguard Center"

In this chapter, I examine the emergence of Black feminism in the second wave, a movement that grew out of changes in the Civil Rights and
Black Liberation movements of the 1960s and 1970s. From the 1950s to
the mid-1960s, the Civil Rights movement was predominantly rooted
in local community institutions in the South; women played key roles
within these institutions (Crawford et al. 1990; McNair Barnett 1993;
Payne 1989, 1990; Robnett 1997). But by the mid-sixties, the movement's social base had shifted, becoming younger and more northern;
with this shift of the movement's social base came an infusion of a masculinist version of Black nationalism. Black women were subsequently
discouraged from keeping the positions of responsibility that they had
held, and were asked to take "supportive" roles behind the scenes. These
role constrictions sat poorly with many Black women, who argued that
male activists were being influenced by a white middle-class conception
of traditional gender roles, roles that were in any case alien to the Black
community, and which contradicted the revolutionary goals that movement activists espoused. And at the same time as masculinism rose in
the Black movement, white women's liberation groups were becoming
a visible presence on the left. Emerging Black feminists were equally
critical of what they saw as white feminists' preoccupation with issues
that were relevant only to white middle-class women's lives, and thus
Black feminists attributed the limitations of both movements in large
part to their failure to maintain consistent class critiques of injustice.

Black feminists constructed an ideology of liberation from racial, sexual, and class oppression, what I call at various points in this chapter a "vanguard center" approach to politics. Since Black women were at the intersection of oppressive structures, they reasoned that their liberation would mean the liberation of all people (Roth 1999a, 1999b). This legacy of intersectional feminist theory – of analyzing and organizing against interlocking oppressions – would come to have a profound impact on feminist theory as a whole.

As in the chapter on white women's liberation that precedes it, and the chapter on Chicana feminism that follows, in this chapter I focus on Black women's organizations that self-identified as feminist, mindful that African American women's activism during this period did not begin or end in these groups. I first consider what the secondary literature says – and does not say – about Black feminism. I then briefly examine Black women's participation in the Civil Rights movement, and how the changes in the movement prompted Black feminist emergence. I next address Black feminist critiques of the class biases of Black Liberation and white women's liberation, and the construction of Black feminism's "vanguard center" political ideology. In telling this story, I consider the emergence (and decline) of several Black feminist organizations, namely, the Third World Women's Alliance, the Black Women's Liberation Group of Mount Vernon/New Rochelle, the National Black Feminist Organization, the National Alliance of Black Feminists, Black Women Organized for Action, and the Combahee River Collective, drawing on archival records, interviews conducted with former members of these groups, and (very) recent scholarship on Black feminist organizations. I conclude with a consideration of what the Black feminist vision of a "vanguard center" politics meant for other feminists post–second wave.

Where Were the Black Feminists? Looking in the Wrong Places

As mentioned in the introduction, much feminist scholarship on Black women and their relationship to second-wave (white) feminism has focused disproportionately on the question of why African American women were not more eager to identify as feminists and join (white) feminist organizations (Buechler 1990; Evans 1979; Freeman 1975; Lewis 1977; Marx Ferree and Hess 1994); in previous work, I have called this playing "the numbers game" of wondering why there weren't "enough" Black feminists in white feminist groups (Roth 1999a, 1999b). Partially in reaction to this tendency in the literature, another group of feminist and womanist scholars have argued that too much concern with specific labels like "feminist" has led to our missing the inherent feminism of Black women's activism on behalf of their race and their communities, say, on matters of welfare rights, community safety, police abuse, and education (Giddings 1984; Gray White 1999; Hill Collins 1990; hooks 1981; Joseph and Lewis 1981; King 1988; Omolade 1994; Townsend Gilkes 1980, 1994). Both groups of scholars, though, have left out a consideration of actual Black feminist organizing in the second wave, and in the past several years, there has been a small outpouring of scholarship on that subject (Anderson-Bricker 1999; Baxandall 2001; Davis 1988; Gray White 1999; Harris 1999; Omolade 1994; Polatnik 1996; Roth 1999a, 1999b; Springer 2001; White 1984).

Among the first group of feminist scholars looking for Black feminists in mainstream (white) feminist organizations, there are two general kinds of explanations for Black women's supposed distaste for feminism, the first structurally oriented and the second resting on explorations of "ideology." As previously noted in Chapter One, some scholars accounted for Black women's lack of interest in feminism by emphasizing Black women's relative equality vis-à-vis Black men, and their ensuing lack of a mobilizing feeling of deprivation around gender issues (Freeman 1975; Lewis 1977); this argument blames structure for Black women's supposed lack of interest in feminism. But the structural argument ignores available evidence that feminist beliefs can exist quite apart from affiliation with feminist organizations, because at least one survey during the time of Black feminism's emergence showed greater support for feminist goals and ideas among Black women than among white women, and if structure determined consciousness in so simple a manner, the sympathy that Black women felt for feminist *issues* should not have been present.[1]

Arguments about why Black women didn't become feminists also focus on the role that existing ideology played in Black women activists' lives. These explanations posit that Black male activists placed "ideological barriers" in the way of Black women trying to become feminists (Freeman 1975:37–43). Although simplistic, thinking about ideology

---

[1] The 1972 Louis Harris Virginia Slims poll has been cited by several white feminist scholars (Carden 1974:30; Freeman 1975:37; Klein 1987:27). Marx Ferree and Hess (2000:89) note that Black women's relatively more favorable attitude toward feminism continued in surveys done in the 1980s.

at least brings us closer to the movement level, and to looking at the relationship of Black women to Black men in movements in the 1960s. There were unquestionably "ideological barriers" constructed by Black Liberation that stood in the way of Black women's joining white women's liberation, but ideological barriers were erected by white feminists as well to the extent that the white women's movement privileged gender oppression over racial oppression (Marx Ferree and Hess 1994; see also Chapter Five). As will be discussed later in this chapter, there is considerable evidence that Black women did not back down in the face of "ideological barriers" set before them by Black Liberation or white women's liberation; instead, they confronted the barriers by setting up in the interstices of the movements, that is, by making their own feminist groups (Springer 2001).

Black feminist scholars have argued that Black women's activism on behalf of the race showed a feminist component that was both long-standing and deeply held (Giddings 1984; Gray White 1999; Hill Collins 1990; hooks 1981; Joseph and Lewis 1981; King 1988; Omolade 1994; Townsend Gilkes 1980, 1994). For them, looking for the feminism of Black women entails taking the broader view that feminism is inherent in an antiracist struggle. Since the 1830s, African American women have articulated feminist concerns within the antiracist struggle, and they continued to do so in the second wave (Giddings 1984). Black women's organizational allegiances, historically and in the second wave, were complicated by the links that were felt to Black men, and by a nineteenth-century and early-twentieth-century history of uneasy relationships with a white women's suffrage movement that was often actively racist and xenophobic (P. N. Cohen 1996; DuBois 1978). Thus, most of these scholars have deemphasized the importance of having a feminist label or affiliations, and have taken the stance that Black women's activism, for example, in grassroots community service organizations, was feminist in itself.[2] Too much focus on a feminist label meant missing the key role played by community organizations like Daphne Busby's "Sisterhood of Black Single Mothers," founded in 1973, which strategically avoided the "feminist" label so as not to become "embroiled in either feminist or nationalist ideological debates" (Omolade 1994:168).

---

[2] Gray White (1999) is a partial exception, insofar as she recognized distinct tensions created by Black women activists who highlighted gender issues and who rejected the necessity of male leadership in Black organizations.

The work by these African American feminist scholars has done much to turn attention to feminist potential in groups not explicitly defined as "feminist," but there were also Black women who felt strongly enough about gender oppression to organize autonomously from Black Liberation groups as feminists, and from a much earlier point in the second wave than is generally acknowledged. Recent scholarship shows that Black feminist caucuses started within some Black Liberation organizations at roughly the same time that white women's liberation was forming, and at least two Black feminist organizations, the Third World Women's Alliance and the Mt. Vernon/New Rochelle group, had emerged by 1968 (Anderson-Bricker 1999; Baxandall 2001; Cade [Bambara] 1970a; Davis 1988; Gray White 1999; Harris 1999; Omolade 1994; Polatnik 1996; Roth 1999a, 1999b; Springer 2001; White 1984). Black feminists came out of different organizations, fought different battles, and felt different obligations than white feminists did. By tracing the history of these organizations, this literature has refuted the idea that Black women were uninterested in feminist activism. That some Black women chose to call themselves feminists in the second wave in the face of competing demands on their loyalties and energies was politically significant, and the result of political decisions made in a complex web of social-movement obligations and opportunities. To understand the beginnings of that process, I first consider the roots of Black feminist activism in the changes that occurred in the Civil Rights movement of the 1960s.

Black Women and Changes in the Civil Rights Movement

The Civil Rights movement of the 1950s and 1960s featured Black women activists in prominent roles (Crawford et al. 1990; Giddings 1984; Gray White 1999; hooks 1981; Joseph and Lewis 1981; McNair Barnett 1993; Payne 1989, 1990; Robnett 1997; Standley 1990; Terborg-Penn 1978). Although the most public leaders were men, Black women played significant parts in the movement, both on local and national levels, contributions that were noted within the Black community at the time (see Bender 1969; Thomas 1964). Southern Black women's networks were central to the struggle, since Black women had been active in clubs and other political organizations that agitated on behalf of the race, such as the Montgomery Women's Political Council. Among Black college students, 48 percent of participants in sit-ins and Freedom Rides were women (Prestage 1980); Orum's (1970:72) survey of Black college students' participation in Civil Rights protest found that nearly twice as many women as men in the sample participated in protest (2,047 women versus 1,142 men).

Black women probably participated in the movement in disproportionate numbers (Payne 1990), filling roles that formed the backbone of the movement and exercising leadership "behind the scenes." Women were most often "bridge" leaders (Robnett 1997), using local networks to link new activists to national organizing. Their "invisibility" as leaders within the movement (McNair Barnett 1993) has been exacerbated by the tendency to define leadership as belonging only to those with public-speaking roles. For example, Ella Baker chose a place in the Southern Christian Leadership Conference (SCLC) that was out of the spotlight so as not to threaten male egos; nonetheless, she was a key participant in that organization (at one point its interim executive director) and also helped "midwife" the Student Nonviolent Coordinating Committee (SNCC) into existence. Baker insisted that women's work was at the core of the Civil Rights struggle:

> All the churches depended ... on women, not men. Men didn't do the things that had to be done and you had a large number of women who were involved in the bus boycott. They were the people who kept the spirit going. (Payne 1989:890)

And Ella Baker was not alone. Gloria Richardson, Fannie Lou Hamer, Rosa Parks, Ruby Doris Smith Robinson, Diane Nash, and Jo Ann Robinson form an incomplete list of women who were heroes of the movement, if not as widely visible to the public as someone like Dr. Martin Luther King, Jr. (Brock 1990; Fair Burks 1990; Giddings 1984; Locke 1990).

Much of Black women's energy in the movement was used for stereotypical "female" tasks, but the Civil Rights movement also gave Black women a chance to work alongside men in "nontraditional ways" (Marable 1978; Omolade 1994). Women went to jail (and were beaten there) as they handled bus boycotts, field projects, voter registration drives, and challenges to state and national Democratic party leadership. Cynthia Washington had her own voting rights project in Bolivar County, Mississippi, which she did not consider to be an "exceptional" thing for a woman to be coordinating (Washington 1979:238). Even later Black feminist critiques of sexism within the Civil Rights movement acknowledged that women have been given the opportunity "to do far more significant work than white women in their movement" (Bender 1969, citing Eleanor Holmes Norton). Omolade (1994:124) even argued that "traditional" female work took on new meaning in the "radical context and communal settings" of the movement, enabling women to become not just "wives, mothers, or maids," but also "lovers, friend, and comrades."[3]

Two intertwined changes in the Civil Rights movement of the mid-1960s affected Black women's roles within the movement. First, the social base of the movement shifted; it became younger and more northern. The southern community base that had fostered women's participation became less important to the Civil Rights movement as the student vanguard changed that movement. Second, an ideological program of advocating middle-class, traditional gender roles as a means of remaking the revolutionary Black family developed as part of Black Liberation ideology. Black women who had been active in social protest organizations were asked to become merely supportive and secondary to men.

Black women's roles were delimited as the social base of the Black movement moved from southern communities to northern cities. Southern community-based protest had relied on mature women who were part of previously existing community organizations, churches, and other "movement halfway houses" (Morris 1984:139). Students had been involved in the vanguard of the Civil Rights movement in the South, but the community was the key to student activism; the most active campuses in the South were those situated within stable Black communities (Orum 1970). In the years 1961–1965, fully 71 percent of all movement-initiated events took place in the South, but in the following five-year period of 1966–1970, only 34 percent did; this shift of the center-of-movement gravity northward meant that "strong indigenous links that insurgents had established in the South" were to some extent broken (McAdam 1982:190). In essence, by 1967 Black Liberation was "a new movement with a largely new leadership and social base," located in northern cities where the Civil Rights movement had previously been relatively weak (Young 1977:120).

In any case, the community base for women's participation eroded as the movement momentum left the South. In one example, Bernice Johnson Reagon (1978:24) saw a shift in opportunities for women as students became more central to Civil Rights protest. After her work

---

[3] There is some indication that Black women saw sexism in the movement but deprioritized it (Standley 1990). Washington (1979:239) herself felt that having responsibilities caused her to be treated as "one of the boys" by men who saw her abilities as placing her "in some category other than female." Washington also stated that "the Black struggle for equality blinded us to other issues."

in Albany, Georgia, was done, Johnson Reagon tried to become active with SNCC in Atlanta:

> I tried to get involved in what was happening in Atlanta, but it did not have the community base. The Atlanta movement was student-based, and something that I had gotten from the Albany situation was missing. I worked at the SNCC national office; I went to rallies and demonstrations in Atlanta; and I went back to Albany as much as possible. (1978:24)

Missing from Johnson Reagon's experience was a southern, community social base where women played significant roles in making movement decisions. Accompanying the shift in social base were ideological changes that would make it increasingly uncomfortable for Black women to occupy positions of responsibility in the movement.

The social base of Civil Rights protest became younger as well as more northern. Black students were increasingly likely to go on to higher education as the 1960s progressed, and very likely to be active in social protest. In 1964, there were 234,000 Black college students nationally, 51 percent of whom were enrolled at traditionally Black colleges, but 500,000 Black college students by decade's end; a 1969 study showed that Black students were involved in 51 percent of student protest activities, while making up about 6 percent of the national total college enrollment (Van Deburg 1992:67). SNCC's own northward shift followed both the passage of the Voting Rights Act and the death of most of SNCC's projects in the South (Giddings 1984:296; Stoper 1983:329). By 1966, two-thirds of SNCC organizers were working in urban areas outside the South, Atlanta being the sole southern urban exception (Carson 1981:231). But SNCC did not take hold in the North. It was unable to form alliances with northern groups, its growing militancy scared potential (white) donors, and it failed to recruit, in comparison with home-grown urban groups like Oakland's Black Panthers (Stoper 1983). The nationalist agenda SNCC adopted in order to unite a class-divided northern Black community did not work, perhaps because SNCC's focus grew more concerned with making international alliances at the expense of solving local problems (Carson 1981).

The Black Liberation ideology that accompanied the Civil Rights movement's shift to a northern, younger social base was characterized by what Giddings (1984) has called a philosophy of "masculinism." This ideological development proved crucial to the emergence of Black feminism. By the mid-1960s, integrationist approaches in the Civil Rights movement gave way to Black Power strategies and resurgent Black nationalism, forming the two major ideological components of Black Liberation. Black Liberation as an ideology was more suited to working within urban and northern contexts, and more popular with younger African Americans; sympathy for the "Black Power" slogan was greater among the young and those born in the North, whose southern roots were more attenuated (Aberbach and Walker 1971).

There were initially significant differences between Black Power and Black nationalism, but by the end of the decade, the two were difficult to distinguish from each other. SNCC was instrumental in the development of Black Power ideology; Stokely Carmichael and Charles Hamilton – authors of *Black Power: The Politics of Liberation in America* – were SNCC leaders when they began to formulate their ideas in 1966 and when their book was published in 1967 (Matusow 1971). Black Power political philosophy held that African Americans should strive for self-sufficiency and economic progress. Carmichael and Hamilton, holding up ethnic immigrant groups as models, argued that Black people needed to question the benefits of mere formal equality; to become economically empowered, they needed to turn inward, toward strengthening Black communities. Building on older nationalist ideas of self-sufficiency within the Black community, they expressed frustration at the limits of the Civil Rights agenda.

Carmichael and Hamilton were silent about Black women helping the community to gain economic empowerment. Virtually the only mention they make of women's roles was that of

> another set of leaders in the Black community in Lowndes County. This was a group of middle-aged ladies, who knew the community well and were well known. They were to play a very important role in the political organization of the Blacks. They had considerable influence in the Black community – being staunch church members, for example – but they possessed no power at all with the white community. (Carmichael and Hamilton 1967:102–103)

In contrast to Black Power's silence about Black women, Black nationalism in the mid-1960s was strongly characterized by masculinist discourse and practice.[4] According to the nationalists, the truly "revolutionary" Black woman was a supportive one, who kept house

---

[4] Carmichael himself moved from the neutral position on gender roles of his earlier work to holding Black women accountable for turning their backs on Black men by seeking careers (Marable 1983).

while the Black man kept revolution, so as to allow him to reclaim his public manhood (Marable 1983). Despite the work of Black women in the Civil Rights movements, and the very public presence of a small number of women in Black nationalist organizations themselves (e.g., Angela Davis, Kathleen Cleaver, and Elaine Brown), Black nationalist organizations such as Maulana Ron Karenga's US movement and the Black Muslims advocated restricting opportunities for activism by women (Brown 1992). In this traditionalist take on women's roles, the Black nationalist resurgence of the 1960s differed from the older formulations. Whatever tensions existed between Black men and women in activist groups (see Gray White 1999), older Black nationalism did not seem to require as rigid an ideology of traditional sex roles, as was evidenced by Amy Garvey's strong advocacy of women's equality and the key role she played in the 1920s Garveyist movement (Adler 1992; Gray White 1999; White 1984).[5]

During the 1960s, masculinism was very much present in other parts of the Left and in other parts of the Black community; for example, the traditional gender role ideology of the much-admired Black Muslims added legitimacy to masculinist ideas about delimiting women's roles in the movement (Kashif 1970). However, Black feminists (both then and now) have argued that the masculinist cast of Black nationalism in the 1960s was a reaction to the "Black matriarchy" theory in the 1965 Moynihan report, *The Negro Family: The Case for National Action* (Dubey 1994; Giddings 1984; Gray White 1999; hooks 1981; Murray 1975; see Pittman quoted in Cantwell 1971; Wallace 1996). The resurgent masculinism of Black Liberation was therefore tied to state intervention into the relationships that existed within the Black family; Black feminism in part responded to the aftereffects of this intervention. In reaction to the Moynihan report, Black masculinists attempted to counter the depiction of Black men as the most abject victims of racial discrimination, with Black women putatively better off by virtue of participation in the labor force. The report concluded that the Black family was "matriarchal" and "deviant," because women held an inappropriately large

---

[5] Garveyism was a 1920's-era, urban-based Black nationalist movement that emphasized Black pride and the importance of Africa for Black peoples. The movement's gender politics were characterized to some extent by ideals of "Victorian womanhood" (Gray White 1999:121). Nonetheless, Amy Garvey, the second wife of founder Marcus Garvey, was a key figure in the running of the United Negro Improvement Association, the central organization in the movement, and articulated a gender- and race-based perspective on Black women's position in the diaspora (Adler 1992).

amount of power (this despite the fact that Black women's status as the most economically deprived group in the country was also noted). This "deviant" family structure hindered the progress of Black men, and, by extension, that of the Black community itself (Dubey 1994; see also Marx Ferree and Hess 2000).

Black nationalists condemned the report as racist, but many responded that the patriarchal family had to be reinstituted so as to right the historical wrongs done to the Black male. With this analysis in place, Black nationalist organizations "prescribed clearly restricted roles for black women in the movement" (Dubey 1994:18). The behind-the-scenes roles that women played in the Civil Rights movement were no longer far enough behind the scenes; women were to be supportive and subordinate, producing "male warriors for the revolution" within newly patriarchal families (Dubey 1994:18). Existing Black family structures, which were based on extended kinship networks, and where illegitimacy carried less stigma than in middle-class white society, were to be changed in favor of the nationalist model of a nuclear patriarchal family. This stance on the need to return to "traditional" – even if largely fictional – gender roles in the Black community was also accompanied by calls for Black women to end their use of birth control. At the Black Power conference held in Newark in 1967, organized by Amiri Baraka, an anti–birth control resolution was passed (Ross 1993); the possibility of Black women helping to carry out Black genocide by using birth control would continue to be a hotly contested issue between Black nationalists and emerging Black feminists, as will be discussed later.

In general, then, the Moynihan report was seized upon by many Black male activists as both a manifestation of white racism *and* proof that Black women out of their traditional place were abetting that racism. As Gray White (1999:200) argued, the report "legitimized the perception of black women as unnaturally strong and emasculating." But the masculinist reaction to Moynihan also found itself challenged by Black feminist organizing, as some Black women activists, facing problems in their ongoing struggles as activists, responded by uncovering the contradictions that confronted them.

Black Feminists Respond: Early Organizations

By 1968, Black feminists had responded publicly to the Black Liberationist/nationalist emphasis on traditional gender roles. Their critiques were nuanced ones, directed as much at white society as at the changes in

the Black movement. They condemned advocacy of a patriarchal family structure by Black Liberationists even as they attacked the racism they found in Moynihan's depiction of the Black family. Additionally, Black feminists were staunchly anticapitalist, attributing the shortcomings of existing movements to a failure to carry through on the full implications of revolutionary politics.

The first Black feminist groups grew directly out of Black women's activism within the Civil Rights movement. The Black Women's Liberation Group of Mount Vernon/New Rochelle, New York, was formed out of two networks of Black women activists (Polatnik 1996).[6] Women in New York's Westchester County formed a welfare rights group in 1964 and facilitated a rent strike in protest of poor housing; in doing so, they prefigured the work that Black women would do within the National Welfare Rights Organization (Gray White 1999; Piven and Cloward 1977). In 1966, the Mount Vernon women also organized a Saturday afternoon "freedom school" for neighborhood children. Group members thus had direct roots in the Civil Rights movement, and one of the group's founders, Patricia Robinson, also had close personal links to Planned Parenthood and to white feminists, having "provided counsel and support to a number of New York feminists in 1967–8 as women's liberation groups began to form" (Evans 1979:196n). Robinson had been involved in a New York City group called Black Women Enraged (BWE), which had organized to help the family of assassinated leader Malcolm X; she had actually been in the audience the night he was assassinated (letter to Jordan/Sanchez, December 17, 1966). The members of BWE then turned to antiwar organizing, urging Black men to resist the draft (Evans 1979:196n).

Robinson's involvement with the Mount Vernon Group came after many years of activism within the Black movement, in family planning, and in socialist politics (letter to Jordan/Sanchez, December 17, 1966). She corresponded with Joan Jordan, a white West Coast women's and labor activist (who also used the pen name Vilma Sanchez) from October 1966 through 1971. The two seemed to have mutually influenced each other's thinking, with Robinson quoting Jordan's writings on the position of Black women and their historical role, and Jordan's essays clearly drawing from Robinson's experience as a practicing

---

[6] Baxandall (2001) dates the origin of the group to 1960, when Robinson formed a group to start to address the problem of teenage pregnancy.

psychotherapist (see letter, Robinson to Jordan/Sanchez, January 30, 1967; Jordan 1968). Joan Jordan was part of a group in the Bay Area, Mothers Working Alone (MWA), that was oriented toward helping poor women (Baxandall 2001). Both Robinson and Jordan were eager to apply socialist insights about women's oppression to their activism. Although middle class herself, Robinson faulted her Black militant friends for conflating class oppression with race oppression, and her brand of socialist politics included friendliness to the white women's movement from its inception, since she saw it as one part of the worldwide revolution of the oppressed (letter to Jordan/Sanchez, February 25, 1970). Robinson wrote Jordan/Sanchez that she thought more Black middle-class militant women would be supportive of feminism if they were not "too scared to come out honestly for black women's liberation" (letter to Jordan/Sanchez, April 10, 1970).

The Mount Vernon/New Rochelle Group lasted in one form or another until 1976 (Polatnik 1996). They achieved recognition in the white feminist movement when part of a position paper, originally entitled "Poor Black Women," was published as a "Statement on Birth Control" in Robin Morgan's 1970 collection *Sisterhood Is Powerful* and as a pamphlet. A longer version of the statement, as well as other position papers, appeared in *The Black Woman*, Toni Cade (Bambara)'s 1970 collection of Black women's writings. The statement appears to have been written chiefly by Patricia Robinson in September of 1968 as a response to an earlier one from the "Black Unity Party" against the use of birth control by Black women. Robinson, whose father had been on the national board of Planned Parenthood, had early on personally rejected Black militant claims of birth control as genocide (letter to Jordan/Sanchez, March 1, 1967). In "Poor Black Women," Robinson and her coauthors maintained that the Pill gave "poor Black sisters" the ability to resist white domination.

More pointedly, in an example of early second-wave Black feminist intersectional ideology, the Mount Vernon women accused the anti–birth control Black militants of being "a bunch of little middle-class people" with no understanding of the Black poor:

> The middle-class never understands the poor because they always need to use as you want to use poor black women's children to gain power for yourself. You'll run the black community with your kind of black power – you on top! The poor understand class

struggle! (Black Women's Liberation Group of Mt. Vernon/New
Rochelle 1970:361)

The authors' self-descriptions established their credentials as women
who could speak for the poor. Robinson (housewife and psychotherapist), Patricia Haden (welfare recipient), Sue Rudolph (housewife),
Joyce Hoyt (domestic), Rita Van Lew (welfare recipient), and Catherine
Hoyt (grandmother) criticized middle-class Black militants for irrespon-
sibly advocating that poor Black women dispense with using birth control. The group was dedicated to the dispersal of birth control information because they wanted Black women to have children that were
wanted, and because they felt that children represented their community's future (Polatnik 1996). Continuing a Black feminist class analysis into the early 1970s, Robinson also published a book, *Lessons from
the Damned: Class Struggle in the Black Community*, in 1973 (Baxandall
2001).[7]

A second group with roots in the Civil Rights struggle, the Third
World Women's Alliance (TWWA), was formed in December of 1968
by Frances Beal and other women involved in SNCC (Anderson-
Bricker 1999; Beal 2000 interview). A women's liberation group had
formed within SNCC to address problems that women were encountering (TWWA, "History of the Organization," 1971). As Frances Beal,
one of the TWWA's founders recounted when interviewed, the women
in the TWWA first formed a group they called the Black Women's Liberation Committee. This precursor to the TWWA had politics that were
in many ways consonant with the anti-imperialist, Pan-Africanist politics developing in SNCC as a whole. Beal shared these anti-imperialist
politics, which she developed as a result of having lived in Paris in the
early and mid-1960s. In Paris, Beal met Africans involved in liberation
struggles against colonial powers, met Malcolm X, and read Franz Fanon
(in French). But when she returned to the United States and worked
with SNCC during the summers, and then again when she returned

---

[7] *Lessons from the Damned* is still in print. The book is attributed to a collective
author (See Damned, The, as author in References), and so it is impossible to say
how much of it was written by Robinson or other members of the Mount Vernon
Group. A combination of essays, reprinted conversations, and testimonials, *Lessons*
is decidedly and simultaneously socialist, feminist, and Third World–centric in its
politics.

permanently to the United States in 1966, she became mindful of the contradictions engendered by holding an expansive anti-imperialist politics together with retrograde attitudes regarding gender roles. Putting herself back in her mid-1960s shoes, Beal recalled:

> I've become conscious of the colonial world, of imperialism, of Africa, of all of these various different things, of Vietnam . . . so my consciousness has gone from tiny little Binghamton [where Beal was born], to New York, to a world, to Paris, to a world . . . so that my mind is expanding and becoming very intellectually active, and on the home front, I'm being told to put myself into this little box. . . . And the contradiction becomes just too big. (2000 interview)

As Beal continued to explain in the interview, the contradictions that she saw generated her feminist organizing:

> It all just came together for me. Because, first of all, we're talking in SNCC about freedom and liberation and night-long things about throwing off the shackles of the past . . . but all of a sudden the voice in terms of what women should be doing, is this old one [and] for some of us, that was too much. We said we can't talk about freedom and liberation and talk about putting women down.

As Beal recalled, the formation of the SNCC Black Women's Liberation Committee in 1968 generated controversy within the group, but it felt to her like the logical next step in organizing. She, and the other women in SNCC who formed the group, encountered accusations that they were being "divisive" and overly influenced by white women. Beal and the others disagreed:

> We actually saw our feminism emerging from our personal lives and from our experiences in terms of taking up the struggle against racism. 'Cause on the one hand, a lot of Black women were asked to do things that they had never been asked to do before – speak in front of a group, organize a meeting. . . . People left their homes, they went to organize, they had to pull meetings together, they had to sit in meetings and try to discuss politics, often taking a step back . . . but people were being trained in a new way of life, and then when it was explicitly put in an ideological form that

women should step back . . . that was a problem . . . for some of us, not for everybody.

According to Beal, the Black Women's Liberation Committee went through several name changes on the way to becoming the TWWA. It next became the Black Women's Alliance, and then the Third World Women's Alliance as a result of having Puerto Rican and Asian American women come into it.[8] Throughout all the name changes, the group engaged in what Beal characterized as an explicitly political process of "consciousness raising":

> We began to talk about our roles – I'll never forget this, we sort of said "what does it mean to be a Black woman or a Puerto Rican woman?" And we said, "Well, we're certainly citizens, right, of this society in a broad sense. We take part in society as a whole. We're workers. That is certainly a strain that unites us. We're certainly mothers and family."

Through their consciousness raising, members of the eventual Third World Women's Alliance developed a politics self-described as "the radical tradition of the anti-racist movement": explicitly anticapitalist, and critical of the "middle-class style" of the Black Liberation movement (TWWA 1971). The TWWA was adamant in their insistence that Black militant men were being "white" and middle class when they enforced middle-class gender roles and expected Black women to be "breeders" for the revolution. Members argued that organizing Third World women across racial/ethnic groups to fight capitalism would "enhance" the national liberation struggle of Black people, by attracting "women who might not ordinarily be reached by male–female organizations" (1971: no page given). Thus, the TWWA established early the concept of Black feminist organizing as intersectional, with Black women constituting a "vanguard center" whose liberation would mean the liberation of all.

This intersectional stance was taken in the group's most well-known position paper, Beal's "Double Jeopardy: To Be Black and Female"; it was written in 1969 and published in 1970, in both Toni Cade (Bambara)'s *The Black Woman* anthology and in Robin Morgan's collection *Sisterhood*

---

[8] Beal recounted that some Black women were lost when the group became multicultural in this fashion; as will be noted later, Beal saw definite limits to the making of multicultural alliances among feminists (2000 interview).

Is Powerful. According to Beal, the concept of the intersection of race, class, and gender in the essay was a collective effort, although she was the principal writer and was therefore assigned authorship (2000 interview). It was written at the behest of Morgan, who wanted some sort of statement from Black women for her anthology of the women's movement. In "Double Jeopardy," Beal and the TWWA laid responsibility for the cultural ideal of Black "manhood" squarely at the feet of American capitalism. They argued that the construction of masculinity and femininity was driven by the need to sell products; Black women, who had historically worked outside the home, could not conform to the idea of a "typical" middle-class woman, staying home and buying consumer products. It therefore made no sense, argued Beal and her compatriots, for the Black community to support a system that was not designed for them, for male Black Liberation activists to take their guidelines for gender analysis "from the pages of the *Ladies Home Journal*" (Beal 1970:92). Beal and the collective that contributed to "Double Jeopardy" were sympathetic to Black men's suffering at the hands of white society, but nonetheless maintained that the Black woman had been "the slave of a slave," and that Black women's dignity and sexual personhood had always been as much under assault as Black men's (1970:92). Consistent class analysis by the Black movement required recognition that Black Liberation needed to purge itself of white middle-class goals for gender relationships, and that Black women's groups needed to come in to steer the movement's course straight.[9]

Another TWWA member, Maryanne Weathers, published position papers in which she simultaneously lambasted the Moynihan report and the masculinist desire to restructure the Black family along middle-class, patriarchal lines. In "An Argument for Black Women's Liberation as a Revolutionary Force" (Weathers 1968a:2), she argued that forming a Black women's movement was the correct strategy for building an all-encompassing movement that would liberate men, women, and children, a movement that would be "pro-human for all peoples." Such a movement would need to take into account all Black women from different classes, older women and professional women included. In her work, Weathers also challenged the "birth control as genocide" argument made by nationalists, arguing, as the members of the Mount

[9] Beal, when interviewed in the summer of 2000, noted that she now considered some of the analysis in "Double Jeopardy" to be simplistic. But as an early articulation of "vanguard center" Black feminist politics, many (including me) believe it holds up pretty well.

Vernon Group had, that the liberalization of abortion laws was a means for Black women to gain control over their lives (Weathers 1968b).

In the late 1960s and early 1970s, TWWA had adherents in New York City and Cambridge, Massachusetts, and links to other activists in Detroit; in November of 1970, the group reportedly had about 200 members and was in the process of setting up chapters in other parts of the country (Hunter 1970). TWWA members participated in the 1970 Women's Equality Day March, sponsored by white women's liberation groups (Hunter 1970), and they published a newspaper, although for how long and how consistently is not clear. Elements of the group's manifesto that appeared in the March 1971 issue of their paper *Triple Jeopardy* were reprinted and distributed by other women's groups (e.g., Seattle Radical Women). In 1971, the New York–based chapter of TWWA held weekly consciousness-raising groups, with men invited to every other meeting (Beal 1970). The group was active on behalf of TWWA member Kisha Shakur, who, when seven months pregnant, was taken into custody in New York City and held as a material witness in a case involving a member of the "Panther 21." TWWA's Bay Area chapter, also explicitly socialist in its politics, existed from about 1971 through 1980 (TWWA c. 1971). By 1980, the group had changed its name to the Alliance Against Women's Oppression, a multiracial group with a "strong class analysis on capitalism and the oppression of women" (Johnson 1980:9).[10]

Both the Mount Vernon Group and the TWWA incorporated fierce critiques of the injuries caused to women of color by intersecting systems of domination, capitalism among them. As Black feminists, they found fault with what they saw as middle-class biases on the part of both Black Liberation and white women's liberation; these linked critiques helped to justify the need for an independent Black feminist movement. Only a Black feminist movement, the vanguard at the center, could liberate the community as they worked on behalf of women oppressed by sexism, racism, and class domination.

---

[10] Beal, who had moved to the Bay Area by the late 1970s, dates the end of the West Coast TWWA to 1978, and was critical of the move to include white women (2000 interview). According to Beal, the group's politics were attractive to many white radical women in the Bay Area who wanted to organize with feminists of color. But she felt that organizing with white women in a historical moment in which white women were still so much more privileged than women of color was not sound politics, and also felt that the group's priorities shifted considerably after the white women were included.

The Black Woman, *Black Liberation*, and *Middle-Class Style*

The members of TWWA and the Mount Vernon Group were not entirely on their own; Toni Cade (Bambara) (1970a:107) wrote that in the late 1960s, it seemed "that every organization you can name has had to struggle at one time or another with seemingly mutinous cadres of women getting salty about having to man the telephones or fix the coffee while the men wrote the position papers and decided on policy." By 1970, the voices of the "mutinous cadres" of women described by Cade (Bambara) were gathered into her watershed edited collection entitled *The Black Woman*. Conceived as a dialogue with the Black movement – but unable to avoid some dialogue with white women's liberation – the book was organized out of her "impatience" with the lack of real information about the lives and politics of Black women (1970b:10). The contributors to the collection were primarily writers and activists who spoke as members of older women's groups, Black liberation groups, Civil Rights groups, New Left groups, and no groups at all.

As might be expected, many of the pieces in *The Black Woman* were characterized by concerns over Black Liberationist/nationalist reactions to the Moynihan report, and the specific failure of those reactions to maintain revolutionary consistency regarding gender roles. As noted, Beal's "Double Jeopardy" appeared in the collection; one of the Mount Vernon Group's position papers appeared, entitled "On the Position of Poor Black Women in this Country" (which, like "Statement on Birth Control," was widely reprinted and distributed throughout the white women's liberation movement). In this piece, Robinson and her group continued criticism of middle-class Black leaders as a self-interested elite leading poor Blacks down the garden path of capitalism, linking class, gender, and racial oppression as belonging to one grand package:

> Capitalism is a male supremacist society.... All domestic and international political and economic decisions are made by men and enforced by males.... Women have become the largest oppressed group in a dominant, male, aggressive, capitalistic culture.... Rebellion by poor black women, the bottom of a class hierarchy ... places the question of what kind of society will the poor black woman demand.... Already she demands the right to have birth control, like middle class black and white women.... She allies herself with the have-nots in the wider world and their revolutionary struggles.... Through these steps ... she

has begun to question aggressive male domination and the class society which enforces it, capitalism. (Robinson et al. 1970a:196)

Robinson and the group argued for a united front of middle-class Black and white women who would join poor Black women in continuing to expose male oppression. At the "bottom of a class hierarchy," poor Black women in concert with others would be able to lead this united front toward liberation for all exploited people (1970a:196).

The anticapitalist critique of American society and the Black Liberation movement was present in other contributors' work in *The Black Woman*. In her essay, Gwen Patton (1970) also argued that capitalism was at the root of what she called the "Victorian Philosophy of Womanhood." According to Pam Allen, herself an activist in the Civil Rights and white women's liberation movement, Patton sent Bob Allen (Pam Allen's husband) a draft of her piece for the collection in August of 1968; Pam Allen thought it should be published because "it would be the first time we (or perhaps any paper) have printed a black woman's objection to women assuming supportive roles to black men" (Allen 1968b). Arguing that Black male militants should be more savvy about the intent and impact of the Moynihan report, Patton chastised Black male activists for not seeing through the report:

> Black men . . . respond[ed] positively toward Black Power and could assert their leadership, which included a strengthening of their masculinity. . . . Black women will now take the back position. . . . [A] victory for the capitalistic system! Black men are now involved with keeping their women in line by oppressing them more, which means that Black men do not have time to think about their own oppression. The camp of potential revolutionaries has been divided. (1970:146–147)

Patton recommended that Black women challenge Black men directly, so that the Victorian philosophy "of men on top, women on bottom" (1970:147–148) could be destroyed and the road could be cleared for real revolution.

Besides Patton, other contributors to *The Black Woman* wrestled directly with the Moynihan report, with the Black Liberationist "manhood" preoccupation that was restricting Black women's activism, and with the effects of capitalism on the Black community (Cade [Bambara] 1970a; Carey Bond and Perry 1970; Lincoln 1970; Lindsey 1970).

Kay Lindsey's essay in *The Black Woman* echoed the idea that Black militants had been seduced by capitalist promises, and that the "Black middle class" were "pseudo-escapees into the mainstream" who had assumed "many of the institutional postures of the oppressor, including the so-called intact family" (1970:86). Lindsey argued that white establishment efforts to "encourage the acquisition of property among Blacks via Black Capitalism . . . would probably serve to further intensify the stranglehold on women as property" (1970:86–87).

And contributors also had concerns about Black Liberation's anti–birth control stance, following the stance first articulated by the Mount Vernon Group. Black Liberationist anti–birth control politics did not stop at rhetoric; in 1969, Black nationalists from the United Movement for Progress closed down a birth control clinic in Pittsburgh, which was subsequently reopened by community women (Lindsey 1970). Cade (Bambara) (1970c:163–164) wrote of attending a workshop given by a Black Liberation group that degenerated into a diatribe against birth control. She described how "one tall, lean dude . . . castigated the Sisters to throw away the pill and hop to the mattresses and breed revolutionaries and mess up the man's genocidal program." One of the women present responded with a question about the "dude's" financial responsibility in this: "[W]hen's the last time you fed one of them brats you been breeding all over the city, you jive-ass so-and-so?"

The writings contained in *The Black Woman* represented a polyphonous response to the traditional gender ideology that Black Liberationists were espousing as revolutionary; in other places, Black feminists were agreeing that Black Liberation's sexism was rooted in their unquestioning adoption of middle-class values alien to the Black community. On the West Coast, in Seattle, Nina Harding, then a thirty-one-year-old Black Studies major at the University of Washington, a mother, and an employee of the Seattle Opportunities Industrialization Center, wrote a position paper entitled "The Interconnections Between the Black Struggle and the Woman Question," which she presented at the annual conference of the Seattle Radical Women in February 1970. In it, Harding also argued that Black Liberation, otherwise critical of capitalism, had accepted traditional ideas about women's roles, and she blamed these retrograde attitudes on unquestioning acceptance of the Muslims; but she was also critical of Black "bourgeois sisters and silent sisters," who hold to "WASP standards, be those standards interpreted by the Muslim or Nationalist advocates" (1970:4). Other Black feminists in other cities echoed the idea that Black Liberation was importing white middle-class values into the heart of the Black community (Holmes Norton 1970). When interviewed by a *Los Angeles Times* reporter in June of 1970, Margaret Wright, a member of the Los Angeles Black women's liberation group, declared it impossible for Black families to be shaped like white ones because of class domination:

> [T]he black man is saying he wants a family structure like the white man's. He's got to be head of the family and women have to be submissive and all that nonsense. Hell the white woman is already oppressed in that setup. (1972:608)

On both coasts, then, Black feminists rejected attempts by Black Liberationists to use middle-class gender ideology to bolster Black male "manhood."

Not surprisingly, voicing feminist sentiments within and to the Black Liberation movement engendered backlash. As Black movement activist Luisa Teish (Anzaldúa 1981) and Cade (Bambara) (1970b) noted, there were many attempts by Black feminists to incorporate feminist demands into the agenda of Black Liberation movements, and these efforts were met with a great deal of resistance. When well-known artist Faith Ringgold and her daughters, including Michelle Wallace, tried to guarantee that a Black art show in New York City would have 50 percent representation of women (and that it would also include the work of art students), the men present at the meeting discussing the show walked out (West 1971). Wallace later wrote that increasingly, she, as a Black activist woman, was having "newfound freedoms . . . stripped from me, one after another":

> No I wasn't to wear makeup but yes I had to wear long skirts that I could barely walk in. No I wasn't to go to the beauty parlor but yes I was to spend hours cornrolling my hair. No I wasn't to flirt with or take shit off white men but yes I was to sleep with and take unending shit off Black men. No I wasn't to watch television or read *Vogue* or *Ladies Home Journal* but yes I should keep my mouth shut. I would still have to iron, sew, cook and have babies. (1982:6)

The attitudes that Wallace describes about Black women's appearance representing their politics were widespread and sometimes codified. "Alafia," the author of a 1969 pamphlet entitled "Black Woman's Role in the Revolution," advised Black women not to wear makeup, not to straighten their hair, not to drink, not to smoke in public and not to wear anything but "African attire" (1969:17).[11] A properly presentable Black woman would therefore be more inclined to participate in a real Black woman's role, which involved stepping back into the home and helping Black men to "*feel like men*" (1969:4; emphasis in the original).

Regardless of what Black feminists were wearing, their organizing represented a threat to the Black Liberationists, insofar as men in mixed-gender groups contemplated the withdrawal of Black women's energy and loyalty (D. H. King 1988; Smith and Smith 1981). But the masculinism of Black Liberation politics made it difficult for women challenging contradictions within the movement to argue their case, and the emphasis on traditionalism in the family was particularly difficult for Black lesbian feminists, who saw no place for themselves in the largely homophobic Black movement (Allen Shockley 1983; Clarke 1983; Lorde 1982, 1984; B. Smith 1983). Lesbianism (along with male homosexuality) was considered counterrevolutionary, a view shared by many Black militant women as well as men; lesbianism was envisioned as coming from outside the Black community, much like an infection or contagious disease caught from white women (Marable 1983).

This briefly summarized view of many Black Liberationists, that Black feminist organizing was antirevolutionary and diversionary, did not stop feminist organizing by some Black women. But neither did it drive those Black women into the political arms of white women's liberationists. Black feminists were equally critical of the neglect by white women's liberation of race *and* class oppression, and even though the political rejection of white women's liberation by Black feminists was never total – as indicated by some of the relationships noted between Robinson and Jordan/Sanchez, between Beal and Morgan, or between Patton and Allen – relationships with organized white women's liberation groups were troubled ones for Black feminists, for the reasons I now address.

Responses to White Women's Liberation

Black women did hold ambivalent attitudes toward white women's liberation as an organized movement, although, as noted, their general

---

[11] Alafia is particularly harsh – and homophobic – when it comes to "western attire," stating that pants and other kinds of non-African clothing "were designed by white faggots for devil women" (c. 1969:16).

hostility to feminist issues has been greatly exaggerated (Cantwell 1971; Conley 1970; Ferguson 1970; Morrison 1971; Smith Reid 1972; Washington 1979). An unsigned editorial on feminism in Chicago's *Daily Defender* (1970) made the split clear; one Black woman is quoted as saying that Black women cannot remain outside the feminist movement because of its importance, while another states that women's liberation has no significance for Black women. In mainstream accounts, Black women's ambivalence to feminism became a kind of trope, such that Black women hostile to feminism were always quoted along with the views of well-known "liberal" Black feminists, such as civil rights lawyer Flo Kennedy (see "Blacks v. Feminists," *Time*, March 26, 1973).

In fact, the ambivalence of Black activist women toward organized white feminism was just that: a hesitancy to work with white women exclusively on gender (and not race, and not class) oppression. This resistance to organizing in white feminist groups was exemplified in Inez Smith Reid's *"Together" Black Women* (1972). She interviewed 202 self-defined "militant" and mostly college-educated Black women from all parts of the United States, selecting them for their "reputation in the community for militancy" (1972:x). Although many of Smith Reid's respondents were in favor of more "egalitarian" gender roles in the Black movement, they were wary of white women's liberation (1972:70). Respondents feared the "co-optation or subordination of Black liberation goals through a merger of interests with women's liberation," since this would mean abandoning efforts on behalf of Black liberation (1972:53). They also feared that women's liberation could undermine relationships between Black men and women. Nonetheless, Smith Reid's respondents emphasized support for some goals of the white women's movement, especially those "which touch[ed] on the functioning of the total American system" (1972:54). They felt that any rationale for joint work between white and Black women would have to be built on bread-and-butter employment issues, and they were rather less concerned with the "personal" kinds of debates that white women were seen to be engaged in over the cultural meaning of womanhood.

Other Black women activists were sympathetic to the feminist struggle but leery of white feminists themselves. What Steven Buechler (1990:134) has termed white feminists' "class" and "race unconsciousness" was repeatedly raised by Black women activists as a hurdle to organizing with white feminists, and the personal cost of having constantly to reframe issues and reeducate white feminists about the reality of life in the Black community was more than many feminist-identified

Black women wanted to take on. Althea Scott, a feminist-identified radiology technician and local television host interviewed by the *Los Angeles Times* in 1973, said that she preferred to meet with Black feminist friends because racism was a daily part of her life, and she had no desire to seek out more in political work, telling her interviewer, "[i]f I called them out every time they [white feminists] hurt me, we wouldn't get anything accomplished" (Liddick 1973:16). Scott's view was that she could be allied with white feminists while working apart from them: "We don't have to be Siamese twins to be sisters." And she emphasized the existing class divide between white women and Black women, arguing that "[w]hite women were groomed to be ladies. I came from a history of women groomed to be workers."

The idea that white women's liberationists could not shake the class privilege of "ladydom" was earlier argued by Toni Morrison (1971). She saw white feminists as blind to the material reality of Black women's lives, oblivious to the fact that white women wanted the kind of "freedom" – to work, to be responsible for themselves – that Black women had always had. But as critical as Morrison was, she speculated that the appearance of prominent Black women within the ranks of white women's liberation might broaden the movement so that it would one day be fighting for a more broadly based set of rights, which included economic survival. Survival issues proved compelling enough so that many Black women activists in the 1960s simply chose to organize around class issues rather than primarily over issues of gender, or even race. The National Welfare Rights Organization (NWRO), which held its founding convention in 1967, drew poor Black women whose primary identification was as poor women (Gray White 1999). The NWRO was headed for most of its life by a Black man, George Wiley, although the membership was primarily Black women, who saw the main purpose of the group as advocacy for the poor, who happened to be disproportionately Black and female. But the NWRO experienced fatal schisms when those poor Black women asked for greater power within the group, and the tensions engendered by those requests contributed to more feminist interpretations of power dynamics by the time Johnnie Tillmon took over as executive director in 1973. Unfortunately, with Tillmon at the helm, private donations by "foundations and church groups" dried up, and the NWRO was basically moribund by 1975 (Gray White 1999:242).

Black women activists who did begin to identify and organize as feminists addressed themselves to white feminists' class and race unconsciousness in several ways. First, Black feminists argued that the white feminist agenda did not link gender oppression with other kinds of oppression. Second, Black feminists saw white feminists as overly concerned with cultural change at the expense of economic change. Third, many Black feminists criticized white feminist conceptions of the need to alter the nuclear family as insufficiently cognizant of how many in the Black community saw the Black family itself as threatened (especially in the aftermath of the Moynihan report).

Most Black feminists saw white women's liberationists as having failed to make the links between gender and race and class oppression that Black feminists were intent on making; regardless of how many Black feminists may have come from middle-class backgrounds within their own communities, they were disadvantaged vis-à-vis the white middle class, and thus they repeatedly cited white feminism's middle-class character as a reason for Black women to form their own groups (Hunter (1970).[12] The perception that white feminism lacked a class critique was the key obstacle to a joint Black and white feminist struggle.[13] For example, Black feminist Dorothy Pitman, a community organizer, was sympathetic to women's liberation but felt that "I can't really say I'm a sister to white women, unless they recognize how they also were oppressive in a capitalistic situation" (Cantwell 1971:183). Pitman, who was also critical of Black Liberation, thought that white women needed a class analysis of oppression in order to understand how their class privilege contributed to the oppression of Black women; without such an analysis, Pitman argued, white women would not be able to do much for Black women's liberation. Sisters Barbara Smith and Beverly Smith (1981) saw class privilege as responsible for white feminist insensitivity to the hardships that even so-called middle-class Black women endured. The Smith sisters especially challenged what they saw as some white middle-class women's "arrogance" in seeing downward mobility as a measure of the correctness of their politics, arguing that material comfort had a very different meaning for Black women, who had to struggle for it and did not take it for granted (1981:113).

Related to the criticism of white feminists' class unconsciousness was the Black feminist perception of the tendency in white feminist politics

---

[12] As noted in Chapter One, there was a postwar narrowing of individual Black and white working women's income; but by 1970, the median money income of all Black female workers was still 15 percent lower than that of white female workers ($3,285 and $3,870, respectively) (U.S. Bureau of the Census 1975:304).

[13] There were white socialist feminist groups who were unfairly tarnished with the class "unconsciousness" brush. The failure of white socialist feminist and Black feminist groups to link up can be explained in part by the second-wave ethos of "organizing one's own," which will be furthered explored in Chapter Five.

to elevate cultural complaints over economic issues. In a satirical "play," Lorna Cherot (1970:16), a self-described "'straight' black woman," critiqued what she saw as the obsession of the white women's movement with body image, women loving women, and the like. Her response to the calls for sisterhood – calls that she agreed with in principle – was "I'll love you when my belly is full, there's clothes on my back and shelter over me." And in articles that appeared in the Philadelphia women's liberation newsletter *Women* (Philadelphia Area Women's Liberation 1970), Black feminists criticized the (white) women's liberation program of abortion on demand, divorced from other issues of reproductive rights that were directly tied to class and racial status: involuntary sterilization, life circumstances that compel poor women to abort, and the possibility that women on welfare would be forced by the state to have abortions. The author(s) argued that if white feminists really cared about having an impact in communities of color, they would expand reformist policies into a commitment to destroy the economic system.

Lastly, Black feminists were ambivalent about white women's liberation because they had very different perceptions of the meaning of struggles surrounding the family (Polatnik 1996). Many white feminists wanted to take the nuclear family apart; Black women and Black feminists saw a Black family under attack via the Moynihan report. The white feminist movement was seen as trying to destroy a family structure that Black feminists were trying to protect, even if their vision for the family differed from the patriarchal version espoused by Black Liberationists (Dubey 1994; Ferguson 1970; hooks 1984). Unlike white women, many of whom experienced family obligations as a primary locus of exploitation, most Black women found that the family was the least oppressive institution in their lives and constituted a refuge from domination by white racist institutions outside (White 1984). Middle-class white feminist demands to work outside the home did not resonate strongly with Black women, who had never been excluded from the privilege of working to support their families (Lewis 1977). Additionally, as bell hooks (1981) noted, it was easier to deconstruct the family when outside institutions (i.e., government) were on one's side. Black women, poorer as a group, could not rely on such institutional support, nor could they rely on class privilege that could buy middle- or upper-class white women out of the responsibilities of family by hiring other (poor, nonwhite) women to do the work for them (hooks 1981; Morrison 1971).

As a result of race and class oppression, motherhood itself had different meanings for Black and white women, and thus for Black and white feminists (Polatnik 1996). Middle-class, suburban white feminist activists saw becoming a mother as tantamount to being doomed to living a 1950s-style suburban housewife role. Coming from less prosperous and more urban backgrounds, Black feminists knew that alternative styles were possible; in the urban Black community, "othermothering" and a generally more communal style of child rearing existed. Black feminists did not reject the positive role for Black women as the mothers of future Black generations (accepting part of Black Liberation's emphasis on the importance of producing Black children); instead, they argued for choice and control over motherhood, in the manner of the Mount Vernon/New Rochelle Group.

Thus, rather than being uniformly hostile to feminism, Black feminists were sympathetic to some aspects of white feminist struggle, but not terribly interested in organizing within (or, really, even with) white feminist groups on the basis of what they saw as problems with white feminist politics. They were wary of joining white women's liberation groups that paid insufficient attention to the links between gender, racial, and especially class oppression. Critical of the middle-class bias of both liberation movements, Black and white, Black feminists therefore found themselves maneuvering in the interstices between the two (Springer 2001). Having developed a political ideology of countering race, class, and gender oppression, Black feminists had to decide how to organize "the vanguard center," and I turn to these efforts next.

Black Feminist Organizing Within/Outside the Black Movement: Questions of Autonomy

Black feminists faced a "quandary of . . . how best to distribute their energies among . . . issues and what strategies to pursue [to] minimize conflicting interests and objectives" (Murray 1975:357). They had constructed the ideological rationale for autonomous organizing – positing Black women as being at the center of interlocking oppressions of race, class, and gender. Since Black women were the most deprived group in the United States, their liberation would constitute the liberation of all, in a way analogous to that of a rising proletariat wiping away the evils of class domination. But while ideological consensus and organizational momentum for forming the "vanguard center" grew, Black feminist activists still found themselves caught between movements, practicing "interstitial politics" (Springer 2001).

As for the white feminists considered in Chapter Two, asserting a feminist politics did not erase political investments that Black feminists had made. As members of an oppressed community with limited resources, they found issues of potential disloyalty and destruction of movement unity particularly acute. Many Black women were able to carve out a role for themselves as female "warriors" within the movement, finessing the space between ideological calls for restricted roles for women with the bottom-line need for women to keep social movement organizations going through daily and hands-on labor (Omolade 1994:166). For example, despite conflict over their roles, many women in the Black Panther Party saw their work within that group as aiming toward a revolution that would free both women and men ("Panther Sisters on Women's Liberation" 1969; F. A. Smith 1970).[14] Feminist practice was certainly not typical of daily Panther life, but feminist ideas made some inroads into the group (perhaps as a result of their socialist politics), and the Panthers adopted a progressive stance on gender oppression and, notably, on gay rights (Newton 1970). The Panthers were also an exception to the "birth control as genocide" Black Liberation credo, although the pro–birth control policy was controversial within the group itself (Ross 1993). In general, though, the Black Panther Party was no feminist haven, despite the presence of strong, committed women. Elaine Brown (1992), who rose to chairmanship of the party in 1974, reported being forced to wait to eat at meetings until men had finished; remarks were made to her about not wearing short skirts, and she was automatically expected to do kitchen duty. As a party member, Brown rejected autonomous organizing by Black women, and noted that Panther women "had no intention, however, of allowing Panther men to assign us an inferior role in our revolution" (1992).[15]

Unlike Panther women, Black feminists who espoused socialist politics felt that Black women's position as the most oppressed members of society mandated autonomous organizing ("Black Women's Liberation Is a Component Part of Black People's Liberation" 1975; "L.D., black student" 1970; Newman 1970; Williams 1970). Maxine Williams, a

[14] See Matthews (1998) for her view that the Panthers' sexual politics were much better than those of other Black Liberationist groups like Karenga's Los Angeles–based US.

[15] In her autobiography, Brown (1992:357) argued that in retrospect, the Panther women who aspired to leadership were seen as "making an alliance with the 'counter-revolutionary, man-hating, lesbian, feminist white bitches.'" Her acceptance of the chairmanship of the party rested on her conviction that she had to "muster something mighty" (1992:357) to keep the Panthers going. She eventually left the group with the conviction that both racism and sexism oppressed Black women, and that therefore both had to be defeated for their liberation.

member of the Socialist Workers Party, wanted an autonomous Black women's movement that would work for the "complete destruction of this racist, capitalist, male-dominated system" (1970:11). To that end, she was not terribly interested in matters of white women's personal racism, stating that "white women sitting around a room, browbeating one another for their 'racism' saying, 'I'm a racist, I'm a racist' . . . is not doing a damn thing for black women. What is needed is action." Williams's writings were reprinted with those of Pamela Newman, a member of the Black Students Union at Overbrook High School in Philadelphia, who agreed with Williams's take on Black women's autonomous organizing, and argued that such a movement could destroy capitalism and male chauvinism at the same time:

> The total working class must be liberated, including the women, and of course the black woman shall have to be liberated **first** because of the multi-oppression which she suffers. . . . Black women's liberation could not and will not be a diversion from the liberation of our people. The organization of black women to fight for our needs as well as the needs of all black people will intensify the struggle. (Newman 1970:15; emphasis in original)

Williams and Newman represented the "harder" formulations of Black feminism as the vanguard center of liberation. Milder conceptualizations of "vanguard center" Black feminism leaked through to both the mainstream press and Black press. In 1971, *Essence* magazine, whose editor Sheila Young would be quoted in *Time* magazine in 1973 as dismissing the class-bound focus of white feminism, published an interview with Aileen C. Hernández, the second president of NOW and a longtime activist in labor politics and civil rights policy (Lewis and Hernández 1971). Hernández, who was one of the first commissioners of the federal Equal Employment Opportunity Commission, used the interview to argue for a serious Black feminism that would incorporate the issues women had as workers. The vision of Black women seeking an end to the intertwined evils of racial and gender oppression surfaced even when reporters sought to explain Black women's supposed hostility to feminist organizing (Liddick 1973; "Blacks v. Feminists," *Time*, March 26, 1973). In the early 1970s, then, activists and others saw a space existing for Black feminist organizing, even if it was not the most comfortable one possible.

In May of 1973, the National Black Feminist Organization, or NBFO, was founded to fill the Black feminist space. Its founding and relatively short life constituted the most ambitious attempt at Black feminist organizing up to that point. The NBFO grew out of a series of meetings of about thirty Black women in New York City who wanted feminism to speak directly to the multiple sources of oppression that Black women faced (Buechler 1990:155–156; Davis 1988; Freeman 1975; Giddings 1984:344; Lewis 1977; Springer 2001). In August of 1973, the group held a press conference to announce its existence (Adams 1973; Davis 1988; Fulman 1973; Springer 2001). According to a number of sources, the NBFO received more than 400 phone calls after announcing their formation (Davis 1988; Galvin-Lewis 2000 interview; Springer 2001). Flo Kennedy, Gloria Steinem, and Aileen Hernández of NOW were reported by the NBFO to be in support of the group's formation (NBFO 1973a).

The announcement of the NBFO – which was, in fact, not at that point a national organization, or any sort of organization at all – touched a serious nerve, and the response was tremendous. Many Black women had thought they were alone in their feminist discontent; others had already been talking about the idea of forming a national feminist organization, like NOW, for Black women (Davis 1988; Eichelberger 1999a interview; Galvin-Lewis 2000 interview; Gray White 1999). The response to the formation of the NBFO actually refuted the idea of Black women's hostility to feminist issues and completed a full circle whereby NOW, inspired by those who felt there should be a kind of NAACP for women, further inspired Black feminists connected with NOW to form their own group.[16] NOW itself had participating minority members, and it elected Hernández, a Black woman, as its second president; still, the organization had trouble reaching Black women. Hernández felt that NOW failed to understand links between sexism and issues of poverty, and that NOW luminaries like Friedan, who "had the right motivations," lacked connections to communities that would enable NOW to form coalitions on survival issues (2000 interview). Moreover, Hernández noted that when she was president of NOW, she had been required to spend her own money to support her activism, and had only been able to

[16] According to Aileen Hernández, "Pauli Murray had been interviewed in New York City by the *New York Times*, about the fact that the commission was not making many decisions on sex discrimination, and what she said was 'well, if women want anything done, they're going to have to organize something like an NAACP to put the pressure on'" (2000 interview). Hernández believes that Betty Friedan and others had read about Murray's statement, and were thus prepared to form NOW when the opportunity presented itself at the Third National Conference of Commissions on the Status of Women in 1966 (Freeman 1975).

do her work because she was a self-employed consultant who could squeeze NOW into the margins as she traveled. As such, NOW's reliance on volunteers in positions of authority was not amenable to the recruitment of Black and other racial/ethnic women from poorer communities.[17] Therefore, the NBFO was organized to fill the breach created by NOW's failure to address the needs of Black women and poor women.

Jane Galvin-Lewis, one of the NBFO's founders, confirmed that the idea of forming a Black feminist group modeled on NOW had been "floating around" her group of feminist-identified Black women in New York City (2000 interview). She and another NBFO founder, Margaret Sloan, discussed having a national Black feminist group, and, according to Galvin-Lewis, they were urged to gather women together by Flo Kennedy:

> One day we went by Flo's – which was always a dangerous thing to do – and Flo said, "I'm so sick and damn tired of hearing you bitches running around here, talkin' about you gonna form something. Form it! Call a meeting!" . . . Then we had some meetings. It was very, very ironic, our first meeting was in a beauty parlor, because one of the women that was in our little core group . . . her cousin had a beauty parlor . . . and it had a big back room, they'd play cards back there. . . . I thought it was wonderful because the beauty parlor has been the hub of Black activity for years. (2000 interview)

The group outgrew the beauty parlor and began to meet in school classrooms and churches. Galvin-Lewis also credited Kennedy with suggesting that the group go beyond these meetings and publicize its existence nationwide: "Flo said, 'Have a press conference! That's what you need to do! Let people know you're there! You all know you're there!'"

According to Galvin-Lewis, Eleanor Holmes Norton was then contacted and asked to write a statement for the August press conference that announced the NBFO. Holmes Norton also made herself available to the press for interviews. After the press conference, Galvin-Lewis reported that the group was in no way prepared for the hundreds of phone

---

[17] On a further note about NOW's class bias, Murray, who had helped to found the organization, broke with NOW over its selection of the Equal Rights Amendment as a primary objective (Hartmann 1998). Murray saw the selection of the ERA as a target as class based, and reminiscent of earlier suffrage battles that had prioritized getting the vote for white women over getting it for Blacks. Although she kept her membership in NOW into the 1970s, she ceased to play a major role in the organization after 1967.

calls they received:

> We thought we were going to have about twenty-five phone calls
> and we said . . . if we could get enough people together, we were
> going to try to have a conference in the spring. If we could get
> enough people, and if we could get the money, maybe we would
> have regular meetings like every other week or something like
> that. . . . The phones rang for about a week. Solid. I mean literally,
> I am not kidding you. [She demonstrates putting down a phone,
> hearing it ring and picking it up, putting it down and hearing it
> ring, and picking it up again.] Unbelievable. And we were shell-
> shocked. I mean we did not know what to do with ourselves. (2000
> interview)

Galvin-Lewis was particularly impressed by calls that came from as far
away as California, and calls that included women who offered to become
local organizers and presidents of NBFO chapters. Many of these women
offered to come to the as-yet-unplanned conference and to raise money
locally. What the NBFO organizers had inadvertently tapped into was
an unorganized, decentralized set of local groups of Black feminists doing
consciousness raising at the local level, like the aforementioned Althea
Scott and her five feminist friends in Los Angeles (Liddick 1973; see
also Campbell 1973). Galvin-Lewis characterized the response and the
new knowledge of the possibility of a mass Black feminist movement
as simultaneously thrilling and daunting: "It was wonderful, but it was
very frightening. . . . And we did have a conference, we had a wonderful
conference at St. John the Divine and it was just glorious and for the
first time, at least, in that century, Black women had a feminist voice."

Among those who were excited about the forming of the NBFO was
Brenda Eichelberger, a Chicago-based public high school counselor, who
in the early 1970s had thought she was "the only black feminist in the
world" until she read about the NBFO in Ms. magazine in May of 1974
(Eichelberger 1999b). In another local example of decentralized Black
feminist activism, Eichelberger had already started a group among her
students to discuss women's issues. She contacted the NBFO in New York
City, in May of 1974, writing Margaret Sloan (letter, May 11, 1974) and
asking to form a Chicago chapter. She noted that

> prior to reading that article, I thought I was the only black woman
> on the planet Earth who felt the way I felt. . . . It sounds ridiculous

to say that, but all the black women at the time, with whom I
came in contact seemed very male-defined, very male-oriented –
all their time was taken up with trying to get a man and get married.
(1999a interview)

New York City NBFO put Eichelberger in touch with other interested
Black women in the Chicago area, as an NBFO chapter in Chicago, with
Linda Johnson as a contact person, had begun to form. Eichelberger and
Johnson had a "long conversation," after which Eichelberger called an
NBFO meeting, drawing from the NBFO list and her own social circle:

> I not only invited women I knew...but I invited women I
> didn't know too well. I invited women who were doing things,
> women who were active ... within the Black community and just
> in general as well. These would be the type of women to get
> involved.... They were already active. (1999a interview)

Eichelberger found much opposition to the idea of creating a Black
feminist group at this first meeting, and minutes from the meeting show
that a great deal of discussion took place about whether or not the
group should call itself "feminist" (NBFO minutes, June 19, 1974). But
Eichelberger herself was adamant that the feminist label was accurate
and necessary; her personal definition of feminism was "just talking about
a person living to the fullest of one's capacity" (1999a interview). By
the next meeting the issue had been resolved, and the group became
engaged in trying to become the Chicago chapter of the NBFO (and, as
will be discussed, the Chicago chapter of the NBFO eventually became
the National Alliance of Black Feminists, headed by Eichelberger).[18]

The NBFO sponsored an Eastern Regional Conference at St. John
the Divine, a large church/community center on the Upper West Side

---

[18] The question of what the label "feminist" meant to Black women was not really as
neatly resolved as Eichelberger may have wished it to be. In order to be recognized
by the national NBFO, a local group had to label itself "feminist"; some present
felt that under those circumstances, joining was not an option. Eichelberger had
to resolve the impasse by promising to "poll" meeting attenders after the meeting
regarding the use of the word "feminist" as part of the group's self-description.
By the next week (NBFO minutes, June 26, 1974), the eighteen women who
attended all agreed to use the word, since "all in attendance were either pro the
term or impartial to it." One has to wonder who did not show up for the second
meeting.

of New York City at the end of November and beginning of December 1973. The organizers invited attenders to address themselves to the needs of Black women in "Amerikkka" (NBFO 1973b), and about 400 women came (Lewis 1977). The membership of the NBFO at that point was diverse and included "women from a wide range of ages and occupations" (Freeman 1975:156–157; see also Davis 1988 on this point). Margaret Sloan and Margo Jefferson, in a letter to *Encore* magazine defending the NBFO from Black critics, characterized the membership of the NBFO as consisting of "students, housewives and a variety of working women, including household technicians [domestic workers], lawyers, artists, students, secretaries, and welfare mothers" (Jefferson and Sloan 1974:46–47). The NBFO's attempts to be inclusive of all Black women showed in the ambitious roster for the regional meeting, which listed workshops on sex-role stereotyping and the Black child; Black feminists and the labor force; the triple oppression of the Black lesbian; Black feminist input in politics; Black feminists and the cultural arts; abortion and forced sterilization; female sexuality; the image of the Black woman in the media; Black women as consumers; the incarcerated Black woman; Black female addiction; Black female self-image; Black female rape; Black women and the women's rights movement; and Black women and welfare (NBFO 1973c).[19]

The Black feminists of the NBFO wanted to remedy the idea that women's liberation was irrelevant to Black women, and to Black Liberation in general. NBFO literature stressed the crucial role that Black feminism could play in helping to achieve real liberation for all Black people. The authors of the group's "Statement of National Black Feminist Organization" (c. 1973; no page given) insisted that Black feminists could "lend enormous credibility" to the women's movement, but would more importantly

> strengthen the current efforts of the Black Liberation struggle in this country by encouraging *all* of the talents and creativities of Black women to emerge. . . . We will encourage the Black

---

[19] The NBFO activist agenda represents a mindfulness of the concerns that Black women community activists generally had (Myers 1999; Naples 1991, 1998a; Omolade 1994; Townsend Gilkes 1980, 1994). Community activist groups also, in some circumstances, drew closer to feminism; see Gray White (1999) and Tait (1999) on the National Welfare Rights Organization members' growing discontent with male leadership and incorporation of feminist analysis into welfare rights struggles.

community to stop falling into the trap of the white male Left, utilizing women only in terms of domestic or servile needs. We will remind the Black Liberation Movement that there can't be liberation for half a race.

The NBFO's politics was also rooted in a "vanguard center" critique of domination, although the NBFO's anticapitalist rhetoric was rather muted compared to that of earlier Black feminist groups like the Third World Women's Alliance and the Mount Vernon Group. Their guide for members, "Standard Questions You Might Be Asked – Suggested Answers That Might Work" (1975a), nonetheless used a class-based rhetoric in addressing what the group considered to be the shortcomings of the "middle-class men" in the Black Civil Rights movement, and their traditional gender-role expectations. The group stressed economic survival issues continuously in its position papers, and committed itself to addressing the problems of working-class and welfare-reliant Black women. Although structurally bureaucratic in nature, the NBFO's central coordinating committee in New York City attempted to run as a collective and make decisions by consensus (Springer 2001). This strategy ended up being extremely difficult for the women involved, and it caused problems for communication with the branch chapters.

The NBFO organizers tapped into localized grassroots Black feminist organizing, but met with some resistance in making the grass roots visible. Reaction to the formation of the NBFO from some in the Black community was swift and negative. Brenda Verner (1974:22), a teacher at the University of Massachusetts, wrote about the 1973 NBFO Eastern Regional Conference for *Encore* magazine, which was hostile to feminist organizing by Black women even before the NBFO press conference, editor/publisher Ida Lewis having been quoted by *Time* magazine as characterizing feminism as "a playtoy for middle-class white women" ("Blacks v. Feminists," *Time*, March 26, 1973:64). Verner's main criticism of the NBFO was that the conference workshops – which seemed to address just about everything – somehow did not pay sufficient attention to concerns within the Black community:

No workshops were listed that were concerned with the Black family, Black nationalism, or Pan-Africanism. Yet there were workshops entitled "Black Women and the (White) Women's Rights Movement" and the "Triple Oppression of the Black Lesbian."

And each workshop was described in the same terminology and manner that White feminists use in their literature.

Verner strongly hinted that most NBFO conference attenders were lesbians, having heard one vocal Black lesbian minister speak at one workshop; seemingly, what lesbians had to say could be dismissed, as they were somehow imports from the white feminist community. Verner accused the NBFO of using a "white" approach, and of existing only to add legitimacy to the white women's movement. As she saw it, since Margaret Sloan – one of NBFO's founders, and a Civil Rights movement veteran – had worked with Ms. magazine, she was in the magazine's pocket. More fundamentally, Verner (1974:23) was critical of any attempts to link Black and white women's fates, since the white women's movement had ignored Black women's survival and community issues.[20]

By October of 1974, the NBFO had elected a Coordinating Council of thirteen women, representing different committees within the group; there were eight local chapters, in Atlanta, Buffalo, Kansas City, MO, Los Angeles, Philadelphia, Raleigh, Washington, DC, and Westchester, NY, with contacts listed for Boston, Chicago, and Detroit (NBFO 1975b). By March 1975, Houston was added to the "contacts" list, and by September of 1975, chapters in New Haven and Baltimore, as well as a new separate chapter from the national office in New York City, had joined the roster. Most of the local chapters reported that "consciousness raising" was a major part of their work. The chapter structure was envisioned as giving individuals the chance to link up with the existing local groups of Black feminists, and members were asked to pay dues on a sliding scale, 20 percent of which would go to the national office in New York City (NBFO c. 1974a). There were fairly elaborate guidelines for chapter formation. First, a local group would have to accept the NBFO's statement of purpose, constitution, and bylaws; they would then have to have a minimum of four consciousness-raising sessions based on principles provided by the central office. The local group would send meeting minutes and chapter by-laws to the national office, and then write the

---

[20] Margaret Sloan and Margo Jefferson were allowed to defend the NBFO against Verner's article (Jefferson and Sloan 1974). Encore published a letter in which Sloan and Jefferson rejected the idea that Black women could not link themselves to other (white) women, arguing that Black feminist figures in the past (e.g., Sojourner Truth) had "understood power, coalitions, and the value of attacking an oppressive system from as many directions as possible" (1974:46).

national office to ask for chapter status. At that point, a national office member would be sent to talk to the chapter; this visitor would hopefully issue a favorable report, after which a six-month trial period of NBFO membership would ensue.

The NBFO as such continued organizing through at least 1975.[21] In March of that year, the national office sent a tentative agenda via its newsletter for a meeting to plan another national conference for late 1975, to take place in Washington, DC (NBFO 1975c). The agenda for that meeting included clarifying the "Purpose and Philosophy of NBFO," "Current and Long Range Goals," and "Directions for the Future." In April of 1975, fifty NBFO members met in Detroit with additional representatives from Oakland, Cleveland, Lansing, and Richmond (newsletter 1975d). In Detroit, the "priorities" that representatives had drawn up for this upcoming convention continued to echo the "umbrella" approach of the NBFO's previous statements of purpose:

1) Self Image (media, sexuality); 2) Education (sex and race role stereotyping, feminist education, child care); 3) Health (abortion, forced sterilization, suicide, etc.); 4) Employment & Economics (decriminalization of prostitution, oppression of household technicians, welfare, etc.); 5) Crime & Law (the battered woman, rape and sexual abuse, the penal system, etc.); 6) Religion (as it relates to the Black woman); 7) The Black Lesbian (triple oppression, lesbian mothers, oppression of Black Lesbians in movements, etc.). Special projects are: 1) Research on Black women; 2) Legislation & lobbying on all levels; 3) Black women's cultural development. (1975e)

However, the NBFO fell apart in late 1975/early 1976. As early as 1974, there had been shifts in the New York–based Executive Board that indicated the existence of schisms among those coordinating the group (NBFO 1974a). In September of that year, the Executive Board of the NBFO wrote local chapters in "an attempt to communicate to you the past, present and future position of the National Black Feminist Organization as accurately as brevity permits." The letter, cosigned by six members of the Executive Board, reported that after the Eastern

[21] Davis (1988) argues that the NBFO continued on in localized fashion until 1979, but she is almost certainly including offshoots like the National Alliance of Black Feminists and the Combahee River Collective.

Regional Conference in the fall of 1973, the board had continued to meet and soon found itself planning a fund-raiser with NOW from which the two groups would split the proceeds. The letter writers described these meetings as "painful": "Questions were raised concerning type of talent, responsibility, leadership and monies. Some of our members resigned at that time or stopped attending meetings. The publicity committee dissolved" (letter 1974a).

The authors of the letter wrote that even in the wake of this crisis, the NBFO in New York City continued to meet and attract new members. But other members also dropped out as a result of "personality clashes, political priorities, conflicts over feminist philosophy, over concern with alliance and coalition with white feminists, and for personal reasons" (letter 1974a). As of the fall of 1974, there were still six women on the board, involved in planning new committees, establishing a clearing-house for exchange of clothing and appliances, setting up a "rap" line, and getting "more concretely involved in the child care issue." The board also wanted to put out a monthly newsletter. Shortly afterward, the national office sent a ballot to members in local chapters asking them to vote for members of a new national coordinating council for the NBFO ("Ballot" 1974b).

There is some indication that the NBFO did not survive much past sending out that ballot because there was a "takeover" of the group; there appears to have been a major reconfiguration of the New York–based executive board in 1975 that led directly to the group's demise, when a new guard came into the national office and "killed" the group through inaction. Davis (1988) recounted a challenge to the New York–based leadership of the NBFO coming from members who continued to at-tack New York members throughout the following year. Galvin-Lewis recalled a shift in the executive board growing out of a convention held by the group in Philadelphia in 1975, whereby a group of women took over – that is, were elected into – executive board seats (2000 inter-view). According to Galvin-Lewis, the original executive board mem-bers ceded to the newly elected ones, with an agreement that the new board members would come by later for NBFO materials, books, and the key to the group's office space on Madison Avenue. The new members never came by for the materials, and the old members, who had been completely unprepared for what their press conference back in 1973 had launched in the first place, were so hurt by "having our baby taken" that they did not come together to restart the group (Galvin-Lewis

2000 interview). The picture here of takeover and turnover is admittedly murky, but it indicates that members were not able to keep differences from becoming unduly personal. Galvin-Lewis remembered that a meeting was held approximately six months after the Philadelphia convention (again sometime in 1975), and that it was filled with further accusations by the newly elected board against the old executive board (who had been nicknamed "The Founding Mothers") about their refusal to turn over records and to cooperate with the incoming officers. In any case, it seems that some rift in board membership occurred, and that this rift caused enough internal struggle so that liaison efforts to local NBFO chapters were neglected and the organization faltered.

Aside from the executive board rift, there were other reasons that the NBFO could not sustain itself for much more than two years. The group's diversity, or more accurately, the heterogeneity of its political concerns, probably diffused energies that might have been better organized around specific, targeted goals. For example, Wallace (1982:31) noted that the group's attempt to prioritize all problems that Black women faced led to members getting "bogged down in an array of ideological disputes. . . . Many of the prime movers in the organization seemed to be representing other interest groups and whatever commitment they might have had to Black women's issues appeared to take a back seat to that." That NBFO members were committed to battling simultaneous oppressions, as well as the attempt to model the organization after NOW, contributed to the umbrella approach, and to subsequent problems involving the group's focus. But the umbrella approach was attempted without real resources; there appears to have been a serious mismatch between the NBFO's ambitious agenda and the actual resources available to act on that agenda.

As noted, the NBFO's founders were in no way prepared for the response they received from the field, and thus they capitalized on local Black feminist strengths badly or not at all. According to Galvin-Lewis, the New York–based NBFO founders had relatively few resources with which to deal with the overwhelming response to their August 1973 announcement (2000 interview). Although NBFO members on the local level desired a strong national office and a bureaucratic structure, the resources to build that kind of entity simply did not materialize. Aileen Hernández, who had by 1973 moved to the West Coast but who knew and kept in touch with a number of the NBFO founders, saw the group's major problem as a failure to raise money for a national level organization before the announcement:

> The National Black Feminist Organization had essentially some
> of the same problems that NOW did. . . . It had a problem because
> it could not raise money to have a national organization . . . so
> what essentially happened was you had cores of people in places
> where there were people who had interest, who had a sort of local
> organization that they operated. (2000 interview)

Although Hernández saw the NBFO as an important conduit for information between local groups, she noted that without resources, action
by Black feminists could not be centrally coordinated. And it is especially important, given later critiques of NBFO's would-be bureaucratic
structure (see Joseph and Lewis 1981; White 1984), to acknowledge how
much NBFO members wanted to work together in a coordinated and
even centralized fashion.

In a further complication regarding the implementation of bureaucratic centralized structure, the New York–based coordinating committee actually tried to run itself as a collective and make decisions by consensus, according to Galvin-Lewis (2000 interview; see also Springer
2001). Galvin-Lewis now regards the committee's attempts to be egalitarian rather than hierarchical in decision making as problematic, and
stated: "I would never structure an organization the way we structured
it again. . . . We didn't want a president or a chair. . . . We were trying
to be totally egalitarian" (2000 interview). The hierarchical structure
that the New York NBFO and other chapters saw as necessary for the organization as a whole was actually not practiced in the center of the
organization, and may have led to the kinds of schisms among members
just outlined.

In another area connected to the issue of resources and central coordination, there was a distinct lack of communication between local
chapters and the national office in New York City, which was particularly
distressing, given how much local chapters wanted leadership from the
national office. Frustrations with the inability of the New York NBFO to
really act as a coordinating committee surfaced in an exchange of letters
in 1974 between Brenda Eichelberger, who chaired the NBFO chapter in
Chicago, and Sandra Hollins Flowers from the NBFO Atlanta chapter.
In August of 1974, Hollins Flowers wrote Eichelberger that Margaret
Sloan, who had been chair of the coordinating committee in New York,
had resigned the previous month, but that the Atlanta chapter still

did not know who the new leader would be, or even who the other officers on the committee were at the national level (Hollins Flowers 1974a). The kind of centralization and coordination that a national office could provide for the NBFO was important to Hollins Flowers; she wrote Eichelberger that "[t]here's *no way* we can be a national organization without establishing a communications network and some universal policy guidelines" (1974a; emphasis in the original). At the same time, Hollins Flowers recommended to Eichelberger that the chapters start to "get it together among ourselves," before dealing with the national office:

> I hate the mutinous nature of this whole situation, but the repeated non-response from NY is making it difficult for me to represent the organization accurately. Right now, Atlanta NBFO is what *I* want it to be. In Chicago, it's what *you* want it to be. In DC, it's up to Jo. And Janet might have something altogether different going in Detroit. And in NY . . . ? At any rate, it's time we had something in addition to the Statement, that "something" being regular communication and policy guidelines. (1974a; emphasis in original)

The very process of incorporating new chapters, although crafted to prevent the kind of localism and "mutiny" that Hollins Flowers alluded to, actually contributed to her discontent. In a letter requesting that the national office green-light some Atlanta projects, Hollins Flowers wrote to Jane Galvin-Lewis of New York City's NBFO that Atlanta NBFO members did not like having a six-month waiting period before becoming an official chapter (1974b). Also problematic was the fact that NBFO bylaws required that local members seeking chapter status sign a statement "indicating support for the goals, objectives and stated policies of NBFO"; Hollins Flowers told the national office that her local group had no statements on NBFO policy to look at, and that "a rough draft of the By-laws in which Article I, Section 2 – where the goals, etc. would be listed – is incomplete" (1974b).

Creating a hierarchical centralized leadership, ideological unity, and a strong chapter structure required resources that the NBFO didn't have (for example, a paid, permanent staff). In the absence of those resources, adhering to bylaws and the like was unsuited to the building of a Black feminist *movement* that could draw on local support. In addition to the Atlanta example, the trajectory of the Chicago chapter is suggestive of

what waiting too long for direction from New York could do to local efforts. In July of 1974, the Chicago NBFO group applied for chapter status
to the national NBFO office (NBFO minutes 1974). The Chicago group
had been meeting regularly throughout the summer with close to twenty
women attending. In October of 1974, the Chicago group was awarded
"chapter status"; only nine women were in attendance at this meeting (NBFO minutes 1974). While we cannot know if this attenuation
process was typical, the Chicago experience suggests that local Black
women's networks were not tapped efficiently by the national NBFO
when the national office put local chapters on probationary periods.
Eichelberger had a master's degree in counseling psychology and extensive professional organizational ties. Since she worked in the Chicago
public school system as a counselor, she had the upcoming summer off,
and with it, time to volunteer for the NBFO. But in July of that year,
she was still writing to Sloan asking for the go-ahead, reporting that
there was a solid core of twenty women who would come to meetings
regularly, and could the national office please send news articles on the
NBFO to the group (letter 1974). May to October, when NBFO Chicago
was awarded chapter status, appeared to be a long time in the life of that
chapter, particularly since its main organizer had to go back to full-time
work after having had the summer off.

The NBFO remained central to Black feminism despite its short and
somewhat troubled life. It gave birth to at least two offshoots that out-
lasted the organization, and a third Black feminist group that organized in the 1970s had some connections to both the NBFO and NOW.
In Chicago, the Eichelberger-led National Alliance of Black Feminists
(NABF) survived until 1979; the Combahee River Collective (CRC)
organized in the Boston/Cambridge area, explicitly breaking with the
NBFO over its politics; and in the Bay Area, Black Women Organized
for Action (BWOA) was founded in 1973.

Eichelberger, along with other members of the Chicago chapter of
NBFO, held their own press conference in 1976 to formally announce
the NABF's formation (NABF 1979). The NABF formed in the wake of
the vacuum of leadership at the coordinating committee of the NBFO,
when as Eichelberger recalled, local Black feminists realized that they
were not getting much from the New York office:

> We weren't getting a lot of structure or guidelines from the national
> office ... and that was something some women were concerned
> about, so people said, "Brenda why don't you just do what we're

doing here? We don't have to be connected with New York, we could still be national." (1999a interview)

According to Eichelberger, the local group kept "National" in the title because many women who lived outside of the Chicago area wanted to be members. She recalled that the group had about 100 paid members at any given time, but that "some people saw themselves as members who never paid a dime in membership."

Generally speaking, the goals of the NABF were not distinguishable from those of the NBFO (NABF 1977a). However, the NABF was more receptive to affiliative strategies in organizing, and proclaimed itself open to "a structure which allowed our supporters who were not Black women to also join us" (NABF 1979). In contrast to the NBFO's insistence that Black women organize on their own, the NABF sought links with Black men and white women, inviting them in as members; the group sought coalitions with white feminist groups, groups of other women of color, and human rights organizations more generally. Eichelberger even recalled a white male volunteer who would come over to the NABF office and donate his time.

During the late 1970s, the Chicago NABF organized to help pass the Equal Rights Amendment (ERA), conducted rap sessions, and ran assertiveness training workshops (NABF 1978). They sponsored at least one conference, called "A Meeting of the Minds: A National Conference for, by and About Black Women" in Chicago in October of 1977 (1977b). Resolutions that emerged from this conference (NABF c. 1977) covered everything from protesting the Bakke decision to working for the freedom of Black women to choose their "lifestyles" (presumably a euphemism for supporting Black lesbians), indicating that the NABF, like the NBFO, was attempting an omnibus approach to feminist issues. The conference also resulted in resolutions on the following topics: protecting Black children being bussed from violence; writing booklets for Black women dealing with the criminal justice system; women's health care and maternity; women supporting other women; media images of Black women; Black women relating to Black men; links to other (non-Black) feminists; getting more Black women in electoral politics; fighting for the ERA; helping adolescents; sexuality; and women in the arts.

The NABF did replace the moderately anticapitalist rhetoric of the NBFO with a more consistently liberal one. The NABF promoted a "Black Women's Bill of Rights" (NABF 1976), which included such Black women's issues as "Accurate Media Portrayal"; "Quality Health

Care"; "Quality Education"; "Economic/Consumer Development"; "Pursuit of Stable Home Life"; "Political Advancement"; "Civil/Criminal Justice"; Cultural participation"; "Quality Child Care"; and "Individual Freedom." "Political advancement," for example, was defined as the right to equitable political representation, the right to unionize, and the right to "lobby for better living standards." Similarly, "economic development" was defined as the right not just to equal employment opportunities, but to "equal access to full participation in the entrepreneurial system."[22]

The NABF was active at least through 1979, organizing an Alternative Education School Program, with open enrollment for men and women in all courses save "female sexuality" in that year (NABF 1979). The "program" was noteworthy for the emphasis its organizers put on the importance of personal growth for collective action, continuing the more liberal bent of the group's efforts:

> [W]e realize that we must develop and grow as individuals[;] the principle of self-help is the basic foundation on which our organization is built. . . . These programs are designed to help foster our personal growth and development, thereby encouraging us to take **individual** action and to help foster societal growth and development by encouraging us to take **collective** action. (Emphasis in original)

By the beginning of the 1980s, the NABF had more or less stopped activities. Eichelberger attributed this to a lack of funding (the price of space in the redeveloping downtown Chicago "Loop" where the group's office was located increased exponentially) and the presence of some "dissension from the inside" (1999a interview). She recalled that internal disagreements focused on whether the group should let white women in as members. It was her feeling that the NABF – whatever coalitions it might broker – should stay Black. According to Eichelberger, Black women needed the feminist message more than white women did, and

[22] Similar in agenda to the NBFO but different in strategy, the NABF also sought to distinguish itself from the former group by creating a new logo. The NBFO logo had been a fist in a Black woman's (distaff) symbol, a design clearly intended to resonate with both Black Liberation and white women's liberation. The NABF changed this to a hand-drawn picture of two female hands breaking through a rope on which was written "racism/sexism," thus avoiding a direct link with 1960s activist symbolism (NABF 1977a).

only a Black feminist group could effectively deliver that message to Black women.

On the East Coast, the best-known NBFO offshoot, the Combahee River Collective (CRC), formed in the Boston/Cambridge area. The CRC became well known for "A Black Feminist Statement," which appeared in Moraga and Anzaldúa's collection *This Bridge Called My Back* (1979) and in former Combahee member Barbara Smith's *Home Girls* (1983). Unlike the NABF, the CRC was intentionally a very different kind of group than the NBFO; its members came together in early 1974, after the NBFO's first Eastern Regional Conference, after they found that they had "concrete differences with the NBFO's seemingly bourgeois political stance and inattention to the issue of heterosexism" (Combahee River Collective 1981:216; see also Harris 1999; Springer 2001:170; White 1984). In the summer of 1974, CRC members decided to become independent from the NBFO and to organize collectively, as most members had been active in lesbian and socialist feminist groups. The CRC added an explicitly pro-lesbian, anti-homophobia stance to Black feminist vanguard center politics, arguing that if "Black women were free, it would mean that everyone else would have to be free since our freedom would necessitate the destruction of all the systems of oppression" (CRC 1981:215).

Members of Combahee stressed the need to take on simultaneous oppressions through discussion that would enable Black women to better understand their position. Interviewed by Duchess Harris (1999), CRC members like Barbara Smith, Sharon Page Ritchie, Cheryl Clarke, Gloria Akasha Hull, and Demita Frazier stressed the need to link their activism and awareness in a constructive way, and in a safe space. In its focus on intellectual development coupled with activism as a way of life, the CRC was aided by being situated in Boston/Cambridge's extremely vibrant local activist milieu; Demita Frazier described herself as being "thrilled at the chance to be in a city where there seemed to be a lot of discussion. There was a feeling that you could talk about nearly anything, and you could raise issues about anything" (Harris 1999:14).

When she joined the CRC, Margo Okazawa-Rey was an activist living in Cambridge and working as a social worker in the Dorchester section of Boston; she recalled meeting Barbara Smith in and around left-wing lesbian feminist circles. Okazawa-Rey joined the group when Combahee was reforming itself as a study group; various "internal disagreements" within the group – lesbian/straight, and those that resulted from political and class differences – had led to a period of quiescence, out of which the study group emerged in 1976. From 1977 to 1979, the CRC met locally and also held a series of six retreats between 1977 and 1979 in order to think about their efforts as Black feminists (Harris 1999).

Among the work that CRC members read was Cade (Bambara)'s *The Black Woman*. Okazawa-Rey recalled the collection as sparking a commitment to writing and theorizing from group members' own perspectives, and it was this group-centered theorizing that resulted in the CRC's "A Black Feminist Statement." Okazawa-Rey saw the statement as reflecting the group's discussions quite accurately:

> In that group, we weren't just talking about race, we weren't just talking about gender . . . we were talking about class, we were talking about imperialism, and I think that the Combahee River Collective statement really reflects all the ways that we were trying to understand the world, and it's interesting the way the document still pretty much holds up, you know, now . . . twenty-four years later. . . . I'm very proud to have been part of the thinking that went into that. (1999 interview)

Like other Black feminist groups, the CRC placed itself in the difficult space of being critical of other Black community and white feminist organizations. CRC members saw themselves as fighting at the juncture between these organizations, doing so without "racial, sexual, heterosexual or class privilege to rely upon" (CRC 1981:214). As a Black lesbian-identified group, the CRC rejected Black Liberationist politics that could not even admit to the existence of lesbian relationships. At the same time, CRC members rejected lesbian separatism, by the late 1970s a dominant strand in white feminist cultural politics (Echols 1989). CRC members argued that lesbian separatism left out "far too many people, particularly Black men, women, and children" (1981:214).

The question of the collective nature of the CRC has been the subject of some contention (Springer 2001). Clearly, Barbara Smith was both a charismatic leader within the group and one of the key formulators of its politics; her charisma, as well as her subsequent scholarship, has led to the CRC's being recast as "her" group. A separate, and arguably more important, issue for thinking about the collective nature of the CRC was whether or not members acted in coordinated fashion in various political struggles. CRC members were active, for example, in showing support for Kenneth Edelin, a Boston African American physician who was arrested for performing a legal abortion; they became involved in local efforts to assure the hiring of Black laborers for a school being built in the Black community; they championed the case of L. L. Ellison, a Black woman prisoner at Framingham State Prison who had killed a guard in self-defense against sexual assault; and they worked to publicize the murders of a dozen Black women in the late 1970s, charging the city and local media with neglect of the issues (Harris 1999).

Okazawa-Rey remembered members engaging in these struggles more as individuals than as part of the CRC, and she felt that the CRC was on the periphery of these local struggles, rather than at the core. But the CRC as an organization did issue a pamphlet about the Boston murders of young Black women, entitled "Why Did They Die?" (CRC 1979). By June of 1979, twelve Black women and one white woman had been killed. The police failed to act swiftly after the murders; their disregard led to meetings within the affected communities and the forming of an organization called CRISIS, which further publicized the murders, organized self-defense classes, and set up neighborhood watches. The CRC pamphlet was designed to be reproduced without permission; it included self-defense tips along with an analysis of schisms between the organized Black and (white) feminist communities. It was reprinted in *Radical America* in 1979, where the editors characterized the CRC as a minority voice within the Black community that had nonetheless seen success in spreading awareness of Black feminism.

The CRC was never very large, but despite its size and somewhat fractious history, it was an example of Black feminist success on its own terms (Harris 1999; Okazawa-Rey 1999 interview; Springer 2001; White 1984). The efforts Combahee members made toward seeing Black feminism as an important intellectual project led to its revised vanguard center politics – with freedom from heterosexism having been added – being taken up in a serious manner by a growing feminist community. The CRC, perhaps more explicitly than other Black feminist groups, articulated an alternative to universalistic visions of an identity of sisterhood that erased differences between women, and its statements offered a way to think about the proliferation of identities around which feminist (and other) organizing was happening (Harris 1999). As ex-members of Combahee moved into other activist groups and other kinds of alliances, the intellectual work done in Combahee followed them. Okazawa-Rey, who left Combahee in 1979 – and who spent years in Boston afterward working in a number of progressive causes – described Combahee as the place where she developed herself as a theorist, although at the time she never thought she was "doing" feminist theory.

In any case, the "doing" of feminist theory by members of Combahee had long-standing effects. It is in the writings of the Collective that we see a thorough-going attempt to address the import of the kind of inter-sectional politics that the group was developing; members of Combahee called their stance "identity politics," by which they meant a politics that attempts to address simultaneous and overlapping oppressions op-erating in people's lives. As noted, the group was never separatist, and members engaged in activism on a variety of causes in cooperation with others. The members of Combahee, then, meant something very differ-ent by "identity politics" than what some critics of the concept do. For example, Todd Gitlin (1995:141; emphasis added), in his lament, *The Twilight of Common Dreams: Why America is Wracked by Culture Wars*, defined "identity politics" as the endpoint of a process of

> first, the discovery of common experience and interests; next, an uprising against a society that had imposed inferior status; finally, an inversion of that status, so that distinct qualities once pointed to as proof of inferiority were transvalued into the basis for positive distinction. *It is only this third stage – where the group searches for and cultivates distinctive customs, qualities, lineages, ways of seeing, or, as they came to be known, "cultures" – that deserves to be called identity politics.*

Ironically, it seems to me that members of the Combahee River Col-lective would only really recognize their identity politics as consisting of points one and two, in as much as the "distinctive customs," and so on, that groups supposedly search for in Gitlin's model would have undoubtedly already been present in the overlapping communities in which Combahee members lived. But the more important point to note is that Combahee's vision and activities – and those of other vanguard center Black feminists – were never intended to stop at the borders of their groups, but were intended to be models for transforming the entire world. If Combahee's version of identity politics has been misunderstood to be about celebration of difference as an endpoint in itself, then appor-tioning blame for that misapprehension should at least include a query as to why it does not seem possible to some leftists that they might be led into new ways of thinking about the nature of oppressions, plural, by Black lesbian women (see RC 1981; Harris 1999).

On the West Coast, a smaller and longer-lasting collectivist Black feminist group was organized in the Bay Area in 1973. Black Women

Organized for Action (BWOA) was founded in January of that year by fifteen women, among them Aileen C. Hernández, Patty Fulcher, and Eleanor Spikes, all of whom had connections to NOW (A. C. Hernández 2000 interview; Springer 2001). BWOA existed in the Bay Area from 1973 to 1980, with about 200 women on the membership list each year during those years; Hernández estimated that BWOA's efforts reached more than two thousand women there during its existence. The group's founders wanted to give African American women a forum for cultivating their own interests, and, as with Chicago's NABF, actually had to negotiate the issue of whether or not to characterize themselves as "feminist." Hernández recalled:

> [W]e were writing up a statement of purpose and we got to the point about whether or not we were going to say that we were feminists . . . and there was a HUGE discussion about whether or not we were feminists . . . so we wound up with a statement which essentially said [about BWOA's members] "some of whom are feminists and some of whom are not." . . . Actually because we said "we don't care about what you call yourself. We're just thinking that we are going to work on issues that are related to African American women." (2000 interview)[23]

BWOA as an organization was committed to giving African American women a chance to nurture their leadership potential, and was collectivist in the sense that leadership was shared and rotating. The group called this leadership rotation "those who share the work, share the power and the glory" (Springer, quoting Fulcher, 2001:182). Hernández (2000 interview) described the structure as ensuring that no one was a leader for more than three months, so that the group had three people in charge, with a rotation of two of those three every three months. Hernández noted that the rotation of leadership was "scary to a lot of people," but that her attitude was that three months was not long enough for one individual to cause much trouble. Additionally, the

---

[23] In my inclusion of BWOA in this chapter on Black feminism, I might be seen by some as expanding the focus of this work beyond looking at self-identified feminist organizations. However, BWOA's finessing of the feminist label did not reflect an antifeminist politics, or desire to distance itself as a group from feminism. Additionally, the feminist organizational lineage of key BWOA members leads me to include it here as part of a Black feminist movement story.

rotation of leadership gave many more women an appreciation of the responsibilities of leadership, that is, that activism was a lot of work. In any event, the rotational leadership structure seemed to have allowed the group to function adequately enough for it to survive a full seven years.

BWOA members engaged in a number of local protests. They initially challenged the San Francisco mayor's Committee on the Status of Women for conducting hearings about the city's women "without including any testimony from Black women" (Springer 2001:173). Members picketed the symphony in San Francisco for refusing tenure to an African American woman tympanist; as Hernández recalled, "BWOA organized a picket line, and we were the best-dressed picket line you have ever seen in your life. We picketed the opening of the symphony in long dresses . . . in mink coats and gloves and everything else" (2000 interview). BWOA protested an impending decision by the city of San Francisco to destroy trees planted on Octavia Street by Mary Ellen Pleasant, an early African American woman resident of the city, and saved the trees. The group put together an employment handbook for young Black women on how to face discrimination and how to look for a job; they cooperated in the San Francisco Women's Coalition, which created the (now defunct) Bay Area Feminist Credit Union. BWOA also gave political endorsements to those running for elective office and sponsored candidates' nights; they tried to broaden their knowledge of international affairs by meeting with women representatives of the United Nations who came through town. The organization also published a newsletter, which was entirely the responsibility of the three women in charge of the group at the time, and was therefore open in practice as well as principle to submissions by virtually any member.

BWOA as an organization was gone by 1980, but Hernández and others couldn't keep themselves away from organizing for long (2000 interview). In 1985, they formed a group of Bay Area women called Black Women Stirring the Waters that was envisioned strictly as a support and conversation network, with some forty or so active participants and about 300 women on their mailing list. However, since 1985, the strictly social network has self-published, in cooperation with a local Black-owned bookstore, two books of essays/personal testimony by members, the second of which contains forty-four biographical essays by women involved in the group (Black Women Stirring the Waters 1997). Although the book's foreword states that the network has "stubbornly avoided any 'call to action' as a group," as Hernández stated in her interview, "It's very hard with these women NOT to do anything" (1997:xiv; 2000 interview).

Conclusion: The Influence of the Vanguard Center

Black feminism arose as an organizationally distinct movement in response to the changes that had occurred in the Civil Rights/Black Liberation movement and to the problems for Black women activists caused by those changes. A resurgent masculinism within the Black movement sought to contain women in the domestic sphere; after having had positions of responsibility and having been behind-the-scenes (and sometimes right-in-front) leaders in the Civil Rights movement, many Black women activists were unwilling to restrict themselves to traditional gender roles. However, white women's liberation was not a natural home for Black feminists, as white feminists were insufficiently sensitive to the importance of race and class oppression in Black women's lives. As a result, Black feminists, beginning in the mid-1960s, and continuing throughout the 1970s, organized as feminists *and* as Black women. Some of these efforts were more collectivist, others more intentionally bureaucratic; some more local in scope and some ambitiously, if only briefly, national. It is safe to say that in various ways and with various levels of intensity, these feminist groups involved several thousand Black women, linking them through discussion, publications, conferences, and work on projects designed to better the lives of Black women living at the intersection of oppressive forces of racial, gender, class, and heterosexist domination.

Thus, Black feminism, with an intersectional, vanguard center vision of liberating politics, emerged into a space created by the inability of both Black Liberation and white women's liberation to incorporate Black feminists as activists. It emerged as white feminism (and as Chapter Four will show, Chicana feminism) was forming; it was a movement that was organizationally and politically distinct and not, as some would speculate, a later variant on white feminism, or a simple reaction by Black women activists to white feminists' personal racism. The sense of difference from white feminists that existed for Black feminists was based on their experiences, their work in the Black movement, and their perception of the failure of white feminism to give enough attention to the economic issues that defined Black women's lives. The very existence of Black feminism needs to be read back into the story of second-wave feminisms, because in very real ways, Black feminists' articulation of

intersectional oppressions of race/ethnicity, gender, class, and sexuality –
and that of a political need to coordinate the struggle against those oppressions – came to have a profound impact on feminism as a whole, and
on other feminisms (see Heywood and Drake 1997; Hill Collins 1990;
hooks 1984; Johnson Reagon 1983; Joseph and Lewis 1981; D. H. King
1988; B. Smith 1979; Spelman 1982; White 1984).

Another group of second-wave feminists, Chicanas living predominantly in the southwestern United States, also addressed themselves to
questions of liberation from overlapping forms of domination, and to
movements that asked them to choose between what they saw as interlocking oppressions in their own communities. It is to their story that I
turn in the next chapter.

"We Called Ourselves 'Feministas'"

Intramovement Experience and the Emergence of Chicana Feminism

We didn't want to be "feminists," we wanted to be women, Chicanas in our own right, even equal partners . . . but it is, it is a feminist line, it's very much the same feminist line that all feminists have . . . we want to be equal partners.

> Leticia Hernández
> Long Beach, California
> 1992[1]

Introduction: "Feministas," Not "Feminists"

The words of Ana Nieto-Gómez and Leticia Hernández in the title of this chapter and the opening epigraph[2] may seem contradictory to the reader. Both women were members of one of the first Chicana feminist groups, Las Hijas de Cuauhtémoc [The Daughters of Cuauhtémoc] at California's Long Beach State University; both women struggled with what being a Chicana feminist meant and what feminist organizing might mean for the Chicano movement. Emerging roughly at the same time as other second-wave feminisms, with the first Chicana feminist organizations being formed in 1969 and 1970, Chicana feminism came out of Chicanas' experiences in the Chicano movement of the 1960s and 1970s.[3] The

---

[1] From Maylei Blackwell's 1992 interview with L. Hernández.

[2] This chapter draws in part on the research and oral histories with Ana Nieto-Gómez in 1991 and L. Hernández in 1992 conducted by Blackwell, particularly regarding the early Chicana feminist group Las Hijas de Cuauhtémoc. See Blackwell (Forthcoming; 2000a; 2000b); L. Hernández (1992); Nieto-Gómez (1991). Quotes from Nieto-Gómez and Leticia Hernández are used with permission of the California State University at Long Beach Oral History Program.

[3] A note on the language(s) in this chapter: "Chicana/o" is the name used by activists in the 1960s and 1970s to describe people of Mexican descent born in the United States. It is a reclaimed, politicized term, having had some pejorative connotations in the past (Aguirre 1971). The term "Mexican American" was seen by Chicana/o activists as less than radical, and as describing a political outlook that did not "recognize any systematic inequalities" affecting the community (de la

year 1968 having been a significant one for feminist organizing in other racial/ethnic communities, Chicana feminists worked in a social movement sector where the possibility of feminist organizing was established, and thus they organized in the face of constraints that were different from those confronted by either Black or white feminists. Chicana feminists maintained organizational distance from white feminists, while being sympathetic to many of the issues raised by white women's liberationists, especially socialist ones. Although many Chicana feminists had contacts with Black women activists, particularly on college campuses, in the late 1960s they did not prioritize cross-racial/ethnic organizing with those women. What Chicana feminists wanted was a greater political presence in the wider Chicano movement, both by organizing in autonomous groups and in women's caucuses within mixed Chicano organizations. To some degree they achieved that, though with difficulty and never as completely as they wanted.

From a sociological perspective, the scant literature on Chicana feminism is descriptive and atheoretical. Chicana feminism as an organized movement does not make an appearance in case studies of white second-wave feminism; these scholars have located feminism in the East and Midwest, and viewed the racial composition of the United States as white and Black, without shades of brown (Gluck et al. 1998).[4] It was left to Chicana/o feminists to write about their movement, and a number did so as the movement was in full swing (see Cortera 1976a, 1977, 1980; del Castillo 1980; Enríquez and Mirandé 1978; García 1990, 1997; Gonzales 1979; Mirandé and Enríquez

Garza 1979:101). In practice, many activists used the terms Chicana/o and Mexican American interchangeably.

Generally, political writing by Chicanas/os in the 1960s and 1970s was characterized by the deliberate mixing of Spanish and English. Because of this, it is difficult to know if mistakes in either language are intentional or not, as for example, activists sometimes did and sometimes did not put accents on Spanish words and proper names. When I believe mistakes to be unintentional, I will use "[sic]." An additional textual problem is that activists may or may not have highlighted or marked Spanish words in a mostly English piece. In most instances, I have opted to preserve the original text to convey the flavor of these linguistic experiments by activists; where appropriate, I have followed Spanish-language usage by translations in brackets. In my own text, I have chosen to italicize most Spanish words on their first usage in each chapter.

[4] For example, Echols's (1989) case study focused entirely on white women's liberationists in the East and made no mention of Chicana feminism; Marx Ferree and Hess (1994:93–97) addressed Chicana feminism very briefly as part of a discussion of the role of "Hispanic" women in the women's movement.

1979).[5] Generally, these authors agree as to the basic historical facts of Chicana feminism; they differ somewhat in their emphases. One group – Gonzales, Enríquez, Mirandé, and Cortera – situate Chicana feminists within a long history of radical social activism on the part of Mexicans in the United States, and see feminism as an indigenous and inevitable outcome of the Chicano movement. The second group, chiefly García and del Castillo, looked at internal processes by which discontented Chicanas demanded a measure of responsibility and respect within the Chicano movement, forming their own organizations upon encountering resistance; they tell stories that more closely resemble those of feminist emergence in other racial/ethnic communities. The story I will tell in this chapter is consonant with this second approach, as I continue to concentrate on understanding how feminists of color made decisions about how and with whom to organize, and about what their links to the activist men in their communities meant.

In this chapter, I focus on how Chicana feminism emerged from the Chicano movement, especially from the student movement, where Chicanas' efforts were central to the success of new organizations on campus (del Castillo 1980). As first-generation college attenders and by means of activism, Chicanas expanded the "traditional" role of women in the Mexican American community. But a masculinist Chicano nationalism grew in the movement, and by 1969, contradictions emerged for Chicana activists. Like their Black activist sisters, Chicanas were asked to take supportive roles in order to preserve Chicano culture and family roles, as emerging "Anglo" feminism was construed to be a threat to the integrity of the Chicano community.[6] Emerging Chicana feminists constructed counterarguments to the idea that feminism was not relevant to, or came from outside, their community. They argued that Chicanas and Mexican women in Mexico had a long tradition of social activism, and that only a gender egalitarian and politicized Chicano family could challenge Anglo domination effectively.

Like Black feminists, Chicana feminists faced calls to choose between gender and racial/ethnic identity in organizing, but there were significant differences in the wider political landscape in which they

---

[5] In this chapter as in others, I draw on archival sources, secondary sources, and interview material. Since I conducted my research, García (1997) has published an excellent documentary collection, *Chicana Feminist Thought: The Basic Historical Writings*; where appropriate, I have drawn from that collection.

[6] The term "Anglo" does not denote English ethnicity; it was commonly used by Chicanas/os to describe both white Americans and white America.

organized. First, in arguing for a reconstructed and politicized family, Chicana feminists were not hampered by the necessity of challenging a government-sponsored attack on their community like the Moynihan report.[7] Second, in contrast to many Black students, Chicanas and Chicanos were isolated on college campuses. There were no historically Chicano campuses to attend, as there were for Black students; instead, student activism took place in settings where Chicanas and Chicanos were vastly outnumbered by whites. College meant an inevitable confrontation with the Anglo world, such that in Chicana feminist arguments about white feminist insensitivity, cultural and class issues became intertwined.

In the following, I first look at the activism of Chicanas in the Chicano movement, particularly in student politics. I next consider the rise of a Chicana feminist critique of Chicano movement politics, focusing on the 1971 National Chicana Conference in Houston, Texas, as a watershed event for Chicana feminists. Backlash against Chicana feminists – who were charged with being *agabachadas* [Anglocized or Americanized] and *vendidas* [sell-outs] – ensued. Chicana feminists countered these charges by arguing that Chicanas had historically always been "feminists" as they struggled for the greater community, and that the traditional roles within the Chicano family needed to be remade to continue the struggle against Anglo domination. I consider the impact of these political counterarguments for Chicana feminist organizing, and I also consider Chicana feminists' relationship to white women's liberation as a movement. I conclude that Chicana feminism shared with Black feminists a vision of gender oppression overlapping with other forms of oppression, but that they mobilized in a movement landscape that both shaped the arguments they made for feminism and that allowed them to stay linked to other Chicano activists in mixed-gender groups. Chicana feminism was thus also an organizationally distinct feminism in the second wave, rather than a mere racial/ethnic variant of general feminism in the era, or a simple reaction to white feminist racism.

Chicanas in the Chicano Movement of the 1960s and 1970s

Chicanos as a people came into being in 1848, when Mexicans residing in what became the U.S. Southwest became a new national minority

---

[7] If anything, the Mexican American family was presented in dominant social science literatures as overly patriarchal; see Sotomayor (1971) for a critique of this simplistic view of Chicano family structure.

(Sánchez 1990). They were linguistically distinct and regionally concentrated, living primarily in rural areas until relatively recently; urbanization of the Mexican American community took place mostly after
World War II (Gómez-Quiñones 1990). As Chicanos were oppressed
by the white-dominated power structure, their activism throughout
the twentieth century showed evidence of the "oppositional consciousness" that characterized the mobilization of oppressed groups (Morris
1992:363; see also Mansbridge and Morris 2001). Chicano activism un-
derwent changes from the early part of the century to the 1960s, since
Mexican Americans' organizational strength grew after conquest. By
the 1920s, the predominant approach was assimilationist, exemplified
by organizations like the League of United Latin American Citizens
(LULAC) (de la Garza 1979). Women had been involved in the founding of these organizations as well as their own groups; early in the twentieth century, Chicana feminists had organized on the U.S. side of the
border, in the wake of the Mexican Revolution of 1910. The Liga Feminil
Mexicanista [Mexican Women's League] was formed in 1911 as a result of
the first Congreso Mexicanista [Mexican Women's Congress] in Laredo,
Texas (Cortera 1976a; Mirandé and Enríquez 1979).

   World War II further accelerated Chicano urbanization and community organization (Gómez-Quiñones 1990); however, as in the African
American community, the egalitarian promise of the postwar years and of
"direct political participation" was not fulfilled (de la Garza 1979:113).
Influenced by the Civil Rights/Black Liberation movement, Chicano
politics of the 1960s and 1970s came to be characterized by militancy
and cultural nationalism, distinct from the more integrationist pursuits
of the previous decades (Gómez-Quiñones 1990). Chicano activism in
the 1960s had several different loci, both urban and rural. On the rural front, the United Farm Workers (UFW), led by Cesar Chavez and
Dolores Huerta (an oft-cited role model for Chicana feminists), organized farmworkers, beginning in Delano, California (Mirandé and
Enríquez 1979; Cortera 1980); women played a significant role in rural
and other Chicano labor movement struggles (Cortera 1977; Mirandé
and Enríquez 1979). The land grant movement in New Mexico, led by
Reies López Tijerina, sought the return of land to *Hispano* families; activists there formed the Alianza Federal de las Mercedes [the Federated
Alliance of Land Grants], later renamed the Alianza de los Pueblos
Libros [the Alliance of Free City-States] (Ludwig 1971).

   Urban community organizing – for example, the Crusade for Justice
in Denver, Colorado, led by Rodolfo "Corky" Gonzales – took place in
cities throughout the Southwest. The Crusade for Justice helped sponsor

the 1969 Chicano Youth Liberation Conference, which was attended by up to fifteen hundred activists, and which issued the Chicano nationalist program, "El Plan de Aztlán" [The Aztlán Plan].[8] The Youth Liberation Conference was also the site of a women's workshop that issued a statement that read in part: "It was the consensus of the group that the Chicana Woman does not want to be liberated," about which more will be said later in this chapter (Flores 1971a:2; "Chicana Regional Conference," *La Raza* 1971:43; López 1977:23–24). In other urban Chicano neighborhoods in the Southwest, the Raza Unida [United Race] Party, which spread from Crystal City, Texas, focused on electoral politics; the RUP ran candidates for a variety of electoral posts, including president of the United States (López 1977).[9] In Los Angeles, high school and university students demanded changes in a school system which they regarded as segregated and racist (G. Rosen 1974). Chicano activists in Los Angeles also protested the disproportionate presence of Chicano soldiers among the casualties in Vietnam, holding protests in favor of a "Chicano Moratorium" on participation in the war (Escobar 1993; Herrera 1971).[10]

Younger Chicano activists in the 1960s were more militant in their politics and confrontational in their tactics; one of the first Chicano student organizations, the "Brown Berets" – California based, but with

[8] Aztlán (sometimes seen without the accent) refers to the area conquered by the United States in the Mexican War of 1846 to 1848, namely the Southwest (California, Arizona, New Mexico, Colorado, and Texas). It is the symbolic homeland of the Chicano people.

[9] *Raza* or *la Raza* refers to Chicanos. The word *raza* literally means "race"; in distinguishing themselves as a race, Chicana/o activists acknowledged the mixed Indian and Spanish heritage of the Mexican people.

[10] The National Chicano Moratorium demonstration, which took place in East Los Angeles on August 29, 1970, was held because reportedly nearly one-third (8,000) of the 27,000 Chicanos who went to Vietnam were killed in action or later died of their wounds. About 25,000 people participated in a parade that was to end in a peaceful rally in a park; violence ensued when police tried to clear demonstrators from the park. Journalist Ruben Salazar, director of a local Spanish-language television station and a writer for the *Los Angeles Times*, was killed by a missile fired into a bar by the police. There was a widespread feeling in the Mexican American community that the police targeted Salazar, and the accident was considered by many to have been an assassination (Herrera 1971:236–240). The Moratorium debacle and police repression of the Chicano movement ended up contributing to the further radicalization of what had been a relatively conservative and assimilationist Mexican American community in Los Angeles (Escobar 1993).

branches in Texas and as far away as Michigan – reflected the younger activists' lack of desire to fit into dominant Anglo society (Ludwig 1971). The culturalist and separationist approach of movement activists in the 1960s was in sharp contrast to earlier assimilationist programs; this approach emphasized "pride in our heritage, our language, and the humanistic values governing our personal relationships," all of which were seen as lacking in Anglo culture (de la Garza 1979:113–114). Students and other young community activists constructed a vision of *Chicanismo* [roughly, Chicano-ness] which put their community culturally and politically at odds with mainstream America. They expressed their dissatisfaction with institutionalized white racism in various ways, most notably in high school walkouts, which took place in Los Angeles and other communities in the Southwest throughout the late 1960s and early 1970s (Ortego 1971; G. Rosen 1974).

As they found themselves in growing numbers on university campuses, Chicana/o students worked for their rights, for Chicano studies curricula, and for greater links between the university and the community. They formed organizations like United Mexican American Students (UMAS) and others, most of which later changed their names to Movimiento Estudiantil Chicano de Aztlán, or MEChA [the Chicano Student Movement of Aztlán] (Gómez-Quiñones 1990; G. Rosen 1974). By May of 1968, UMAS already had ten chapters at Los Angeles–area colleges and universities; but as noted in Chapter One, Chicanos remained severely underrepresented in higher education throughout the 1960s and 1970s.[11] Student groups helped to alleviate feelings of alienation that Chicana and Chicano students experienced:

> I went to school in the sixties at the state university in Northridge, California, in the part of the San Fernando Valley which was all white. Looking across that campus I would never see a Mexican or a black person or anybody of color. . . . [I]n the university system Chicanos had no presence. . . . The *Movimiento* [movement] gave me a place to focus . . . and affirm the fact that I wasn't crazy. (Judy Baca, interviewed by Neumaier 1990:257)

Ana Nieto-Gómez, a founder of one of the first Chicana feminist groups, Las Hijas de Cuauhtémoc, spent two years at a community

---

[11] Of the more than 83,000 students enrolled at major public universities in the Southwest in 1968–1969, only 3,370 (less than half of 1 percent) were Spanish surnamed (Ortego 1971:168).

college in San Bernardino, California, and was recruited through Educational Opportunity Programs (EOP) to Long Beach State in 1969 (Blackwell interview with Nieto-Gómez 1991).[12] But once at Long Beach, Nieto-Gómez felt extremely isolated and became depressed. She recalled seeing another Chicano student carrying a sign that said "Chicano," and she sounded the word out to herself because she had never seen it written before. The first UMAS meeting that Nieto-Gómez attended helped her to know that her loneliness was not unusual. Another member of Las Hijas, Leticia Hernández, also recruited to Long Beach State through EOP, at first eschewed Chicano activism, dismissing UMAS as "not for me, because I'm here to study" (Blackwell interview with L. Hernández 1992). But attending an Anglo-majority college provided the first encounter with overt racism for Hernández, who had been raised within a residentially segregated Chicano community and had attended a largely segregated high school; the racism of white students in dormitories ultimately drove her to involvement in UMAS.

Chicanas played significant roles in the student struggle, helping to found and develop Chicano campus organizations (del Castillo 1980). Chicana students seemed to have participated in the student movement in high numbers (P. Hernandez 1980), and for many young Chicanas, the opportunity to work within a political movement expanded their sense of the traditional female role (as did college attendance in the first place). According to Nieto-Gómez, women probably enjoyed "proportionately" more freedom than men by going to college, since high school and community roles had been more constricted for them (Blackwell interview with Nieto-Gómez 1991).

However, with the freedom that Nieto-Gómez spoke of came a set of contradictions when Chicano student organizations followed the trend toward exclusively male leadership that was typical of many of the older national Chicano organizations (del Castillo 1980). The movement philosophies of Chicanismo and *carnalismo* [brotherhood] led many male (and some female) activists to argue that Chicano cultural preservation

---

[12] In the early 1970s, Lopez and Enos (1972: Appendix P-2) reported that in California, 43 percent of Chicano students in the California State University and College system, and 72 percent of Chicano students at the University of California, were there through EOP, an affirmative action program that was often negatively viewed by the majority of (white) college students.

required that men play strong public roles, and that women support them in private.[13]

Chicana leaders were actually hidden from Rudolfo "Corky" Gonzalez when he came to speak to one student organization (del Castillo 1980); in another case, a Chicana student activist at San Diego State University who had held numerous leadership positions within MEChA rejected her election to the position of secretary, arguing that women were seen as capable only of doing such clerical tasks; she was elected treasurer as a result of her complaint (P. Hernandez 1980). Other Chicanas found themselves ignored when they spoke as individuals in meetings (Baca Zinn 1975). Increasingly, the influential female activist was the woman who was in agreement with and loyal to men considered movement "heavies" (del Castillo 1980; "El Movimiento and the Chicana," *La Raza* 1971). Thus, Chicanas in the student movement began to experience contradictions in their expected and desired roles in the movement. On the one hand, college attendance and social movement experience expanded their sense of their own capabilities; on the other hand, masculinist versions of Chicanismo focused on traditional sex roles, a situation analogous in some ways to that which Black feminists experienced in the mid-1960s. In a further complication, it was in fact true that Mexican American women's labor force participation, in contrast to that of Black women, was relatively low, such that familial role models of working mothers – as opposed to the strong central figures of domesticity that some "revolutionaries" were calling for – were less common (see Chapter One, Table 1.2; also Cooney 1975).

It would be a mistake, however, to overemphasize the differences between masculinist versions of Chicanismo and the gender politics present in other 1960s and 1970s left social movements, especially student movements. Much of what activist Chicanas were expected to do for the sake of "revolution" was very much what leftist women were asked to do in other movements. As was the case for Black feminists, Chicana feminists faced these problems while white women's liberation was ascendant; by the 1970s, the white women's movement was the

---

[13] I have translated *carnalismo* as "brotherhood," although it carries with it a slightly different meaning than the standard Spanish word for brotherhood, *hermandad*. The word *carnal* (or *carnala*, for a woman) refers to a "brother" in the sense of someone from the neighborhood that one grew up in; the English slang equivalent, which is not exact, might be "homeboy."

most visible and vibrant part of the white Left. Rejecting the Chicano movement's traditionalist gender ideology, Chicana feminists began to address the obstacles blocking full participation by women in their own movement.

Early Organizing by Chicana Feminists

The call by Chicano cultural nationalists for the preservation of traditional gender roles for the sake of Chicano culture was countered, in the words of longtime community activist Francisca Flores, with a cry of "OUR CULTURE, HELL!" (1971b:1). Emerging Chicana feminists countered that only the best part of that culture should be preserved. They argued that *machismo* in Chicano culture was a reaction to Anglo domination, and had to be discarded in the interests of community progress; radical, revolutionary politics required that Chicanas "no longer remain in a subservient role or as auxiliary forces in the movement" (Flores 1971a:i).

While this situation may seem similar to the one that Black feminists faced in the Black Liberation movement, there were crucial differences in how arguments about the need for traditional gender roles were made in the Chicano movement, and therefore how Chicana feminists could respond. Chicana feminists confronted a call for traditionalist gender ideology that was justified on the basis of cultural preservation, and not renovation as in the Black community. Black activists, female and male, were cognizant of the ways in which their relationships did not reflect traditional gender roles, and they saw the Moynihan report as an outside, state-sponsored threat aimed at once again labeling them as inferior. As noted in Chapter Three, Black *feminists* argued that the masculinist turn of Black Liberation was a defensive move against white oppression, if an entirely misguided one.

Chicano cultural nationalists argued that traditional gender roles were an inherent part of what existed between Chicanas and Chicanos prior to and in the face of conquest; Chicana feminists countered these assertions without the shadow of a Moynihan report hovering over their efforts. Since the matter was one of defining what constituted their culture, Chicana feminists could feel that they were equally expert to men on the subject. For example, the aforementioned 1969 Denver Chicano Youth Liberation statement about Chicana women not wanting to be liberated was met with a swift and, for the most part, unapologetic bout of feminist organizing by Chicanas (Mirandé and Enríquez 1979;

Nieto-Gómez 1971).[14] Chicana feminists challenged the idea that cultural preservation entailed their submission to male leadership, in part by presenting themselves as supportive of the family, and not at all hostile to men. In fact, early Chicana feminist organizing was characterized by the express desire to stay linked to men and to existing Chicano organizations while promoting a greater role for women in service to the Chicano cause.

In 1969, Chicana student activists formed Las Hijas de Cuauhtémoc at Long Beach State University (later California State University at Long Beach), named after an early Mexican revolution–era women's rights group that had chapters on both sides of the border. The Long Beach State group started as a consciousness-raising group that was also researching the history of la Chicana (Blackwell 2000a, 2000b; Blackwell interview with L. Hernández 1992; Blackwell interview with Nieto-Gómez 1991; García 1997; Gluck et al. 1998). Naming themselves after this group was a conscious attempt by the Long Beach Chicana feminists to link themselves to a historical tradition of activism in the community, and it had the effect of making the women feel less selfish about their efforts. In a movement context in which any feminist activism was characterized as petty, studying history gave feminism a kind of weight that went beyond the individual (Gluck et al. 1998). Nieto-Gómez made clear that studying their history made the women feel that their oppression as women "was a result of policy, of policy that could be changed" (Blackwell interview with Nieto-Gómez 1991).

Since the group saw itself as having the political education of the Chicana as its main purpose, in January of 1971 members disseminated the first of what would be several issues of a self-named newspaper that was distributed both on and off campus. Las Hijas took on a variety of tasks, as a group and as individuals, that would come to be typical of Chicana feminist politics; they did campus work to support Chicana students through counseling; they helped recruit Chicana (and Chicano) students to campus through EOP; they refashioned and created curricula for Chicano studies; they participated in the underground abortion movement; and they worked on community welfare rights struggles, with

---

[14] There were different interpretations as to what exactly was meant by the Denver statement. Longauex y Vasquez (1970) and Cortera (1977) both saw the workshop statement as a specific reaction to Anglo feminist preoccupations; Vásquez (1977) argued that it was a reaction to attempts by leftist white groups to influence the Chicano movement. In any case, the statement itself had no dampening effect on Chicana feminist organizing, which proceeded apace.

local Chicano community centers and with other left-wing Chicano groups like Catolicos [Catholics] for La Raza (Blackwell interview with Nieto-Gómez 1991; Gluck et al. 1998). Members of Las Hijas helped to organize a regional conference of Chicana feminists that took place prior to the May 1971 Conferencia de Mujeres por la Raza/First National Chicana Conference, thereby creating national communication networks. Later, in 1973, the newspaper *Las Hijas de Cuauhtémoc* was revived as a national Chicana studies journal, *Encuentro Feminil* [Women's Encounter/Meeting], edited by Nieto-Gómez and Adelaida del Castillo (Gluck et al. 1998).

Las Hijas were emphatically not separatist; as Nieto-Gómez put it, the group wanted "to involve the Chicana in the struggle of her people by identifying and dealing with the problems of the Chicana," and this stance was echoed by Leticia Hernández (Blackwell interview with L. Hernández 1992; Blackwell interview with Nieto-Gómez 1991). The members of Las Hijas debated whether or not they should organize as women, and consciously decided to keep their credibility intact by supporting the campus UMAS/MEChA group through fund-raising and other day-to-day organizing activities. Despite these efforts, the group's very right to exist was challenged by male activists. Nieto-Gómez recalled that men in UMAS/MEChA either ridiculed the Chicana feminist groups that were popping up all over the Southwest, as trivial, or alternately, took feminism to be a threat. As Leticia Hernández recalled, when the group's newspaper came out

> we were ridiculed . . . "all that slop and all that ridiculous feminist bullshit and ha ha ha . . . oh here come the feminists, they're trying to be white women." . . . It was hell. And I think that all the rest of us . . . to begin with, were having a hard time fitting into campus, and the only place that we did fit in, we were being ridiculed . . . for having our own beliefs. (Blackwell interview with L. Hernández 1992)

Apparently, the newspaper's article on machismo, "Macho Attitudes," drew the most attention despite the presence of many other pieces on Chicana/o history, education, community organizing, Chicanas in prison, and issues involving the family (*Encuentro Feminil* Editors 1997 [1973]).

Long Beach male MEChA activists were particularly abusive of Nieto-Gómez's leadership. Nieto-Gómez was actually elected president of Long Beach State MEChA, and was only the second female president of one of the chapters. The male loser of the election organized others against her, arguing that having a woman president was detrimental to the Chicano cause. As Nieto-Gómez recalled, he took his argument a step further:

And so he had them [other MEChA members] hang me in effigy outside the MEChA trailer, and they had the *teatro* [theatrical group] . . . do a mass, a burial for me and *Hijas de Cuauhtémoc*. . . . I had already put out the first newspaper of *Hijas* . . . so there were three crosses, me, Corrina and Norma [other members of the Hijas collective] I suppose, and they buried us. (Blackwell interview with Nieto-Gómez 1991)

Leticia Hernández corroborated the vehemence with which male activists opposed Nieto-Gómez's leadership (Blackwell interview with L. Hernández 1992). According to Hernández, the men in the group

were upset that so many of us felt that Ana could do a good job. I think it was okay when Ana was vice-chair, and it was okay if she was secretary or treasurer, but it wasn't okay that she would be the chairperson of the organization. I think the guys wanted to be in charge and in control of everything all the time.

After the effigy incident, Las Hijas continued, unwilling to let what happened to Nieto-Gómez shut them down (Blackwell interview with L. Hernández 1992). But Hernández felt that the group was too beset by the tensions generated by strong egos in an intense setting for them to stay together. She left to become more involved in Chicano cultural activism, which she regarded as a relatively safer port in the storm than organizing could be. Nieto-Gómez moved on to the Chicano Studies Department at California State University at Northridge and to publishing *Encuentro Femenil*. Other members graduated and/or went on to community work.

Beyond college campuses, the Comision Femenil Mexicana [Mexican Women's Commission, or CFM] formed in October of 1970 when women attending the National Mexican American Issues Conference (NMAIC) in Sacramento, California, issued a resolution based on discussions during a "Workshop on Women" held at the conference (CFM 1971a; Cortera 1976a; Flores 1971a, 1971b; Mirandé and Enríquez 1979; Vidal 1971a). The resolution was both critical of the Chicano movement's treatment of Chicanas and adamant about the need to work together with men to achieve liberation. It read in part:

> The effort and work of Chicana/Mexicana women in the Chicano
> movement is generally obscured because women are not accepted
> as community leaders either by the Chicano movement or by the
> Anglo establishment. . . . THEREFORE, in order to terminate ex-
> clusion of female leadership *in the Chicano/Mexican movement* and
> in the community, be it RESOLVED that a Chicana/Mexican
> Women's Commission be established . . . which will represent
> women in all areas[;] that the Comision direct its efforts to orga-
> nizing women to assume leadership positions *within* the Chicano
> movement and community life. (CFM 1971a; emphasis in original)

The resolution directed the CFM to concern itself with the dissemination of information about "the work and achievement of Mexicana/
Chicana women" and with the promotion of "programs which specifically lend themselves to help, assist and promote *solutions to female type
problems and problems confronting the Mexican family.*" A last task the
CFM founders assigned themselves was "to support and explore ways
to establish relationship[s] with other women's organizations and movements," thus seeing themselves as a potential liaison to other women's
groups who were part of other movements.

According to Francisca Flores, a CFM founder, the group voted to become an independent organization affiliated with the NMAIC, and welcomed sympathetic men into the group (Flores 1971b); CFM established
chapters in various California locales and later linked itself formally
with another Chicana feminist organization in the Bay Area, Concilio
Mujeres [Women's Council]. CFM established the Chicana Service
Action Center (CSAC) in Los Angeles, a social services center that was
one of the few "run for Chicanas by Chicanas" and which ran "the first
employment center to provide meaningful employment opportunities
and job training for Mexican-American women" (Cortera 1976a:181).
The CFM also made its voice heard on electoral issues, for example, petitioning then President Nixon to replace a Mexican American
woman treasurer of the United States (Romana Banuelos) on the
grounds that she exploited Mexican women workers who worked in her
businesses, and urging Nixon to replace Banuelos with another woman
of Mexican American descent (CFM 1971b).

Concilio Mujeres (CM) was also formed in 1970 by a group of
Spanish-speaking women at San Francisco State College. At the center
of the group was Dorinda Moreno, a single mother of three, who had

grown up in the Bay Area and returned to school after being in the work-force for many years (2000 interview). Moreno had a history of involve-ment and activism that dated back to her high school days in the Mission District of San Francisco. She had come to San Francisco State through EOP, and saw CM as a place for Raza women in higher education to gain support. CM members wanted to encourage Raza women to enter higher education and go into professions; they also wanted to be a support group for women doing so. CM published a journal called *La Razon Mestiza* [the "Mixed" – i.e., Chicana – Cause], and in 1975, the group put out a sixty-four-page special edition of *La Razon* in honor of International Women's Year called *La Razon Mestiza II*. CM members formed a *teatro* called Las Cucarachas [the Cockroaches], which had ties to the Chicano activist theater network, Teatro Nacional de Aztlán [the National Theatre of Aztlán] (CM 1974, c. 1975b). CM members also sponsored a monthly television project on educational television called *Pa'Delante Mujer* [roughly, "Go Forward, Woman"] which featured Latinas talking about their lives and community issues (CM "Biography," no date; CM *La Mujer en Pie de Lucha* [Woman Ready for the Struggle], no date).

CM members came to see as their primary mission the propagation of Chicano culture and the dissemination of information about Chicanas; as was the case with Las Hijas and with the CFM, members felt that one of the goals of Chicana feminism had to be just getting information out about the very *existence* of Chicanas as a group of oppressed women with a history in the United States. In 1973, CM opened an office in the Mission District, San Francisco's Latino population center (CM c. 1973). A 1974 letter that went out to "friends of La Raza women," listing Dorinda Moreno as the director of CM's "Library Collection," solicited funds for a library/clearinghouse project.[15] Letters written in 1975 continued to solicit donations of both money and materials for the clearinghouse, later renamed the "Chicana Collection Project" (c. 1975a). The Chicana Collection Project was described in CM letters as designed to let the broader movement know about the lives of Raza women, and was a key focus of efforts by CM members for a number of years.

---

[15] Much of the material collected from left organizations for the clearinghouse project sat uncatalogued in the State Historical Society of Wisconsin files when I did the archival research for this project. In my 2000 interview with Moreno, I discovered that these papers had come back to her from the State Historical Society, and our interview took place in her living room, which was crowded with actual boxes of the material. Moreno was, at that time, looking for a new home for the collection.

Moreno argued that gathering "sufficient data collected in archives and accessible to the public regarding the history of women and their lifestyles" would go a long way toward eliminating the "ignorance, fear and confusion" that shape people's actions toward women in the current era (CM c. 1975a:1). Essentially, Moreno argued for an approach to Chicana liberation where activism over cultural and historical knowledge would come first. In a paper written while she was a master's student in communication at Stanford University, entitled "Colonization and the Mestiza, a Framework for Discrimination and the Chicana," Moreno reasoned that the Chicana who was concerned about liberation must free herself from within her own culture but not from it:

> Sexual equality is inherent in racial equality. History has relegated to Chicanos, both male and female, a mutual oppression. Our mutual culture has been our survival mechanism. Therefore priorities and direction can only be established through our mutual quest towards overcoming the inequities existing in the total society. (Moreno 1975:2)

In this view, the need for liberation within the cultural sphere would therefore necessitate Chicanas' cooperation with Chicanos; that approach largely deprioritized Chicana feminist work with white feminists, especially if white feminists wished to attack the Chicano as the root of Chicanas' problems.

CM maintained affiliations with other Chicana feminist groups, such as Comision Femenil Mexicana, helping to put together what they called a "resource bank" of information to be used for networking. But by 1975, CM was having difficulty raising money for its projects and getting members to attend meetings on a regular basis. A letter from September 1975, addressed to "Estimada Hermanas" [Esteemed Sisters], informed others that turnout at a recent meeting had been disappointing, and that CM was unsure if there was the commitment necessary for maintaining the group. By the beginning of the 1980s, CM had completely faded as an organization for a number of reasons. Moreno left San Francisco to start a master's in communications at Stanford, and fell ill in the late 1970s with hepatitis, which forced her to withdraw from activism (2000 interview). Looking back, she also attributed the demise of the group to the changing political context of organizing, in particular to the need to institutionalize activist concerns. For Moreno, feminist and community organizing became too corporate and less familial, in a way that led to enervation: "Organizationally, we were just depleted. We spent too much time and money on paperwork proving what we were doing for the community."

The 1971 Houston Conferencia de Mujeres por la Raza/ First National Chicana Conference

Following on the heels of early Chicana feminist organizing, a national conference of Chicana feminists, the Conferencia de Mujeres por la Raza – the first National Chicana Conference, was held at the Houston YWCA from May 28 to 30, 1971, and attended by up to six hundred women (Bennett 1971; Blackwell 2000b; Cortera 1980; Flores 1971a; López 1977; Nellhaus 1971; Vidal 1971a, 1971b). The conference was a watershed moment for emerging Chicana feminism, as it solidified existing links among feminists and created new ones, as local feminist activists worked together in a series of regional conferences prior to the event. The conference was widely viewed as a success despite a walkout by a substantial number (possibly half) of the participants, who objected to the use of the YWCA venue (Nellhaus 1971). Walkout participants charged the YWCA itself with racism, unresponsiveness to the local Chicano community, and heavy-handed treatment of conference participants.[16] Those who walked out went across the street and met in a park, drawing up their own set of resolutions for the conference members to consider; they eventually came back in and read those to the reconstituted group (Vidal 1971b).

Regional conferences of Chicana feminists met in order to prepare for the national one ("Chicana Regional Conference," La Raza 1971). An unsigned article in La Raza, a Los Angeles–based Chicano movement magazine, reported that the Los Angeles–based regional conference in May of 1971 was a

successful organizing attempt by women from three different colleges to bring Chicanas together to discuss their role in the movement. An estimated 200–250 Chicanas attended the

[16] The YWCA venue became controversial, but I have not found any data that suggests that conference organizers anticipated the controversy, or even as to why the Houston YWCA offered itself as a venue. Medal (1971) reported that several conference organizers worked in social service capacities for the organization, which might explain why it was available. Presumably, hosting the Chicana gathering was seen as congruent with the Houston YWCA's mission, or at least with the outlook of some of its Chicana employees.

conference, along with a handful of interested Chicanos. . . . Six
workshops were organized for the regional conference in the areas
of philosophy, education, welfare, the pinta [female prisoner],
political education, and communication. ("El Movimiento and
the Chicana," 1971:43)

The author of the article noted that despite the Denver statement negat-
ing the need for Chicanas' liberation, the high attendance at the regional conference was evidence of the Chicano movement's maturity,
of its ability to reckon with the new roles that men and women would
have to play to fulfill their revolutionary potential. The author acknowledged that some Chicanas attending the regional conference worried
about Chicana feminist activism splitting the movement, but saw an
even greater problem in the disillusion felt by activist Chicanas at being stymied in their activism within the movement itself. The article's
author was at once critical of Chicanas who were skeptical of feminist
organizing *and* wary of Chicana feminists:

It can't be denied that a good part of this Regional Conference
remained at the level of bitching about male oppression, without
taking into account that the Chicano is equally enslaved to cultural
indoctrination. He too is victim of the constant reinforcement
of sexual stereotypes which are perpetuated by the educational
system, the media, and even la cultura mexicana [Mexican culture].
All stereotypes are perpetuated to keep the movement divided
against this racist and oppressive system. (1971b:44)

Thus, Chicanas were admonished to "carefully analyze the situation,"
so that they could work in concert with Chicanos (1971b:44).
    At the Houston conference, attenders focused on a number of issues,
some of which were specific to their movement/community context and
some of which clearly echoed feminist concerns in other racial/ethnic
communities. Conference resolutions called for the termination of the
"exclusion of female leadership in the Chicano/Mexican Movement and
in the community," and the establishment of a commission to direct the
organizing of women within the community (Flores 1971a:3). Much
of the conference was turned over to workshops involving what might
be thought of as "the personal is political" issues. Reportedly, the two
largest workshops at the conference were on "Sex and the Chicana" and
"Marriage – Chicana Style"; the conference produced calls for free, legal
abortion and birth control by Chicana-controlled community clinics,
and free twenty-four-hour child care (Vidal 1971a). Taken as a whole,

the conference workshops and resolutions focused less on matters of cultural knowledge about Chicanas, as the early feminist groups had. But the Chicanas' meeting in Houston took on the "traditional" role of the Chicana woman with an assertion that "women are oppressed both as women and as part of La Raza" (Vidal 1971a:10).

As mentioned, the conference was not free of tensions, nor were all conference-goers eager to assert Chicanas' need for liberation. While the reason for the walkout was disputed, it laid open rifts among Chicanas about the wisdom of feminist organizing. One account of the walkout tied it to a specific racist incident at the YWCA, using the incident itself as an argument against deprioritizing Chicano nationalism. Tomasin Medal, who wrote about the conference for a San Francisco–based Chicano movement journal *El Tecolote* [The Owl], reported that the walkout against the YWCA happened after "(a) sister bought a writing pad at the Y gift shop. Later, she returned for a pen. The girl at the desk said: 'You people can only think of one thing at a time, huh?' Later that night the walkout began" (Medal 1971:8). It was clear that from Medal's point of view, the incident was payback for the Houston conference being merely reformist – that is, merely feminist – and organized by "six Raza women employed in various titles as social service workers by the YWCA in the Chicano community" in Houston itself (1971:8). Medal also took exception to the keynote speaker, whom she called "una gavacha del Houston Y" [a white woman from the Houston Y], and to what she saw as "preferential treatment given to media men (sí, gavachos [whites] who were given programs while sisters had to wait for theirs)."

Attenders who were pro-feminist, like Mirta Vidal, saw the walkout as disingenuous and divisive.[17] According to Vidal,

the protest action divided the conference, which had more impor- tant business to carry out. The majority of Raza women had come

---

[17] Vidal herself was an Argentinean immigrant, who was raised partly in the United States; she was also a committed member of the Young Socialist Alliance and, later, the Socialist Worker's Party. In 1971, when she reported on the Houston conference for *The Militant,* she was the national director of Chicano and Latino work for the Young Socialist Alliance. Although not Chicana, she became active in the Chicano movement for about three years at the behest of the party, and chiefly due to her ability to speak Spanish. The cited pamphlet, *Chicanas Speak Out/Women New Voice of La Raza,* was widely circulated, and was recently reprinted in part in García's (1997) documentary collection of Chicana feminist writing. In a 2000 interview, Vidal noted that although she came from outside the Chicano community, she felt at home in the movement and welcomed by the Chicanas and Chicanos with whom she worked.

here from all over the country to meet and discuss issues that were relevant to us as Raza women. We were not here to reform the YWCA. (Vidal 1971a:10)

Vidal argued that the YWCA focus of the protest was a ruse, and that the women who walked out "were opposed to the concept of Chicanas getting together around their own specific demands" (1971a:10). She also felt that the resolutions the protestors developed were not "demands of particular relevance to Chicanas," that is, to Chicanas as women. Nonetheless, Vidal put a positive spin on the protest, reporting that the protestors "were welcomed and heard in the spirit of unity. A new term arose among Raza women this weekend – Hermanidad! (Sisterhood!)" (1971a:10).[18]

Ana Nieto-Gómez also believed that the walkout was planned before the conference by women sent from nationalist groups who had paid for their expenses (Blackwell interview with Nieto-Gómez 1991); however, Nieto-Gómez recalled that the walkout actually began as Maria Villanueva, the editor of El Grito del Norte, a New Mexico–based Chicano movement journal, was speaking about the United Farm Workers and castigating conference attenders for their selfishness in focusing on women's issues. Nieto-Gómez remembered that she was among the speakers who asked women not to walk out as the event itself was happening, and that her words and those of other conference organizers from Houston did stop some women from leaving the hall.

Despite the tensions made manifest by the walkout, Houston gave Chicana feminists who were already committed the opportunity to make links with more localized groups, and it gave Chicana feminists in those local groups a tangible achievement to point to upon their return. For example, Francisca Flores was able to bring back important news to California about the conference and helped to articulate it as a success. In her report on the conference, "Conference of Mexican Women – Un Remolino [Commotion]" written for Regeneracíon, a Los Angeles–based Chicano movement journal, and in an editorial that appeared in the same issue, Flores emphasized the necessity of Chicanas'

[18] Even the term hermanidad was controversial among Chicanas. Leticia Hernández felt that the use of this word for "sisterhood" was not good Spanish, and argued instead for the use of hermandad [brotherhood]. Hermanidad was invented to bring to mind the word hermana [sister], but Hernández, a self-described "Spanish language purist" thought that word made Chicana feminists "sound stupid" (Blackwell interview with L. Hernández 1992).

self-determination, and analogized women's right to self-determination and freedom to that of the Mexican people (Flores 1971a, 1971b). She specifically equated Chicanas' self-determination with control over their own bodies, and argued that traditionalists who wanted to preserve Mexican culture were trying to preserve their control over women's bodies:

> Beneath the rhetoric . . . were the fundamental issues of . . . the right of self determination by Mexican [i.e., Chicana] women over questions affecting her body. The issue of birth control, abortions, information on sex and the pill are considered "white" women's lib issues and should be rejected by Chicanas according to the Chicano philosophy which believes that the Chicana women's place is in the home and that her role is that of a mother with a large family. Women who do not accept this philosophy are charged with betrayal of "our culture and heritage." OUR CULTURE HELL! . . . IF A WOMAN WANTS A LARGE FAMILY . . . NO ONE WILL INTERFERE WITH HER RIGHT TO HAVE ONE. . . . [T]o stipulate this right as a tenet of La Causa [the cause] for all women of La Raza is to play a dangerous game with the movement. It means – stripped of its intellectual romanticism – that Chicanas are being condemned to wash diapers and stay home . . . something which the girls in college are not doing and yet some of them are the ones insisting that their hermanas de raza [race sisters] do so because this "is their role." (1971a:1)

Dismissing ideas that Chicanas organizing around women's issues would be diversionary to movement goals, Flores argued for the absolute right of Chicanas to organize as they saw fit, since the "problems faced by women are best served by their own effort through their own organization within the total movement" (1971a:4); these women's organizations working with the larger Chicano movement on mutually agreed-upon issues would then strengthen the movement as a whole.

Chicana feminist efforts before and after Houston encountered resistance precisely because of the wish to remain linked to the larger movement. Thus, Chicana feminists articulated a set of concerns about Chicanas while simultaneously critiquing flaws in the Chicano movement. Next, I turn to the kinds of critiques that Chicana feminists made of their movement regarding the effects of machismo on women's abilities to be active in the struggle.

Challenging the Machismo in Chicanismo, and
Other Chicana Feminist Concerns

A "minisurvey" – whose number of respondents and exact time is not given – was done at the Houston conference (Flores 1971a). Eighty-four percent of the women present – women mostly in college or college-educated – felt that "they were not encouraged to seek professional careers and that higher education is not considered important for Mexican women" (1971a:3). A similar percentage agreed that women did not receive equal pay for equal work, and 68 percent felt that women did not receive the type of job training needed to move into skilled or semiskilled positions in industry. All the survey respondents agreed that Chicanas were subjected to a double burden – expected to take care of the house no matter what kinds of outside obligations of work or school fell on them. Most (again, 84 percent) agreed that the problems of Chicanas were different from those of other women, although this difference was unspecified. And fully 72 percent of respondents felt that there was discrimination against women in the Chicano movement.

The attitudes expressed in the minisurvey are recognizably feminist and do not seem strikingly different from the agenda of other feminists in other racial/ethnic communities. Then exactly what did Chicana feminists confront that was particular to their community and their movement? As noted, Chicana feminists encountered a masculinist bias against women's full participation in the movement that was cast as an internal problem. They saw their organizing as necessary in order to counter the effects that machismo had on their activism and on their lives; feminism as such was therefore not a mandate to leave the movement and join up with white (or, for that matter, Black) feminists.

Chicana feminist characterizations of machismo and its effects varied somewhat, from "liberal" visions of machismo impeding the advancement of individual Chicanas, to more radical and structural analyses. An example of the former approach came from Bernice Rincon, a founding member of CFM, who in her 1971 article for *Regeneración*, was less concerned than many Chicana feminists with the deleterious effects of machismo on the Chicano movement itself. Rincon took an individualist view of the problems that machismo created for Chicanas, challenging what she saw as cultural roles that would not work in contemporary Anglo society. In her vision, ideas about the active woman as "la mujer mala" [the evil woman] and the ideal woman as "la hembra" [the womb] were dooming the Chicano family, and Mexican American women workers, to economic failure (Rincon 1971:15–16). More so than many radical activists, Rincon saw Chicanos as "Americans" whose best solutions lay in taking the best of both worlds, keeping the Mexican American "corazon" [heart] as a counter to American "materialism" (1971:17).

In more radical Chicana feminist formulations, machismo was a result of the white power structure giving the oppressed Chicano dominion over his family so as to keep the entire community in line. In this critique, machismo was an imported and outmoded "colonial" set of ideas about subordinating women, and Chicanos who accepted it uncritically played into the oppressors' hands:

> When Chicano men oppose the efforts of women to move against their oppression, they are actually opposing the struggle of every woman in this country aimed at changing a society in which Chicanos themselves are oppressed. . . . [T]hey are doing just what the white male rulers of this country have done. The white male rulers want Chicanas to accept their oppression because they understand that when Chicanas begin a movement demanding legal abortions, child care, and equal pay for equal work, this movement will pose a real threat to their ability to rule. (Vidal 1971a:6–7)

Chicana feminists, therefore, took the cry of some male activists – "el problemo [sic] es el gabacho, no el macho" [the problem is the white man, and not the Chicano] – and argued that the problem was el macho who failed to recognize how much his behavior benefited el gabacho (del Castillo 1980).

According to more radical analyses by Chicana feminists, machismo had a number of specific deleterious effects that led to the diminution of women's effectiveness in the movement. First, and this point will be further elaborated, machismo kept women subordinate and confined to the family. When Elma Barrera, publicity chair and one of the organizers of the May 1971 National Chicana Conference, spoke with a reporter from the Houston Post, she attributed Chicanas' subordination within the family to unrecognized macho attitudes:

> The woman still waits on the man. . . . She often eats after the man has eaten. And she's so dependent on his whims that he can walk into the room while she's watching a TV show and switch the channel to another station without asking her. . . . Most Chicanos swear machismo doesn't exist. (Bennett 1971:12)

Barrera felt that it was difficult for Chicanas to face their domestic subordination by Chicano men, because "they [the men] are already put down so much by the rest of society."

Second, outside the family itself, Chicano movement machismo led to the silencing of Chicanas in public settings. As Dorinda Moreno recalled, "at San Francisco State [College], the guys were real *machistas*. They were pushed out of shape if you spoke up" (2000 interview). This issue of silencing women in Chicano movement organizations came up repeatedly in the writings of Chicana feminists (as it did in that of feminists in other racial/ethnic communities), and in interviews with them. One reaction to the machista style – one means of being heard – was the strategic co-optation by Chicana feminists of the "street" language of male activists. Both Irene Blea, a Chicana feminist activist and poet who in the 1970s was living in Colorado (2000 interview), and Nieto-Gómez (Blackwell interview with Nieto-Gómez 1991) in Long Beach countered what they saw as the intimidating style of Chicano nationalist men by swearing and using sexualized language of their own. Both women discovered that this language had to be countered to gain voice, if not acceptance, for a feminist agenda.

Blea was born in rural New Mexico, but raised in Chicano *barrios* [neighborhoods] in the industrial town of Bessemer, Colorado. She recalled that she had to make herself heard in the movement by engaging in swearing and sexual banter with male Chicano activists:

> I was street smart . . . and so when they'd say something sexist I'd be very confronting. . . . I wouldn't back down. . . . [T]hey were really sexist macho guys but they were also great human beings if you called them on their sexism. . . . And you know, they cussed and I cussed. . . . And you know, you grow up in a steel town . . . and there were all these bars and bar life and you get to be pretty tough. (2000 interview)

For Nieto-Gómez, swearing was the key to seeming as though she had street smarts (since, unlike Blea, she saw herself as coming from a sheltered background). Nieto-Gómez recalled that "one of the most empowering experiences I had being a woman in UMAS was learning to cuss" (Blackwell interview with Nieto-Gómez 1991). For Nieto-Gómez, "fuck was a very powerful word, an empowering word," and using it allowed her to finally be heard by the men in the group: "[F]inally I said, I think that idea is fucked. . . . The room was silent, quiet . . . and all of a sudden I had everybody's attention. That may have been the first public power that I had ever experienced." Using "the language of the heavies" (especially in Spanish) was "the only way to stop the dudes, the only way to get them to listen to you."[19]

Third, machismo was seen as leading to a sexual double standard within the Chicano movement that unfairly burdened Chicanas. Jeannette Martinez (1971:18), who described herself as "a young Chicana," criticized the situation of sexual oppression that a Chicana faced if she became involved in the movement:

> When I became involved in the Movement, I began to hate men (MACHOS).... A typical Chicano set up: a few words of Movimiento talk (if you're lucky), and then (he thinks) we go to bed. If you're good, I'll probably call again. Well, if you're smart? Who gives a damn? If I want to talk about barrio problems, why do I need a Chicana.... The majority of Chicanos think of Chicanas in sexual terms only.

The author of an unsigned article in *La Raza* argued that aggressive male sexuality left women in the movement in a double bind:

> If the hermana [sister] has an open mind about pre-marital sex, she is turned off to the movimiento because she values herself as a human being.... [S]he wants to be recognized as an individual who has brains and the ability to use them.... She does not want to be used as a sexual object but does want to be involved in all aspects of the movement. This the guys don't like. They distort her actions and make foolish accusations of strong women being dikes [sic].... Estas [these] Chicanas find themselves dating few of the guys in the organization. She is socially ostricized [sic] from the group. When she brings up the issue of machismo, the other hermanas silently agree but do not say anything to support her. So she is labeled a personality problem. ("El Movimiento and the Chicana," *La Raza* 1971:41)

Thus, while emerging, Chicana feminists took care not to "blame the victim" for machismo. They firmly believed that it was an "obstacle

---

[19] Clearly, not everyone was willing or perhaps able to adopt male street style in order to be heard. Baca Zinn cited the experiences of Jennie Chávez, active in a Chicano student organization: "As soon as I started expounding my own ideas the men who ran the organization would either ignore my statement, or make a wisecrack about it and continue their own discussion. This continued for two years until I finally broke away because of being unable to handle the situation" (1975:23).

to revolutionary struggle" (Baca Zinn 1975:23), insofar as it stymied women's activism and kept them from realizing their full potential within and for the movement.

Chicana Feminist Organizations in the 1970s and the Problem of Backlash

Throughout the 1970s, Chicanas mobilized around feminist issues, with the establishment of groups at both state and elite universities in the Southwest and programs within the community. Cortera (1980) presented a (probably partial) list of thirty-six conferences, workshops, seminars, and meetings from 1970 to 1977 on both the local and national level; by decade's end, there were at least ten newspapers and magazines dedicated to Chicana feminism, and other popular Chicano movement journals published feminist writings. Emerging Chicana feminists engaged in an ongoing debate about the organizational possibilities open to Chicanas, facing in many cases a dilemma over what to do with personal and organizational ties and loyalties that might be damaged by feminist organizing. They also wrestled with whether or not organizing as feminists meant taking something away from the Chicano struggle. Nonetheless, they came to challenge the Chicano movement to incorporate a vision of liberation from sexist domination along with liberation from racial domination (García 1990). This feminist challenge to modify Chicanismo engendered ridicule and a "loyalist" reaction against feminists.

So-called loyalists in the movement were openly hostile to feminist organizing (García 1990). Movement loyalists argued for the primacy of racist over sexist oppression, and felt that women's problems were best resolved in mixed-gender groups; they distrusted the intersectional and feminist solution of simultaneous struggle against both racism and sexism, and the formation of Chicana-only groups to do so (García 1990; López 1977). Those Chicanas who pressed on with feminist activism were met with accusations of being sellouts, of being infected with an outside Anglo ideology, as feminism was painted by loyalists as politics for white women only (García 1990).[20] Loyalists singled out Chicana lesbian feminists for special attack, since their activism was seen as a

---

[20] The charge of feminism as a "foreign import," and the consequent need to assert feminism's indigenousness to particular social settings, is also present in the dynamics of feminist organizing in Latin America; see Alvarez (2000:39).

double threat to the family. The loyalist backlash against feminist organizing was particularly unfair, given how conscious Chicana feminists were about the need for doing the work of Chicana *and* Chicano liberation. As Blea noted in her 2000 interview, her feminist activism was informed by her need to liberate her *entire* people:

> I think that the main track was Chicanismo and Chicano Power. And every once in awhile, I'd run into some kind of barrier that revolved around gender and . . . then finally one day [I remember] just getting really angry and saying "I want this issue of women on the agenda."

Blea was already an activist when she arrived on the scene as a graduate student at the University of Colorado at Boulder in the mid 1970s, having established herself as a campus leader at her undergraduate institution, Southern Colorado State College (now the University of Southern Colorado). At Boulder, she became increasingly unwilling to "back-burner" feminist issues:

> When I got to Boulder, I would go to UMAS and the guys were just really sexist, and they were, they kind of like didn't have respect for what I was saying. . . . Here I am a campus leader . . . I was not a "Johnny-Come-Lately," and there was little or no respect for me and finally I said "it's because I'm female, huh? 'Cause I'm a chick." . . . And they would cop to it. . . . The dialogue really revolved around empowering Chicano people, and me saying things like "Chicanas are people, too. And if we don't empower the women we can't empower our people, because we're at least fifty percent."

As Leticia Hernández noted when interviewed in 1992, the reactions by men against the formation of Las Hijas de Cuauhtémoc at Long Beach State were hard for her to understand, given how much Las Hijas were seeking to help the men:

> We [the women] don't want to take over and we don't want to wear the pants, we don't want balls, we just want to help you, we want to be side by side, and be equal partners. . . . We all over the place had the same enlightening kind of experiences that made us start to form women's groups . . . to rally the women to be more involved so

that we could be an active voice and participants in the MEChA organization. I don't think at any point that we wanted to be the ultimate leaders . . . or to take over and to feminize. (Blackwell interview with L. Hernández 1992)

In other examples of an explicitly stated desire to stay within the movement, Comision Feminil Mexicana, which had functioned since the 1970s as an autonomous, feminist presence in the Chicano community, held its first constitutional convention on June 2 and 3, 1973, in Santa Barbara, California; a pamphlet issued in April 1973 (CFM 1973) advertised the upcoming convention, and it highlighted the links that CFM had been making with members of the rising Mexican American political establishment and the labor movement. Speakers scheduled for the conference included State Assemblyman Richard Alatorre, Marta Cortera (described as a "librarian from Crystal City, Texas"), actress Carmen Zapata, Margarita Flores from the United Farm Workers, and Ruth Miller representing Chicana workers on strike at the El Paso factory of Farah Pants. Workshops for the convention were scheduled to cover issues such as education, employment, child care, sex education, and family planning. And in the Bay Area, it was a point of pride for Moreno and other Concilio Mujeres members that some male activists in the Chicano movement supported the group:

> When men talk about Concilio it's with respect and admiration. They see us as bringing unity and clarity to the movement, probably because we have not a militant feminist approach. In fact, I don't think many of us identify as feminists. We've taught women's classes, and may have bumped heads with the feminist approach. . . . I'm very nationalistic, and I'm not a racist, but I don't believe white people can theorize for us, lead us, or direct us; they can only work with us. (Moreno, quoted in Garcia 1975: no page given)

This assertion by Moreno is something at odds with her recollection of male Chicano activists at San Francisco State [College] as "machistas," but the statement reflects the intention of CM members to locate and work with sympathetic men wherever they existed.

What the positions of Las Hijas, CFM, and CM show is the centrality of the Chicano movement to Chicana feminist organizing. Their statements also hint at the serious backlash that Chicana feminist organizing experienced. Loyalists did not take to heart Chicana feminist intentions to remain linked to the movement, and instead constructed feminism as an Anglo-spawned, divisive distraction from the real cause throughout the 1970s (García-Camarillo and de la Torre 1976). Given that the Chicano movement asserted independence from Anglo influences, loyalist claims that Chicana feminism was a "gringa [white female] invention of *liberacion de las mujeres* [women's liberation]" was the ultimate rejection of feminism's significance (Morton 1975:16). Feminism was not only foreign to the Chicano community; it was actually a kind of deadly disease.

Following monist logic, feminist Chicanas were asked by loyalists to choose between being women and being Chicana. As Nieto-Gómez (1976:3) noted in writing about the resistance that Chicana feminism met within the Chicano movement:

> [T]here is a lot of intimidation in our community . . . against people who define themselves as Chicana feminists. It sounds like a contradictory statement [that] if you're a Chicana you're on one side, if you're a feminist, you must be on the other side. They say you can't stand on both sides.

Nonetheless, Nieto-Gómez (1976:4) insisted that women fighting for their rights in the Chicano community, and for more attention to issues involving "race, welfare rights, forced sterilization," would prevail and force the Chicano movement to "live up to its Carnalismo [brotherhood] and community responsibility." And, consistent with the feminist analysis of machismo as the problem for the movement as a whole, Nieto-Gómez (1971) and others argued that resistance to feminism was the truly divisive force in the movement. In her article for *Regeneracion*, Nieto-Gómez made clear that characterizing unhappy Chicana activists as crypto-Anglos did make Chicanas, or the movement, stronger:

> Being compared with the Anglo woman has been the greatest injustice and the strongest device used to keep Chicanas quiet. Nobody liked to be called a traitor in a [cause] she feels she would die for. And no Chicana who has worked in the movement deserves to be compared with any Anglo woman. . . . These comparisons are divisive and threatening to the strength of the movement. (1971:9)

Backlash could take very personalized forms, as the aforementioned example of hanging and burning Nieto-Gómez in effigy showed. Somewhat later in the 1970s, Irene Blea was seriously harassed while at the University of Colorado at Boulder as a result of a 1977 conference on Chicana feminism that she had organized, a conference which attracted about three hundred people and included nonfeminist Chicana activists (2000 interview). After the conference, the level of abuse that Blea was subjected to as a feminist increased:

> Up until that [conference], the hostility had been mostly name-calling – "bitch," "whore," "ball-buster" – things like that. But after that it escalated to vandalism. . . . There's nothing worse in a Colorado winter than having somebody egg your car and then "t.p." it and then have it freeze. . . . It was that kind of stuff. And then one night, they actually attacked my apartment and broke my window . . . It woke me up with my daughter at three o'clock in the morning, the phone rang, and they said "we're coming right over you blank, blank" and I hung up the phone and five minutes later, all of my windows and my two doors are being knocked on . . . and there were names being called.

Blea had windows broken, was "chased across parking lots," and received threatening letters in response to her public professions of Chicana feminism. She noted in retrospect that some of the harassment may have come from the garden-variety right wing, generated in response to a speaking tour with Angela Davis that she had done. But according to Blea, although it never became all that easy to be a feminist in the Chicano community, she persevered as a feminist because "I come from a long line of people that have persevered . . . and perseverance for me has been a strategy. . . . Just hang in there."

Arguably, backlash, specifically the argument that Chicana feminists were Anglicized sellouts, had productive effects for Chicana feminists, as it stimulated feminist Chicanas into arguing for their place within the movement and making concrete political counterarguments defending their feminism. I next turn to the two main counterarguments that Chicana feminists used to justify their organizing: the existence of the "historical Chicana feminist" in Chicano and Mexican history, and the need to remake the family for struggle against Anglo domination. Taken together, these counterarguments by Chicana feminists asserted the differences that existed between themselves and Anglo feminists; this difference was strategically emphasized at the same time that Chicana feminists' "Chicana-ness" was celebrated.

Counterarguments: The Historical Chicana Feminist and the Need to Remake the Political Family

As outlined in the previous section, the loyalist backlash against feminist organizing in the Chicano movement was serious and widespread. As was the case with white women's liberation and Black feminism, organizational emergence by Chicana feminists required debate and the construction of arguments for the necessity of feminism, since Chicanas were situated in an oppositional community. While Black feminism focused on the "vanguard center" approach of the Black women's position as being the key to universal transformation of oppression, and while a very different picture of a universalist sisterhood was the chief argument of white women's liberationists for the importance of feminism (as will be discussed in Chapter Five), Chicana feminists made arguments about the necessity of their feminism that were specific to their movement context. Drawing on culturally specific ideas about the Chicano community's history and current constitution, Chicana feminists countered loyalist backlash with two main counterarguments: the existence of the historical Chicana feminist and the Chicano family's political familialism, and the further necessity to remake the politicized family for struggle.

Chicana feminists looked for feminist role models in Chicano and Mexican history, much as Chicanos generally looked at Mexican history for inspiration (Gluck et al. 1998). They drew on historical role models in order to counter charges of the "outside" nature of feminism; they used the theme of an indigenous Chicana and Mexicana feminism to justify their struggle as feminists. As Nieto-Gómez commented, using Chicana history to find role models "made it [discussion of women's issues] more like a national issue as opposed to an individual issue – which made us feel less selfish" (Gluck et al. 1998:47). Names that continuously reappear in the formulation of the historical Chicana feminist range from the unfairly maligned sixteenth-century Indian princess Malintzin (mother of the Mexican people), to seventeenth-century Mexican nun and writer Sor Juana Inez de la Cruz; from Doña Josefa Ortiz de Dominguez, active in the Mexican independence movement in the early 1800s, to the soldaderas [female soldiers], "Las Adelitas" of the 1910 Mexican revolution; from Mexican bourgeois feminists of the 1920s and 1930s to

Chicana labor organizers in the United States from the 1930s to the 1960s, such as Dolores Huerta of the United Farm Workers (Blackwell 2000a; Cortera 1976a, 1976b, 1977, 1980; Enríquez and Mirandé 1978; García 1997; Gonzales 1979; Martínez 1997 [1971]; Mirandé and Enríquez 1979; Murphy 1971; Nieto-Gómez 1976: Rincon 1971). These historical figures were recast as feminist *and* indigenous Chicana figures (even if Mexicana rather than Chicana), such that women's participation in the ongoing Chicano nationalist struggle had roots that could be found in pre-Columbian Mexican society, and that this participation was inherently feminist (Cortera 1976a). The academic concern over possibly using the word "feminist" anachronistically did not very much concern activists; as Elizabeth Martínez noted, "Many Latinas might not have defined themselves with a term like 'feminist,' but their lives expressed great strength and defiance of male restriction" (1998:163). This intrinsic feminism was precisely what Chicana feminists celebrated, and in choosing positive feminist models from history, they countered the tendency in the Chicano movement to celebrate icons of "traditional Chicana womanhood" (Moya 2001:447).

Chicana feminists took strength from these rediscovered role models while at the same time recognizing the ideological resource that they represented. The author of a report on the 1971 Houston conference for *La Raza*, the Los Angeles–based Chicano movement journal, argued that male activists who made themselves aware of the historical role of the Chicana in previous struggles would want to work together with women in the interests of unity:

> La Mexicana has been an active revolutionary throughout history, and she will continue to be active in the future – but only through a united struggle, the Chicana and Chicano side by side, will we be able to make a meaningful contribution to la revolucion. ("El Movimiento and the Chicana," *La Raza* 1971:44)

Marta Cortera, who was probably the Chicana feminist who spent the most energy articulating the history of the Chicana feminist, explicitly acknowledged the strategic value of enlightening men as to the existence of historical Chicana feminism:

> That's a really neat argument – we had to use it in the Sixties when the guys said, "Get back home – yo en las conferencias, yo haciendola más bonita, y tu en la casa" [Me at the conferences, I

do it better than you, and you at home]. That's one of the reasons we need our history – to fall back on in these situations. (Cortera 1976b:16).

Cortera's work influenced other feminists; for example, Nieto-Gómez credited Cortera with showing that those who argued for Chicana feminists' being *vendidas* were very much mistaken:

> Marta Cortera wrote an article several years ago saying that feminism is not an Anglo idea. I resent the usual remark that if you're a feminist you have somehow become an Anglo or been influenced by Anglos. . . . [W]e are only supposed to be repositories – everything we say is either his idea or the white anglo "her" idea, but not *our* idea. (Nieto-Gómez 1976:3; emphasis in original)

By using examples of historical Chicana feminists, second-wave Chicana feminists could reassure loyalist men (and women) that feminists were indigenous, not alien, and that they belonged within the Chicano movement. The unearthing of historical Chicana feminists became an important form of Chicana feminist expression in organizing. In 1975, Moreno and other members of Concilio Mujeres produced a film for public television called "*La Mujer en Pie de Lucha*" [Woman Ready for the Struggle] (Moreno c. 1975). An excerpt from the film script showed the historical Chicana feminist approach, as *en pie de lucha* was translated by CM as meaning "to overcome the oppression of the Spanish-speaking woman in a self determined action against bondage." The script included a dramatization of the fighting done by *Las Soldaderas*, "the guerilla women fighters who fought alongside Pancho Villa and Emiliano Zapata, in the Mexican Revolution of 1910." And in the excerpt that follows, it is clear that Concilio Mujeres' theater group, Las Cucarachas, saw its mission as depicting "the role of Raza women in the movimiento" historically:

> Las Cucarachas works to depict and relate the Chicano message and also to be supportive of all Raza women's struggles. Our priority is to devote perpetuation of the concept of the united family. Also the introduction of Mestiza (Latina y India) mujeres who have participated in the liberation of pueblo [people] both historically and in contemporary times. (CM flyer, c. 1975b)

Although effective as an argument for feminist mobilization, from time to time the counterargument of the historical Chicana feminist was subject to intense ridicule. Cortera herself was attacked for her ideas in the very Texas-based movement magazine, *Caracol* [The Spiral], that printed them. In April 1976, Reyes Cárdenas defended machismo in an ambivalent fashion in his "The Machismo Manifesto (humorous article)," but very much took Cortera to task. "Since none of you tienen los huevos [have the balls] to speak up," Reyes wrote, he would take issue with Cortera's admiration of

> [a]quella puta Sor Juana Inez de las Piernas-cruzadas [that whore Sister Juana Inez of the Crossed Legs], certainly a masochist product of shitty Catholicism; la mamasota [the big mama] should have found herself a chavo [guy] instead of Jesús. (Cárdenas 1976:7)[21]

Cárdenas and the like aside, the unearthing of the historical Chicana feminist served to sufficiently differentiate Chicana feminism from the "Anglo" version so that by the late 1970s, the idea of Chicana feminism as a completely internal phenomenon, untouched by any white feminism, had crystallized. Cortera, Gonzales (1979), and Mirandé and Enríquez (1979) argued that

> Chicana feminism is not impervious to Anglo feminism, but its roots are in Mexican-Chicana feminism. There is thus no need to go outside of Mexican-Chicano culture and traditions to explain its emergence. (Mirandé and Enríquez 1979:234)

There is much truth in this statement if we take it to mean that Chicana feminist organizations came from within the Chicano movement. But

---

[21] Cárdenas's writing here illustrates, by way of contrast, the much milder critique of the Catholic Church that came from Chicana feminists themselves. While feminists were very critical of the stereotypes of the good, passive, virginal woman and the bad, active, sexual woman that they saw coming from Catholicism, there isn't much systematic critique of the Church as an institution (Alarcón 1991; Anzaldúa 1981; "Chicana Regional Conference," *La Raza* 1971a; Rincon 1971). For example, criticism of the church is completely absent from Cortera's work on historical Chicana feminism. Chicana feminists may have felt distanced enough from the church not to attack it directly; they may not have wanted to alienate others in the community by attacking the church; and/or they may have seen the church as partly encouraging some leftist activism by both nuns and priests (see Basso 1971).

the assertion of utter indigenousness – of an indigenous origin, and therefore indigenous "character" – for Chicana feminism was strategic in its overstatement; note the word "impervious." Asserting indigenousness for Chicana feminism itself was a counterclaim to charges of feminist *vendidismo*, and thus was useful regardless of whether or not it was true in all parts.

The need to restructure the family in order to aid community struggle was a second counterargument that Chicana feminists used, since loyalists argued that Chicana feminism disrupted traditional male/female roles that were crucial for the preservation of Chicano culture. Emerging Chicana feminists argued that familial relationships within the colonized community had been changed by the struggle against oppression, and that in actuality, they needed to change even more. This counterargument about reforming the political family in and for struggle accepted the idea of Chicano cultural differences from Anglo culture (and with it the truth of the supposed antifamily stance of white middle-class feminism), but took an opposite view on the need to preserve traditional gender roles.

In 1975, the Chicano academic journal *Aztlán* published Maxine Baca Zinn's "Political Familialism: Toward Sex Role Equality in Chicano Families." Baca Zinn argued that given racism and internal colonization, Chicano activists should regard the family as the real locus of resistance that it was; the community needed to recognize that such "political familialism" was strong within the Chicano community, and that it was an asset (1975:16).[22] She attacked the notion that more egalitarian roles between women and men necessarily meant an imitation of the Anglo family, and noted that Chicano loyalists ignored the "changes in the relative position of men and women" that struggle had already brought about (1975:21). For Baca Zinn, gender egalitarianism was and should continue to be the result of struggle against an oppressive mainstream culture; Chicana feminists, in taking egalitarianism further, were acting in the interest of community progress.

In naming "political familialism" as both a feature of, and a goal for, the Chicano community, Baca Zinn recognized a model of activism already present in the Chicano movement. Dolores Huerta (1975:21)

---

[22] See Naples (1998a, especially Chapter 5) for an extended discussion of the related concept of "activist mothering" of community women in the 1960s–1980s, and the importance of the family as a locus of resistance in communities of color.

commented on the nature of communal struggle among farm workers:

> It's really kind of old fashioned. Remember when you were little you had always had your uncles, your aunts, your grandmother and your comadres [godmothers] around. As a child in the Mexican culture you identified with a lot of people, not just your mother and father like they do in the middle class homes. When people are poor their main interest is family relationships.

The familial model of activism extended into local chapters of UMAS and MEChA (Sotomayor 1971). The idea that the Chicano family was a locus of resistance to "Anglo" cultural domination was part of "El Plan Espiritual de Aztlán," drawn up at the aforementioned 1969 Denver Youth conference. "El Plan" read, in part, that "our cultural values of home and family will serve as powerful weapons to defeat the gringo dollar system and encourage the process of love and brotherhood" (Baca Zinn 1975:16).

Chicana feminists shared this emphasis on the family in the movement against oppression, and argued for an activism that showed commitment to maintaining families. This emphasis can be seen in CFM's platform, and in Concilio Mujeres' stress on "perpetuation of the concept of the united family." In another example, Longauex y Vasquez (1970:384) wrote that Chicanas' activism should focus on

> a total commitment of a family unit living what it believes to be a better way of life in demanding social change for the benefit of humankind. When a family is involved in a human rights movement, as is the Mexican-American family, there is little room for a woman's liberation movement alone. . . . The Raza movement is based on brother- and sisterhood. We must look at each other as one large family.

And in preparation for the Houston conference, Las Hijas at Long Beach State asserted that

> [t]he family relationship and involvement with the movement should not be separate. *Chicanas y hombres* [women and men] must work together and try to educate themselves to new roles in order to meet the responsibility of building a nation. (Ugarte 1997 [1971])

The political familialism model helped Chicana activists who were placed in difficult new roles outside the community, as Chicana students negotiated new demands engendered by absence from home for the first time (see P. Hernandez 1980). At the same time, familial models of activism that reproduced traditional gender roles were recognized by Chicana feminists as limiting. The author of the 1971 La Raza article "El Movimiento and the Chicana" argued that recreating the family within the student movement would be problematic for women, since men were sometimes overprotective of women who agreed with them politically. The author wrote that men in the movement sometimes took an obliging woman and set her up as an example of being a good Chicana, "the queen or Azteca princess of the organization" (1971:40). Instead of making princesses, Chicana feminists wanted Chicano student organizations to learn from the example of strong women within the community. The idea that community Chicanas were strong and independent women because of struggles against Anglo oppression was echoed by Nieto-Gómez:

In my mind, I was acting like my mom, like my aunts, like the Chicanas from San Bernardino, and I always look at that ... the women of my era ... and we were all just like I am.... We were independent, we weren't really all that traditional ... we were kind of like a blend of all the good things. (Blackwell interview with Nieto-Gómez 1991)

The Chicana feminist counterargument for the continued remaking of the political family derived its power for fighting backlash from Chicanas' and Chicanos' self-understandings about the centrality of family to their culture. Loyalists had one picture of the ideal revolutionary family, and Chicana feminists quite another, but feminists were able to argue for Chicanas' liberation by using consensual values internal to the Chicano movement. Restructuring the political family meant taking family very seriously while at the same time challenging roles within it, because "[l]a familia [the family] is part of La Causa because if there were no familia there would be nothing to fight for" (García-Camarillo and de la Torre 1976:10). As in the making of the "historical Chicana feminist" counterargument, the Chicana feminist focus on reconstituting the political family served to distance their feminism from supposedly anti-family "Anglo feminism"; holding the family as a central value also allowed Chicana feminists to emphasize feminism's importance to the movement as a whole. As Eliana Rivero argued,

> no hay que renunciar a la cultura de nuestros mayores, sino hacerla más humana, enriquecerla con el concepto de igualdad personal nuestro núcleo de cohesíon" [We don't have to reject the culture of our ancestors; instead we have to make it more human, and enrich it with the concept of personal equality as our cohesive center]. (1977:7)[23]

Chicana Feminism's Relationship with White Women's Liberation: Sympathies Versus Sisterhood

Chicana feminists saw themselves as having a very different set of problems from white feminists, despite having similar sets of priorities. Like Black feminists, they understood their struggle as simultaneously one against sexism, racism, and class oppression, although class received less consistent attention as an axis of oppression than in most Black feminist writings. They were not particularly interested in organizing with white feminists, despite general acknowledgment that they shared issues. For example, Chicana feminist Elma Barrera gave a speech at a national abortion rights conference in New York City in July of 1971 in which she argued:

> I have been told that the Chicana's struggle is not the same as the white woman's struggle. I've been told that the problems are different and that . . . the Chicana's energies are needed in the barrio [Chicano community] and that being a feminist and fighting for our rights as women and as human beings is anti-Chicano and anti-male. . . . But let me tell you what being a Chicana means in Houston, Texas. It means learning how to best please the men in the Church and the men at home, not in that order. (Vidal 1971a:12)

Barrera's view contains both assertions of similarity and difference in conceptualizing the position of white and Chicana feminists, which was

[23] The question of who was left out in holding the heterosexual family as central to the Chicano struggle has been addressed by a number of Chicana lesbian feminists; see Alarcón, Castillo, and Moraga 1993; Anzaldúa 1999 [1987]; Castillo 1994; Moraga 1983; Pérez 1991; and the contributors to Trujillo 1991.

largely typical of Chicana feminist writings. The desire to stay linked
to activist Chicano males shaped the way that Chicanas saw their feminism. Distancing themselves from white feminists, Chicana feminists
continually asserted that the proper site of Chicana feminism was the
Chicano movement, whether or not feminists worked in all-women or
mixed-gender groups. There was also little emphasis in Chicana feminist
writings of the early 1970s on coalition building with other women of
color, it should be noted. Feminists participated in cross-racial/ethnic
efforts on campus to institute racial/ethnic studies (Blackwell interview
with Nieto-Gómez 1991; Moreno 2000 interview); beyond that, forming coalitions with Black women in university settings was described by
Blea in her 2000 interview as problematic due to the "fragmentation"
of the Black movement in the early to mid-1970s.

Many Chicana feminists felt that a mostly white, middle-class feminist movement could not help Chicanas trying to maintain their
community's cultural integrity, and could not aid them in working for
"restoration of control over a way of life, a culture, an existence" (Sosa
Riddell 1974:163). And certainly, as indicated in Blea's opening quo-
tation for the introduction of this book, many white feminist organizations in practice developed a monist political view that asked Chicana
feminists to choose their gender over their cultural identity in their
activism. But also important in generating distance between Chicana
feminism and white feminism was the dynamic of argument and counterargument in the Chicano movement. Loyalist backlash and charges
of vendidismo generated Chicana feminist counterarguments aimed at
asserting utter indigenousness for Chicana feminism and thus loyalty
to the Chicano movement. In the "harder" forms of these arguments,
Chicana feminists claimed that they were uniquely *uninfluenced* by white
feminist ideology. This assertion of indigenousness in terms of ideas was
clearly a result of the fact that loyalists used the white women's movement as a specter to haunt feminists in their midst: "We didn't say that
we were feminist. It was the men who said that. They said 'Aha! Fem-
inista!' And that was a good way they didn't have to listen to her and
her and her" (Cortera 1976b:15).

The idea that Chicana feminists organized without paying any attention to Anglo feminism – or in fact, without having any sympathy
with parts of its agenda – had at its root the strategic purpose of re-
assuring those within the Chicano movement that Chicana feminists
were not vendidas, and it should not be taken at face value. Clearly,
even the Denver statement that asserted that Chicanas did not want

to be liberated was inconceivable except in the response to a growing (and feared) white feminist movement (Cortera 1976b). Even those who argued for the indigenousness of Chicana feminism were mindful of what Anglo feminists advocated, and sometimes were admiring of what white feminists did; Cortera actually contradicted the idea that Chicana feminism emerged without a relationship to white feminism, noting that "Chicanas realized that Anglo women were advocating for greater rights and privileges" (1976b:159). And Enríquez and Mirandé (1978) stated that disillusioned Chicanas did in fact turn to the emerging white (and Black) women's movement, where they found women of other ethnicities to be more sympathetic to their problems than were Chicanos.

A distinction needs to be made between indigenousness in terms of organization and indigenousness in terms of ideas, as Mirta Vidal noted in her 2000 interview. For Vidal (and as noted in this chapter), there is no question that Chicana feminism had indigenous Chicano movement origins; it "was something that came from the Chicano movement itself."[24] But asserting that Chicana feminism was uninfluenced by any other set of feminist ideas negates the power of the Chicana feminist critique of white feminism's blinders, and makes Chicana feminists seem much less discerning than they were about the politics of second-wave feminisms. For example, Ana Nieto-Gómez (Blackwell interview with Nieto-Gómez 1991) never saw herself as part of the mainstream women's movement, but she did read literature put out by the white women's movement, some of which she characterized as "very important to me." It was attending NOW meetings that led Nieto-Gómez to her conclusion that the distance she felt from white feminists was the result of their middle-class status insulating them from the risks of activism. Irene Blea (2000 interview) read white feminist literature, liking Gloria Steinem, and not being too compelled by Friedan's arguments in *The Feminine Mystique*. Echoing Nieto-Gómez, Blea felt that communicating with local white feminists in the Denver/Boulder area was difficult; she found the Anglo domination of the 1975 United Nations–sponsored women's meeting in Mexico City hard to take, but she *went*. Distance from white feminists on the grounds of racism and cultural insensitivity is a theme that runs through the work of feminist Chicana writers Cherríe Moraga and Gloria Anzaldúa, and through the work gathered

[24] Blackwell (2000a, 2000b) has come to the same conclusion about the roots of Chicana feminism being in internal Chicano movement struggles.

in their edited collection, *This Bridge Called My Back: Writings by Radical Women of Color* (1979); but as Moraga (1983:106) noted:

> [I]t is perfectly acceptable among Chicano males to use white theo-reticians, e.g. Marx and Engels, to develop a theory of Chicano op-pression. It is unacceptable, however, for the Chicana to use white sources by women to develop a theory of Chicana oppression.

As del Castillo (1980) and García (1990) showed, Chicana feminists were aware of sexism within their movement and the liberation promises of Anglo feminism (see also Gluck et al. 1998). Del Castillo argued that "Anglo" feminism provided the conceptual tools for Chicanas battling sexist practices in nationalist organizations:

> Feminist consciousness jelled primarily through subjective en-counters with it and through deficiencies in organizational func-tion and structure which denied them equal participation . . . [I]t was difficult for women to articulate these observations with-out a conceptual point of reference with which to explain sexism. . . . Eventually, however, the popularity of the Anglo femi-nist movement served as an important impetus in the articulation of sexism in the Chicano Movement. Within the context of Chi-cano struggle for liberation, women saw a major contradiction in the subordination of the Chicana woman. (1980:11)

Awareness of white feminism – and to a lesser extent of Black feminism – helped Chicanas formulate their feminism on the basis of culturally specific ideas about women and men in Chicano activist culture. These ideas helped them coordinate their organizations much more closely with the broader Chicano movement – that is, men – than was the case in either white or Black feminism. Chicana feminism's successful mobilization was therefore linked to the presence of white feminism, although not in the simplistic ways that the loyalists imagined.

Some Chicana feminists did feel that working with white feminists would actually be dangerous to the Chicano movement. Sylvia Gonzalez (1975: no page given), at the time an assistant professor at San Jose State University, painted a picture of Chicanas as being attracted to the white women's liberation solely to escape oppressive Chicano men in her report on the United Nations–sponsored meetings in Mexico City. Not surprisingly, Gonzalez thought this approach mistaken, and that the fulfillment of Chicanas' "unique needs" could only be reached by working with Chicanos within the movement. But she need not have worried too much; Chicana feminists were ever mindful of questions of cultural distance in their dealings with the white feminist movement. One interesting example that illustrates what some organized Chicana feminists saw as the white feminist movement's inability to cross cultural differences is the attempt by the Boston Women's Health Book Collective to involve Concilio Mujeres in creating a Spanish-language edition of *Our Bodies, Ourselves*. In an unsigned article entitled "Body Language – A Cultural Ms.understanding," which appeared in Concilio Mujeres' 1975 publication *La Razon Mestiza II*, the controversy over developing the Spanish version of the book was chronicled from CM's point of view.[25] CM members argued against a straight translation into Spanish of *Our Bodies, Ourselves* on the grounds that the experiences of white women upon which the book was based would not be useful to U.S. Latinas. CM suggested instead that an entirely new edition of the book be created using the experiences of Latinas, and CM members even suggested that this special edition be in English, which in their opinion would reach more Latinas than a Spanish-language version.

The Women's Health Book Collective apparently agreed to this, but asked CM to collect the experiences of Chicanas and Latinas for them. The author of the article accused the Collective of being high-handed in its treatment of CM:

> [W]e applaud the work that the collective has done. But we urge for a more sensitive approach to promoting an atmosphere of equality, and not the same authoritative, classist treatment of the past; it is oppressive and degrading. It's your book, but you want our experiences. We demand respectful interaction for our cooperation and support. (CM 1975a: no page given)

There was a meeting between a number of CM women and the two Spanish translators that the Collective had hired in May of 1975. However, one translator was leaving the country, and the other admitted to not having much familiarity with the Latino community. CM members felt that the Collective failed to understand that a translation into Spanish without awareness of the differences between white women and Latinas in the United States was insupportable. According to the author

[25] The article was published with an accompanying letter that had been sent to the Health Book Collective by CM and "some 10–12 Chicana educators and community leaders."

of the article, no response came from the Book Collective up until the publication date of *La Razon Mestiza II*.[26]

In fact, Chicana feminists exercised selectivity in orienting toward white feminism as they argued for the continued existence of autonomous Chicana feminist organizing. A number of Chicana feminists have noted the greater pull that socialist feminism had for them, as they conceptualized themselves and their movement as working class (Blea 1992; García 1990; Orozco 1976; Pérez 1991). But Chicana feminism's emergence from an oppositional community of activists meant that sympathies did not dictate association. Even when the Chicano movement "ignored the needs and priorities of Chicanas and therefore excluded us" or restricted Chicanas "to stereotypical sex roles – in the kitchen or at the typewriter," it was the movement that mattered to young Chicana feminists (Orozco 1976:6). Knowing what we know about the transplantation and pollination of leftist ideologies in the 1960s and 1970s – the influence of other movements was in fact welcomed by many in the Chicano movement (Martínez 1998) – it is important to understand that Chicana feminists took on the burden of "proving" that they were not associated with others who were deemed a threat. Taking on this burden of proof may have been good strategy initially, but ultimately, insistence on indigenousness in ideas as well as origins may have delimited strategic choice for Chicana feminists, insofar as it became difficult for Chicana feminists to say that they used some concepts articulated by white feminists. The idea that Anglo feminism did not at all influence Chicana feminism recapitulates the "either/or" logic that loyalists used to accuse Chicana feminists of vendidismo, and ignores the way in which Chicana feminists took an active part in fashioning a movement that suited their vision of liberation.

---

[26] A Spanish-language version of *Our Bodies, Ourselves* was published in 1976, and approximately 50,000 copies were distributed (Berger 2000). Many of these copies were actually given away through social service agencies, as the Spanish language version "never caught on" with Latinas in the United States. In 2000, Seven Stories Press of New York published *Nuestros Cuerpos, Nuestros Vidas* [Our Bodies, Our Lives], a version of the original with about half of the actual material in the book changed to better reflect Latinas' sense of themselves and their connections with others in their families and communities. The effort to not just retranslate but to really remake the book took ten years, with substantially rewritten chapters (especially about reproductive rights and sexuality) and photos and personal accounts drawn from the lives of Latinas. It would seem that the women in Concilio were right to be concerned about the wisdom of translating *Our Bodies, Ourselves* without paying attention to cultural differences.

Fitting into the Struggle: Chicana Feminist
Organizing Through the 1970s

By the mid-1970s, Chicanas had developed autonomous feminist organizations, maintained an ideology of working in tandem with the Chicano movement, and distanced themselves from white feminist groups. Chicana feminist groups grew in number throughout the 1970s, and in contrast to the feminist movements thus far considered, much Chicana feminist work occurred as part of Chicano organizations, whether in caucuses of larger groups or as affiliated projects (Cortera 1980). The most important consideration for many Chicana feminist activists was the good of the community as a whole, shown in this comment on the fight for the Equal Rights Amendment:

> I was not very interested in this issue until recently. In the Movimiento there is the feeling that when we move, we all do it together. . . . Time and energy put into a cause like ERA is even said to detract from other causes which require more urgent attention. I think there's something in that attitude, but now [that] I know a little about ERA I'm in favor of it. Why? Because it's going to crucially affect thousands of Chicana household heads. It's more than an issue of dignity and human rights – for many women it's a survival issue. (García-Camarillo 1976:15)

Chicana feminist projects were established within Chicano community organizations. For example, the Chicana Rights Project (CRP) of the Mexican American Legal Defense and Education Fund (MALDEF) was formed in June of 1974 with a grant from the Ford Foundation (MALDEF 1974; Mirandé and Enríquez 1979). The CRP was meant to be an arm of the organization that focused on the needs of Chicanas, particularly educational and employment issues, "designed to counteract the dismal civil rights litigation record" on behalf of the Civil Rights of Chicanas; the 1974 MALDEF report noted that there were only "53 Chicana organizations, 86 Chicana law students and 86 Spanish-surnamed attorneys up to this time" nationally (1974:1). Activities planned or carried out by the CRP included helping to coordinate the Sixth National Conference on Women and the Law, and conducting a workshop there on the legal issues of Chicana women; providing counseling and information on legal issues to Chicanas; working with the Equal Employment Opportunity Commission and the Department of

Housing and Urban Development to stop housing discrimination in San Antonio, Texas; looking at Chicanas' lack of representation on the grand jury in Bexar County, Texas, which the CRP hoped to use to point out "the limited participation of Chicanas in the mainstream of American democracy"; suing to stop the California Department of Education from instituting regulations to eliminate child-care eligibility for poor women residing in "target poverty areas"; and litigating on a number of employment discrimination suits involving Chicanas (MALDEF 1974:3).

Another important site for Chicana feminist organizing was as part of the political party La Raza Unida [The United Race]. The RUP, which began in Crystal City, Texas, was fairly hospitable to women's organizing from its inception, and this hospitality was certainly facilitated in part by Chicana feminist organizing in the wider movement, as well as by the existence of women community leaders. At the RUP's first national convention in September of 1972, women led the delegations of six of the eighteen states represented, namely, California, Illinois, Kansas, Maryland, Wyoming, and Oregon (La Raza Unida Party 1972). In April of 1972, the Women's Caucus of the California RUP passed a set of resolutions to be presented to the statewide gathering of the party in July of 1972 (La Raza Unida Party 1972). Approximately fifty-four women participated in drafting the resolutions, which called for Chicanas to be accepted as "a vital part of the Chicano community" (1972: no page given). To that end, the RUP was urged to recognize the importance of "la hermanidad" [sisterhood] in organizing Chicanas and that it "not condone, accept, or transfer the oppression of La Chicana"; that "Chicanas be on all policymaking and decision-making bodies concerning La Raza; that party literature include articles, poems, etc. written by Chicanas"; that "Chicanas be represented in all levels of the Partido [party] (leadership, decision-making, organizing, representation)"; that Chicanas run as RUP "candidates in all general, primary and local elections" (1972: no page given).

The Women's Caucus of the California RUP also set out an agenda for the RUP regarding the alleviation of the stressful conditions for women's work, including the guarantee of equal pay for equal work, changed conditions in the garment industry, unionization of Chicana workers, job and skill training, and paid maternity leave. Interestingly, the Women's Caucus urged that prostitution not be legalized, on the grounds that prostitutes were exploited workers, and that legalizing prostitution would only lead to more poor women becoming exploited in a similar manner.

They argued for safe, legal abortions and an end to sterilization abuse:

> Whereas we, as Chicanas, have been subjected to illegal, de-
> huminizing [sic] and unsafe abortions let it be resolved that we
> endorse legalized medical abortions in order to protect the human
> right of self determination. Be it also resolved that Chicanas are
> to control the process to its completion. In addition, we feel that
> the sterilization process, must *never* be administered without the
> full knowledge and consent of the individual involved. (1972: no
> page given; emphasis in original)

Other resolutions urged the RUP to demand "controlled clinics that
would give medical services"; "child care programs to be established
in 'nuestra [sic] barrios' [our neighborhoods] and run by 'nuestra raza'
[our people]"; "bilingual drug abuse programs"; and "Chicana classes
educating the Chicana, Chicano and community [that] should deal with
existing problems faced by the Chicana as a wife, mother, worker and
as a member of 'La Raza'" (1972: no page given). The list of Women's
Caucus issues then included a combination of emphases on economic
matter, reproductive rights, and Chicano cultural maintenance.

Women in the RUP tended to be critical of autonomous feminist
organizing, a somewhat ironic development given that Marta Cortera,
one of the key chroniclers of Chicana feminism as a movement, was
also an RUP activist. RUP member Amparo Aguilar's (1975) report on
the International Year of the Woman conference held in Mexico City
in the summer of 1975 made clear that she did not consider herself to
be solely a Chicana (that is, only a feminist) at the conference but a
representative of the RUP. Aguilar bemoaned the lack of consideration
given to nongovernmental groups at the gathering adjunct to the official
conference; though she blamed *gringas* [white women] for these difficulties, she was also critical of those women representatives who did not
see the necessity of staying affiliated with the RUP:

> [T]wo girls from California sent us a position paper that they had
> prepared [but] the women in California didn't know what they were
> going down there for. They thought they were going to México to
> represent women and Chicanas, not the Partido [party]. And so
> did the people from the Midwest. . . . The papers we received didn't
> have an onda [thing] that had anything to do with the Partido,
> but were only concerned with women. (Aguilar 1975:11)

And Aguilar was even less enamored of other Chicanas at the conference, whom she called *Chicanas con Ondas Gringas* [Chicanas with White "Trips"]:

> Right from the beginning we started meeting Chicanas from different states and different organizations. . . . We all got together, and from that meeting we started realizing that a lot of them were really lost as far as our ideology goes. . . . Their only onda [trip] was how to develop the woman. They didn't think about how the woman develops with her environment. . . . We made them aware . . . that we were Raza Unida, that we followed the Partido's ideology, and that our stand was based on that principle. . . . So we started having hassles with them. And people may have heard about a meeting in which our delegation walked out. That was the problem; they were on a weird onda [trip], and we couldn't compromise. (1975:11)

Whether Aguilar liked it or not, Chicana feminist offshoots of the RUP started in the 1970s. The National Chicana Political Caucus (1973) had links to the RUP, even while it was clearly affiliated with the National Women's Political Caucus. About fifty Chicanas, the majority of whom belonged to the RUP, attended the annual Texas Women's Political Caucus Convention in San Antonio, Texas, August 17–19, 1973. They elected Texas representatives to national Chicana organizations and passed a resolution that supported the rescinding of the Texas Constitutional Welfare Ceiling and the development with the Texas Women's Political Caucus of new welfare legislation, arguing that two-thirds of those living in poverty were women, 39 percent of poor families in Texas were headed by women, and South Texas had the lowest per capita income in the nation in 1973 (with its 85 percent Chicano population). The newsletter for the group reported that groups of Chicanas were involved in electoral political organizing in Houston and San Antonio, Texas, and in Illinois, California, and New Mexico.

Conclusion: Organizationally Distinct Chicana Feminism in the Second Wave

Chicana feminism needs to be understood as an outgrowth of Chicanas' participation in the Chicano movement at a time when other feminisms were organizing, part of a process internal to the Chicano movement as that movement to alleviate racial/ethnic oppression developed alongside others. Chicana feminists saw their purpose as involving "the Chicana in the struggle of her people by identifying and dealing with the problems of the Chicana" (Blackwell interview with Nieto-Gómez 1991); they encountered resistance from Chicano movement loyalists, who saw feminism as a threat from the Anglo outside. Loyalists argued that traditional gender roles were part of Chicano culture; feminists countered that machismo was not worthy of Chicanismo. Chicana feminists countered charges of vendidismo by arguing for the necessity of feminist organizing for the community's liberation; they saw themselves as the latest incarnation in a long history of nationalist struggle by Chicanas, and saw gender egalitarianism as a way to make the Chicano political family more effective in the struggle. Developing a sometimes sympathetic, sometimes conflictual but ultimately distant, relationship with the white women's movement, Chicana feminists ultimately chose to organize in ways that brought them closer to the Chicano movement.

While Chicana feminists shared with Black feminists a politics that linked gender oppression with other axes of oppression, they mobilized (rather quickly and extensively) in a different movement landscape than did Black feminists, and views of Chicana feminism as another, later racial/ethnic variant of either white or (intersectional) Black feminism neglect this terrain. The perceived Black/white racial/ethnic hierarchy gave Chicana feminists a bit of organizational room to move even while it dictated that many early Chicana feminist efforts were aimed at simply letting others know that they existed as a group. Chicana feminists organized without the pressure of a Moynihan report or the reaction that report engendered in the oppositional Black community. Moynihan's report may have had an effect on the Chicano movement, but an attenuated and maybe even positive one; if it did engender a renewed masculinism among Black Liberationists, and if this masculinism did influence Chicano male activist styles, it may have contributed to contradictions in the Chicano movement for women in activist roles, contradictions that generated a feminist response. And in tackling Chicano movement masculinism, and loyalist claims about traditional gender roles constituting Chicano culture, Chicana feminists were well positioned to argue otherwise. Chicana counterarguments to the charges that they were sellouts to white feminism were swift and unapologetic, and made especially strong use of internal Chicano movement values; both the counterarguments of the historical presence of Chicana activism and the argument for the political family seemed to be effective in mobilizing Chicanas in a widespread manner. As they organized throughout the 1970s, Chicana feminists took care to align themselves with the Chicano movement, and to distance themselves from white variants of feminism, claiming a different space for culturally contextualized feminist values.

Taken together, what the three stories of feminist movement emergence show so far is patterns of interaction within movements that were situated in a larger and complex terrain of left-wing politics. These left movements, which Black, Chicana, and white women's liberation joined as social movements, challenged the state and the public to acknowledge a host of inequalities and oppressive realities in daily life. Up until this point, I have told stories about internal developments within left social movements that led to feminist emergences, though mindful of how each racial/ethnic feminism could potentially influence the others. But in considering racial/ethnic feminisms in the second wave, there remains one more crucial aspect to consider, that of the overall social movement milieu. We need an understanding of the way in which 1960s and 1970s left movements competed for and made claims on women's energies; we need to consider how ideas circulated among political movements and how those ideas helped to shape left political culture; and we need to think about how these factors led feminists in different racial/ethnic communities to make political decisions about how to organize effectively. In the next chapter, I consider how these intermovement political struggles influenced decisions that feminists made about how to organize and with whom.

CHAPTER FIVE

Organizing One's Own

*The Competitive Social Movement Sector and the Rise of
Organizationally Distinct Feminist Movements*

No one has invented an "ism" that works for everybody.
Dorinda Moreno
Concord, California
July 2000

Introduction: The Intermovement Level and Feminist Emergences

In the previous three chapters, I have narrated the emergences of feminist movements from different racial/ethnic communities such that
it might be hard for the reader to imagine that feminists would have
had any choice but to form organizationally distinct movements. Since
left feminist movements came from other social movements, and since
"recruitment to a movement follows the lines of pre-existing social relationships," the existence of organizationally distinct feminisms organized
along racial/ethnic lines seems to have been "natural," and inevitable
(Gerlach and Hine 1970:44). But the commonalities that feminists
shared with those in their parent movements were not straitjackets.
It was also the case that there were contacts among emerging feminists in different racial/ethnic communities, and that there was cross-
pollination of ideas about gender liberation. The 1960s and 1970s were
years in which social movement politics were fluid and fast-changing;
when new constituencies of activists emerged and agitated; when long-
standing social injustices and cultural mores were challenged, sometimes
successfully; and when people did, at various times, meet and work with
those of other classes and races. Many white feminists encountered and
emulated Black Civil Rights activists in that movement (Evans 1979)
and continued to stay abreast of developments in that movement; a
number of Black feminists had relationships with white feminists, with
Black women represented in the ranks and among the leadership of the
National Organization for Women (NOW) (A. C. Hernández, interview 2000; Marx Ferree and Hess 1994); and as argued in Chapter Four,

Chicana feminists were sympathetic to a large part of the "Anglo" feminist agenda, if not to white feminists themselves (Orozco 1976). Black feminists and Chicana feminists critiqued the racial/ethnic and class biases of white women's liberation, but there was also substantial agreement about the elements of a feminist agenda across all three racial/ethnic communities. Abortion rights and reproductive choice; freedom from the violence of rape and battering; the need for low-cost, quality child care; increasing educational and employment opportunities for women; and the wholesale jettisoning of traditional ideas about gender roles were all items of a general feminist agenda in the second wave. Emphases and specific rallying points differed, but there was room for cross-racial/ethnic feminist organizing if we look at the agenda alone.

But, of course, we cannot look at movements' political agendas and read back from them the shape of actual organizing; we must look at what activists confronted instead. Second-wave feminists worked within specific political contexts that structured their choices about how to organize and with whom. In previous chapters, I have stressed internal movement pressures on emergent feminists; in this chapter, I wish to consider the neglected and undertheorized impact of intermovement politics on the emergence of second-wave feminisms. Social movement activists in the 1960s and 1970s operated in a particularly vibrant extra-institutional political milieu, so much so that many thought American society was on the verge of revolution; the imperatives of negotiating this intermovement milieu profoundly affected feminist choices to build organizationally distinct movements.

In order to understand how intermovement politics affected the choices that Black, Chicana, and white feminists made about organizing, we have to consider the degree to which left social movement organizing rested on the day-to-day work of women activists. It was women activists who did the kind of daily socially reproductive labor that allowed organizations and groups to continue. Women ran things – typed meeting minutes, ran off mimeographs, made phone calls, walked neighborhoods, and yes, made the coffee. The possibility of women organizing around their own issues was seen as a potential threat to the economy of social movement activism, on both practical and ideological grounds. It was, of course, at least hypothetically, the case that feminist agendas could have been incorporated into those of existing organizations. This did happen, although belatedly, in the New Left, as discussed in Chapter Two, and intermittently in Black Liberation and Chicano groups, like the Panthers and the La Raza Unida Party. But the feminist

Table 5.1. *The Crowded Social Movement Sector/Field of the
1960s and 1970s*

Early to mid-1960s
Black Civil Rights Movement
Student Movement/The Free Speech Movement/The New Left
Antinuclear/Antiwar/Antidraft Movement

Mid-1960s to 1970s
Antiwar/Antidraft Movement
Asian American Movement
Black Feminism
Black Liberation Movement
Chicana Feminism
Chicano Movement
Environmental Movement
Gay Liberation
Lesbian Feminism
Liberal Feminism
Native American Movement
Puerto Rican Nationalism
The New Left
White Women's Liberation

"threat" was heightened in male (and some female) activists' minds because of the competitive social movement sector and the proliferation of social movements. In Table 5.1, I list prominent 1960s/1970s movements to give a sense of just how much was going on; if the reader feels that I've left out a movement, that only strengthens the argument about the social movement field/sector being crowded.

The very fluidity and extra-institutionality of the social movement sector may have led to increased anxiety about, and competition for, the "people" resources available to social movement groups; anxiety and competition would be exacerbated during times of large-scale political protest (Tarrow 1988). Certainly, male New Leftists, Black Liberationists, and Chicano loyalists were anxious about the possibilities of women using their energies for their own work – or the work of other movements – and did not hesitate to say so. Emerging feminists were anxious as well about what feminist organizing would mean to their communities, and the record of their debates over how to organize shows these concerns.

In this chapter, I first briefly consider the competitive structure of the social movement sector in theoretical terms. I then explore how social movement activism rested on women's day-to-day work, and how feminist activism threatened both the economy of and the ideological foundations of left movement activism. Feminists countered political arguments made against their organizing with arguments for feminism's necessity. These arguments were different in each racial/ethnic community, and they had differential effects outside those communities. In particular, New Left trivialization of white women's liberation led those feminists to develop a gender universalist notion of sisterhood; this universalization of women's position – which prioritized gender oppression over other forms of oppression and ignored differences among women – mobilized white women's liberationists, but was problematic for Black and Chicana feminist organizing (davenport 1979; Moraga and Anzaldúa 1979; Redd 1983; Spelman 1982). Feminists of color faced not only the monist challenges of men in racial/ethnic movements but also those posed by white women's liberation itself, since the gender universalism of white women's liberation gave male activists in the Black and Chicano movements ammunition in constructing feminism as bad politics. Lastly, I argue that the "either/or" competitive context of social movement activism in the 1960s and 1970s was bolstered by the ethos of "organizing one's own" as the only authentic style of activism; this ethos provided the crucial ideological component that kept feminists in distinct racial/ethnic organizations.

The Competitive Social Movement Sector

Case studies of social movements tend to look at movements as existing independently of other movements (Marx Ferree and Roth 1998). But this approach is inherently problematic, and especially so in periods of widespread social protest. During periods of heightened mobilization, movements interact with one another as they position themselves for action within what has been called by some a "sector" (McCarthy and Zald 1977), composed of formal organizations and their members, plus all those less formally affiliated but nonetheless willing to engage in "disruptive direct action" (Tarrow 1988:432). Others have conceptualized this sector as a "multi-organizational field" (Curtis and Zurcher 1973:56), or more recently, a "political field" (Ray 1999), as the latter concept stresses the role of the state in constructing the boundaries of movement possibilities. Ideas "spill over" and travel across movements and organizations, as do tactics, and people themselves (Meyer and Whittier 1994:277). Boundaries between movements internal to the sector/field are provisional, as activists form shifting cooperative alliances and competitive relationships over matters of recruitment and resources.

In order to understand individual social movements, then, it was necessary to understand the dynamics of the sector, as the dynamics of the social movement sector shaped how effective groups were in the 1960s and 1970s (Tarrow 1988). This insight about movements involved in relationships dovetails well with feminist assertions of the intersectionality of oppression; in both views, a condition of "inherent multiplicity is usual" (Marx Ferree and Roth 1998:626). Just as women's identities are constructed/constituted by intersecting dominations, so too are feminist identities constructed/constituted by "interaction *among* movements" and not just by collective identity work done internally, in movement organizations (Marx Ferree and Roth 1998:628, emphasis in the original).

Although we cannot draw definitive boundaries around the social movement sector/field, there is a sense in which it is limited in its capacity and subject to significant changes in that capacity over time. In general, early in periods of heightened protest, such as the 1960s/1970s, public protests have "demonstration effects" that encourage newcomers to enter the social movement field. After a certain point, however, further protest and organizing within the social movement field becomes counterproductive (Tarrow 1994). As Debra Minkoff (1995) argued, the actual founding of organizations early in a cycle of protest leads to the founding of new ones, as the establishing of organizations shows that extra-institutional activity is possible and provides networks that enable new organizations to form. But it is also the case that the founding of new organizations places constraints on older ones, insofar as they compete for resources and the public's attention. For example, the rise of competing social issues in the last half of the 1960s forced the race-relations problem into a less salient position vis-à-vis public opinion (McAdam 1982); the development of the contemporary (white) women's movement certainly represented competition for the Black movement, itself "trying to survive dramatic changes in their prospects for continued activism" (Minkoff 1995:111).

If there was a limit to the amount of extra-institutional "space" available to those in public protest, what did this mean for the emergence of second-wave feminisms? As I have argued in previous chapters, emerging feminists were enmeshed in a complex and volatile set of political relationships, where loyalties to community and ideology were constantly being tested and reformed. Feminisms' emergences added to the complexity of the social movement sector and established new challenges to existing organizations in the New Left, Black Liberation, and Chicano movements. Activists knew that the political world around them was, by the late 1960s, growing more and more fragmented (Blea 2000 interview; Evans 1979; Omolade 1994); on both the practical and the ideological level, emergent feminist organizing was a threat to existing groups. Women organizing on their own and for their own meant that crucial energies might be withdrawn from mixed-gender groups; on the other hand, incorporating feminist demands into the politics of existing groups threatened existing ideologies and agendas. The two problems were inextricably linked, as feminist activists were ultimately not willing to give their energies to those who disparaged feminist ideas.

The Social Movement Economy and the Feminist Threat

In each of the three movements from which feminist organizing emerged – the New Left, the Black Liberation movement, and the Chicano movement – feminist activity was seen as a drain on activist energies and therefore a threat to that movement's unity and potential for success. Feminism was constructed as at best a diversion and at worst an infection of the oppositional community. The threat of feminism was due, in large part, to the fact that women played key roles in running the day-to-day business of organizations, from clerical tasks to daily chores. Male activists had an interest in keeping women within mixed groups, where they did what Marge Piercy (1970:424) called the "shitwork." Piercy argued that shitwork was denigrated within the New Left, but utterly essential for the movement's continued existence:

> The real basis [of the movement] is the largely unpaid, largely female labor force that does the daily work. Reflecting the values of the larger capitalist society, there is no prestige whatsoever attached to actually working. . . . The production of abstract analyses about what should be done and the production of technical jargon are far more admired than what is called by everybody shitwork.

There is ample evidence for the critical role of everyday organizing that women played in left social movements, and for activists' awareness of that role. Women's efforts were central to the success of the community organizing projects of Students for a Democratic Society (SDS) (Evans 1979). Black women's leadership – "invisible" (McNair Barnett 1993), "bridge" (Robnett 1997), or otherwise – was crucial to that movement, and Black women participated in all aspects of protest, from the initiation of action to the mobilization of resources. Even when pressure was put on Black women to step back from responsible movement positions into the domestic sphere, their domestic work – including the production of future generations of Black "warriors" (Dubey 1994:18) – was still seen as absolutely essential to the viability of the Black movement, and many women accepted arguments for the importance of their continued, delimited participation for that reason (Omolade 1994). And Chicana activists ran movement organizations by doing the essential tasks of coordination:

> Organizational needs welcomed women's willingness to participate by utilizing their secretarial and homemaking skills. Women took minutes of meetings, typed, answered phones, and cooked. They would set up and tend booths at fundraisers and dances, and stayed behind to clean up. Such responsibilities came within the traditional sphere of women's work, and women were expected to perform accordingly. (del Castillo 1980:8)

Thus, feminist organizing was an eminently practical problem for male activists, although making practical arguments against feminist organizing – that is, that women had to continue to do the typing and the housework for the good of the movement – was not exactly respectable politically. Ideological arguments were more accepted responses to the emerging feminist challenge than admitting that it was not as much fun to type one's own minutes and make one's own dinners. Although the practical problem of relying on women's labor was the same in each racial/ethnic movement, the particular ideological picture of the feminist threat and arguments made against it differed. Feminists who attempted to organize within the New Left experienced ridicule and rejection on the level of revolutionary ideology rather than revolutionary roles, which was the argument employed by Black Liberationists and Chicano loyalists; revolutionary women of color were to take on traditional roles as a means of reconstructing the community for revolution (the Black Liberationist emphasis) or preserving culture from Anglo domination (the Chicano version).

Male New Leftists who took feminism seriously – and many did not – did not make arguments about white women's liberationists needing to maintain traditional gender roles for the sake of the oppositional community. Instead, feminist organizing was seen as being a bourgeois distraction from "real" revolutionary politics: Feminists faced accusations of being "bourgeois separatists" (Weinfeld 1970:1), with "all this talk about bedroom and dishwashing a great distraction from the war, the working class, the politics of The Revolution" (Gitlin 1987:371). Even in those groups where male activists were relatively sympathetic to nascent feminism, the political wisdom of feminist organizing was challenged. For example, the formation of a woman's caucus in the New University Conference in 1968 was seen as cause for concern, as expressed by Mel Rothenberg, one of the editors of the NUC newsletter. In an article entitled "One Editor's View of the Women's Caucus," Rothenberg wrote that the formation of a woman's caucus was problematic because it was an "exclusive" caucus, one not based on "political or ideological allegiance." He specifically saw it as a structure that would siphon energy from the NUC and damage the organization's ideological focus in pursuit of what he saw as narrower goals:

> [T]here will be some women who, as a matter of principle, will function in NUC through the women's caucus whose talents and interest will be cramped by the necessarily narrow concerns . . . of the caucus. This will be NUC's loss as well, since . . . a number of our sisters who could and should shape the development of NUC as a whole, [will] devote their entire energies to the promotion and development of the women's caucus. . . . [B]y focusing the attention and energy of NUC women on questions of women's liberation, there will be a tendency for them to de-emphasize ideological and political problems which aren't comfortably encompassed under that heading. (Rothenberg 1968:6)

He also saw evolving debates in women's liberation as leading to "conflicts" that would be carried to the rest of the NUC, which would lead to the group's "refereeing quarrels between different factions of the women's caucus [that] would represent a drain on our resources" (1968:6).[1]

---

[1] In the NUC's September 1968 newsletter, Marlene Dixon replied to Rothenberg's concerns (Dixon 1968). She responded that issues that affected half the world's population could hardly be defined as narrow or sectarian; for Dixon, a women's

As feminist organizational strength grew – and as the New Left itself became more fragmented – women's liberationists came under increasing attack from male activists for distracting the masses from "real" political goals. Pat Galligan, a Boston feminist activist, reported that

> [w]hen I would go out in the streets selling women's liberation literature I was often confronted by people I knew from SDS. And they would attack me for joining the women's movement, tell me that I was deserting the revolutionary struggle, that the women's movement would divide the working class. (Lund 1970:9)

Another Boston feminist, Jeanne Lafferty, reported that men from New Left organizations like SDS and the Progressive Labor Party would come to meetings sponsored by women's liberation groups and tell women to "drop their struggle and fight for socialism" (Lund 1970:10). Not until women's liberation was a major force, circa 1971, did New Left organizations attempt to seriously integrate the liberation of women into an "anti-imperialist" ideology; by then, as noted in Chapter Two, it was too late, since white women's liberationists had largely withdrawn their energy from New Left organizations proper and deposited it into their own women-led groups (see Burris 1971).

Feminists emerging from the Black Liberation movement and the Chicano movement were also subjected to accusations that their concerns were diversionary and disruptive of movement unity, although in these movements, male activists tended to make distinct arguments about women's double obligations of revolutionary politics and revolutionary (i.e., traditional) gender roles. Black and Chicana feminists bore the burden, not shared by white women, that their feminist activism could potentially harm the entire embattled racial/ethnic community. In the Black activist community, for example, it was not just a matter of Black male activists "not want[ing] to lose black women as allies" (Smith and Smith 1981:125); Black men, and as Betty Jean Overton (1970) noted, many Black women, opposed Black women's participation in women's liberation on the grounds that such participation meant diverting attention away from a revolution that was seen by many activists as essential to Black survival in a racist society. The

caucus was precisely the place to address feminist ideological debates. As is argued in this chapter, Dixon's gender universalist view of women's situation typified white feminists' responses to New Left charges of feminism's diversionary character.

idea of Black women's domesticity as crucial to the continuation of the Black community was apparent in Black Liberationist hostility to feminist issues like birth control or lesbianism. This masculinism in Black Liberation, along with the movement's decline in political effectiveness, made challenges by Black feminists doubly threatening (Giddings 1984; McAdam 1982). Ironically, Black Liberation's renewed masculinism had already disrupted the economy of social movement activism by asking Black women to drop roles of responsibility in organizations in favor of domesticity; crucial leadership potential was thus diverted.[2]

As noted in Chapter Four, male Chicano loyalists who charged Chicana feminists with being *vendidas* [sellouts] to Anglo culture based their charges on the idea that Chicano culture was rooted in the complementary arrangement of traditional male and female gender roles (García 1990; Nieto-Gómez 1976). Chicana feminists directly countered the idea that Chicano culture rested on maintaining these roles, and they argued vehemently against the loyalist picture of traditional women. By uncovering Chicana (and Mexicana) women's nontraditional behavior in activism on behalf of the community – "historical Chicana feminists" – and by positing a need to continue to change familial roles in order to better struggle for the liberation of the community, Chicana feminists rejected concepts of revolutionary politics that included constraints on women's ability to participate (Baca Zinn 1975; Cortera 1977; Flores 1971b).

Thus, because women played crucial roles in the day-to-day production of social movement activity, feminist concerns were considered threatening and diversionary on both a practical and ideological level. The arguments used by those hostile to feminism differed in each racial/ethnic community; white New Leftists challenged feminism on the ideological level as being unimportant (or at least not as important as class warfare, etc.); masculinist Black Liberationists and Chicano loyalists emphasized the necessity of constituting revolutionary roles so

---

[2] Significantly, antifeminist Black women like Linda La Rue (1970) argued for Black women's increased participation in Black Liberation and against Black women's participation in the white women's liberation movement. La Rue (1970:4) wanted to see "role integration" – egalitarianism and flexible attitudes toward gendered tasks – in the relationships between Black women and men. It is difficult to separate La Rue's vision of role integration from a feminist one, but La Rue insisted that changing gender roles should ensue from an internal dialogue within the Black community. She might have noticed that such a debate, represented especially within the pages of *The Black Woman*, was already well under way.

as to ensure the survival of the embattled community. Jockeying for position in a crowded social movement sector, the white New Left, Black Liberation movement, and Chicano movement became increasingly monist – centered on one and only one axis of oppression – as the decade wore on. Feminists battling gender oppression in this context required their own compelling ideologies of liberation, as they debated the impact of their organizing among themselves. White women's liberationists found such an ideology by developing a gender universalist analysis of women's oppression; gender universalism led white feminists to monism of a different kind, whereby gender oppression was privileged over other structures of domination. Gender universalism in the white women's liberation movement would then have consequences for Black and Chicana feminist organizing, and so I next turn to the construction of gender universalist ideas about sisterhood and unintended effects.

White Women's Liberation and Universal Sisterhood

As argued in Chapter Two , white women's liberation took a number of years – from about 1965 to 1971 – to separate from the male Left. By the early 1970s, white feminists had generally developed a gender universalist ideology, one that privileged gender oppression above others and that tended to blur racial and ethnic difference among women. Positing a universalist sisterhood in such a manner had implications for feminist organizing in communities of color; simply put, it made feminist organizing in those communities more difficult. But white feminists' gender universalism was not intentionally exclusionary, nor was it constructed out of thin air; it arose as a response to New Left charges of feminism as being diversionary, bourgeois, and individualistic. To counter claims that feminist interests were somehow narrower than those of the working class (or of Third World peoples), white women's liberationists claimed that gender oppression was as fundamental and widespread as racism and class domination. Gender universalism was constructed, then, because it was a strategic answer to concerns that white feminists had about the potentially problematic nature of their new political concerns.

White feminism's gender universalism initially developed from an analogy of gender oppression as being like racial oppression, and then moved toward an assertion that gender oppression was universally experienced by women no matter what their social location. The analogy of gender oppression to racial oppression was an indication of just how seriously emerging white feminists took the struggle for racial justice. They were participants in a social movement milieu that generally saw the Black Civil Rights/Black Liberation movement as the vanguard of left politics, and some of them had actually been in the Civil Rights movement. Analogizing gender oppression to racial oppression underscored how seriously white women's liberationists wanted to be taken. And in continuing to respond to white New Left opposition to women's liberation, feminists moved from using the argument that gender oppression was like racial oppression to an assertion that gender oppression was universal, a rhetorical shift that made the case for feminism even stronger.[3]

The idea of the status of women – white women – as being similar to that of Blacks began in 1964, with Casey Hayden and Mary King's memo "Sex and Caste" circulated to members of SNCC (Baxandall and Gordon 2000; Evans 1979). The following year, Hayden and King circulated the memo to women within the Civil Rights movement and the New Left. Hayden and King wrote of "parallels" (Evans 1979:235) between the status of Blacks and the status of women. They were mostly concerned with reaching a movement audience; by analogizing women's oppression as being like that of Blacks, they were using an effective "frame" for mobilization, one likely to be understood by fellow activists (Snow and Benford 1992). The analogy of "woman as Black" was, in fact, part of academic discourse on the status of women in the United States, and college-educated activists were probably familiar with this discourse. In her proposal for creating a women's center in San Francisco in 1969, Joan Jordan (aka Vilma Sanchez) cited "Appendix 5" in Gunnar Myrdal's work An American Dilemma, first published in 1944, where we see the analogy developed:

> [Myrdal] cites the parallel between the condition of women and that of blacks in this country, pointing out that when a legal status had to be found for the imported slave in the seventeenth century, the nearest analogy was the status of women and children. (Jordan/Sanchez 1969:4)

---

[3] White feminists paid much more attention to the consequences of class than of race, as illustrated by the growth of socialist feminist groups, although Joseph (1981) claimed that socialist feminists were often unable to incorporate into their analyses a specific critique of racism as an independent system of domination. Certainly, many socialist feminists were antiracist activists, but as socialist feminists, they were often working in all-white groups, since by the early 1970s, as I will argue, the left ethos of "organizing one's own" community was firmly established.

In the same proposal, Jordan also cited work by sociologist Helen Hacker, who in 1951 wrote a paper entitled "Women as a Minority Group." Hacker and Myrdal were also cited by feminist Marlene Dixon (1970b) in an article on women's liberation for San Francisco State College's *The Daily Gater*. Dixon also used the work of Everett Hughes, who compared the status of women to that of Blacks, particularly where it concerned white male expectations that members of either or both groups adhere to their traditional roles.

Hayden and King's delimited parallels drawn for a movement audience were taken up by others. Many white feminists began writing about themselves as somehow "Black," vis-à-vis their relationships with white men. In the summer of 1968, Judith Brown wrote, in "Toward a Female Liberation Movement," that SDS men expected women to "continue to function as black troops – kitchen soldiers – in their present struggle" (1968:24). She continued the analogy to describe white women's personal relationships with white men:

> On Southern plantations in the "days of slavery," each member of a wealthy white family had attached to him, often for life, at least one black person who "did for him." In turn, the black derived from the master a commensurate status. Our analysis should be that it is the destiny of most women – no less the radical – to become, finally, some man's nigger. (1968:27)

In 1969, feminist Lyn Wells (1969:2) would also discuss the status of women as being that of slaves to white men:

> [M]uch of our slavery is subtle. . . . When I realized how we've been used and abused, the plight of black people seemed very clear. We are over half of the population and have more at stake in an American revolution than most groups in the country (women have a lower prevailing income than blacks!).

And in 1970, Roxanne Dunbar (1970:483) wrote, in her extended analysis of the "caste" quality of sexist oppression in the United States, that "[t]he clearest historical analogy of the caste status of females is African slavery in English-speaking America."

As in these examples, the "woman as Black" analogy was often stated in the bluntest possible terms, and given the no-holds-barred language common in New Left publications, the use of the pejorative "nigger" to describe women's status was not off-limits. In 1969, Gayle Rubin wrote an article for the *Ann Arbor Argus* entitled "Woman as Nigger"; at Cornell, feminists reportedly handed out flyers about women's liberation entitled "The Chick as Nigger" (see Anderson 1995:317). In fact, some white women's liberationists likened themselves not just to slaves but more specifically to "house niggers," with the implication being that white women were pampered into complacency as those slaves had been (see Piercy 1970; Weisstein 1970). The idea of "woman as house nigger" traveled across to the mainstream press and across national boundaries; a Canadian women's liberation member was quoted in the Canadian women's magazine *Chatelaine* (in an article entitled "After Black Power, Woman Power") as saying that "[h]ere in Canada, we see women as far more complex than house niggers, which is how some U.S. feminists look at women in their present condition" (Batten 1969:39).[4]

Presumably, white women's liberationists used the word "nigger" so freely because the injustice of racial oppression was a clearly delineated aspect of New Left ideology. They also had more sophisticated analyses of their situation in the New Left, at times approaching arguments for women's liberation as a potential revolutionary "vanguard center." For example, the 1968 SDS "National Resolution on Women" actually featured an analysis of the multiplicative effects of various kinds of oppression for those in different social locations, acknowledging that Black women were "uniquely oppressed . . . because as blacks, as workers, and as women, they experience the most compound forms of oppression capitalism/imperialism has devised" (SDS 1968:1). But most of the rhetoric of white women's liberation tended toward the "woman as Black" analogy, as it represented an effective way to hammer home the importance of women's liberation to those activists who resisted feminism. Even the message in the "Resolution" just excerpted was that women suffer "immediate oppression" at the hands of men in much the

---

[4] Other examples of the "woman as Black" analogy include Heather Dean's "The Sexual Caste System," which appeared in a University of Toronto student magazine in 1966; Beverly Jones's aforementioned position paper (1968); Vanauken's (1971: first written in 1968) "A Primer for the Last Revolution," a pamphlet specifically aimed at college students; and Evelyn Goldfield, Sue Munaker, and Naomi Weisstein's (c. 1968) essay, "A Woman is a Sometime Thing." Goldfield et al. actually used the analogy to argue that women's oppression could not be reduced to class oppression; they acknowledged class distinctions among women, but they did not mention that racial differences might also affect the content of women's oppression.

same way that Blacks suffer racist oppression at the hands of whites, even if gender and racial oppression were separate entities. Another variation of the woman as Black analogy – women as a colonized people – emerged in those organizations where Third World liberation struggles and anti-imperialist politics developed. Declaring that women had a "colonial relationship to men" was almost the only way emerging feminists could be taken seriously (Gitlin 1987:370). The "Liberation of Women" manifesto published in *New Left Notes* in July of 1967 (Evans 1979:240–241) characterized women as being in a "colonial" relationship to men in the United States; the authors stated that "we recognize ourselves as part of the Third World." The use by SDS women of the colonialist metaphor worked; it caused a stir within SDS, exciting women and getting men to notice feminist concerns (Evans 1979).

The "woman as Black" analogy survived in the rhetoric of white women's liberation for quite some time (indeed, in my experience, the analogy has not yet disappeared from everyday discourse around feminism). But the analogy came to be intertwined with a new kind of argument: the idea of the universal oppression of women as women and the consequent need for universal sisterhood. This argument by white women's liberationists countered New Left claims that women's liberation was narrow and individualistic. For feminists themselves, thinking of women's oppression in universal terms changed their potential movement audience from movement men to all women (Dixon 1970a). Thus, the development of the gender universalist stance was a crucial mobilization tool, in that it changed the focus of women's liberation from internal movement politics to speaking to women in American society and the world at large.

Many New Leftists simply dismissed the idea that women, much less the white middle-class women who made up the ranks of the New Left, were oppressed (Echols 1992). The trivialization and derogation of women's liberation as bourgeois and/or diversionary resulted not only from a desire to hold onto male privilege and women's energies, but also from a politics in which race and class were enshrined as the privileged categories of radical activism. Women's liberationists had responded by appropriating the logic of Black power and critiques of colonialism to describe women's position and legitimate their struggle; as Linda Seese (1969:71) wrote, women's "awakening could be even more earth shattering than the awakening of blacks." Feminists further developed the idea that women were universally oppressed as justification for forming the women's liberation movement. Given the extent of this universal

oppression, the liberatory potential of fighting for women could reasonably dwarf concerns about "only" race and class. Given the numbers,
women's liberation was potentially the key revolutionary force. The
coexistence of the gender universalism argument with the "woman as
Black" analogy can be seen in the statement by Ellen Willis (1969b:2;
emphasis in the original):

> We must remember that women are not just a special interest group
> with sectarian concerns. <u>We are half the human race</u>. Our oppres-
> sion transcends occupations and class lines. Femaleness, like black-
> ness, is a biological fact, a fundamental condition. Like racism,
> male supremacy premeates [sic] all strata of this society. And it
> is even more deeply entrenched. . . . Male supremacy is the oldest
> form of domination and the most resistant to change.

As can be seen, in constructing universalist gender oppression, white
women's liberationists often posited gender oppression as primordial,
and thus alleviating it became the most radical cause in the root sense
of the word itself. The authors of the "Redstockings Manifesto," who
wished to identify with "the poorest, most brutally exploited women,"
argued that it was logical for the group's (and the movement's) targets
to be men as such:

> We identify the agents of our oppression as men. Male supremacy
> is the oldest, most basic form of domination. All other forms of
> exploitation and oppression (racism, capitalism, imperialism, etc.)
> are extensions of male supremacy: men dominate women, a few
> men dominate the rest. All power structures throughout history
> have been male-dominated and male-oriented. Men have con-
> trolled all political, economic and cultural institutions and backed
> up this control with physical force. They have used their power
> to keep women in an inferior position. *All men* receive economic,
> sexual, and psychological benefits from male supremacy. *All men*
> have oppressed women. (Redstockings 1970:535; emphasis in the
> original)

The members of Redstockings were joined by many in their gender universalism, sometimes in surprising ways. For example, Celestine
Ware, a Black woman, wrote *Woman Power* (1970), in which she defended the universalist stance of emerging white feminists. Ware was

especially opposed to making class distinctions in considering women's oppression; in her book, she took the Boston-area Bread and Roses to task for their socialist leanings, maintaining that a group would only be truly feminist "when it states that women of all classes are equally oppressed and that racism will be ended by women working together to end their exploitation as women" (1970:69). In Ware's view, those who did not acknowledge the existence of universal gender oppression and the need for universal sisterhood were still being influenced by outmoded New Left ideology, which was entirely passé.

Seeing women's oppression as universal was important for white feminists organizationally, since it meant that the audience of potential recruits had moved from movement men to women in general. Much as Civil Rights activists had envisioned a true brotherhood among those of different races as necessary to overcoming racism, so women's liberationists saw that a universal sisterhood was needed to end gender oppression. And envisioning universal sisterhood had a mobilizing effect on white feminists. Writing about the socialist Bread and Roses collective of which she was a founding member circa 1969, Annie Popkin (1988:21) noted that the concept of sisterhood helped build internal cohesion for groups like Bread and Roses, because "differences among women were minimized in the interest of building a cohesive group." Popkin's observation, based on her experiences, fits with theory about a group's establishing a "collective identity" as a prerequisite for joint sustained action (Melucci 1989). The intensity of efforts to form a collective identity may be directly related to a group's heterogeneity (Morris 1992); women, half the world's population, constituted such a heterogenous group.

White feminists' desire for universal sisterhood stemmed from attempts to legitimize themselves within the New Left, and was built on the analogy of gender oppression to racial oppression. Their universalist ideas about the nature of gender oppression grew out of further attempts to argue against others who saw feminism as disruptive and diversionary to radical politics. Unfortunately, ideological formulations that were compelling to one group of feminist activists caused considerable problems for other groups, namely, feminist women of color. The gender universalist stance galvanized white women's liberationists, but it had an unintended negative effect: By blurring racial/ethnic and class differences among women, the universalist stance of white feminists made it difficult for feminists of color to defend feminism to the men in their communities. In short, given the imperatives of the competitive social movement sector, white feminism's universalism came to be one of the wedges that kept feminists of different racial/ethnic backgrounds in organizationally distinct movements.

"Either/Or" from Everywhere: African American and Chicana Feminist Responses

White feminists' universalism helped to render white women's liberation untenable for African American and Chicana women who were struggling to organize as feminists. Privileging gender oppression over other kinds alienated many women of color sympathetic to feminism, precisely because of the attempt to "create an empowered sisterhood through erasing our differences" (Sandoval 1990:65). And although white women's liberationists took racial oppression seriously, some white feminists made decisions early on not to complicate their organizing with the politics of race. In part of a transcript that Alice Echols (1989:369–377) reproduced from the Sandy Springs conference in August of 1968, white women's liberationists discussed the pros and cons of making contacts with radical Black women. Disagreement about the wisdom of such a move centered directly on keeping the politics of women's liberation focused on gender oppression. Echoing earlier concerns about feminist organizing, certain women who were present voiced concerns that Black women would derail the women's liberation agenda with a critique of racist and classist politics, taking up time and energy in the process; that is, some women argued that a simultaneous focus on other oppressions would be diversionary. In the end, the group at Sandy Springs decided to contact Kathleen Cleaver regarding a future conference on Black women's and white women's liberation, a conference that never materialized.[5]

This example aside, most white feminists did not adhere to the idea of a universalist sisterhood in order to exclude women of color; on the contrary, white women's liberation groups desperately wanted women of color to join *them*. But gender universalism did lead to the neglect of issues raised by racial/ethnic feminists regarding racist domination.

---

[5] A subsequent conference of white women's liberationists held in November of 1968 in Illinois appeared to have had no organized discussion of issues that might arise from racial/ethnic differences among women (Women's Liberation, Washington, DC, 1968). In contrast, a workshop on "Caste [i.e., gender as a caste] and Class" was included among the eight or so covered in the conference summary.

By asserting the universalist nature of gender oppression, white women's liberationists would actually focus politically on what Black and Chicana feminists saw as exclusionary political goals. An incident from the August 26, 1970, Liberation Day March exemplified the problems that Black feminists had with what they felt was the narrow focus of white feminism:

> Taking part in the demonstration was the Third World Women's Alliance.... Led by Frances Beal, the Alliance brandished placards about Angela Davis.... Naturally there was great concern about Davis at a time of increasing violence against Black radicals, but that concern was evidently not shared by some leaders of the feminist movement. "We had signs reading 'Hands Off Angela Davis,'" Frances Beal recalled, "and one of the leaders of NOW ran up to us and said angrily, 'Angela Davis has nothing to do with women's liberation.' 'It has nothing to do with the kind of liberation you're talking about,'" retorted Beal, "'but it has everything to do with the kind of liberation we're talking about.'" (Giddings 1984:305)

The exclusionary politics that universalism promoted was a result of the erasure of difference, as gender universalism proved to be a new kind of monist political ideology. This erasure of difference has been characterized as the result of the "unconsciousness" of white women's liberationists regarding other dimensions of oppression, particularly race (Buechler 1990:134). However, unconsciousness as an explanation for universalism is problematic, as is arguing that white feminists could not have recognized their own neglect of other issues due to their relatively privileged social positions. In addition to the Sandy Springs example – which directly contradicts the idea of white feminist unconsciousness regarding other kinds of oppression – the widespread use of the "woman as Black" analogy and the actuality of many white feminists' experiences in the Civil Rights movement belie the idea that they were not cognizant of racial issues. The opposite case can be made, which is that a concern with the politics of race liberation was at the heart of the emergence of white women's liberation as a movement. A la Sandy Springs, it makes more sense to think of the exigencies of making a strategic argument about feminism's importance, and the exigencies of forming viable feminist groups. To put it bluntly, white feminists did not ultimately need a discourse of racial oppression to organize as feminists.

Moreover, a critique of unthinking gender universalism was heard from some white feminists and from Black women activists at the time, facts which further negate the unconsciousness argument. Pam Allen, an early white women's liberationist, wrote in a 1968 draft of a paper called "Memo to My White Sisters in Our Struggle to Realize Our Full Humanity" that she had questions about

> our motives for drawing the numerous analogies we do and secondly the conclusion that we can form alliances with a male-dominated, black power movement. . . . I question our motives precisely because we are white and middle-class. What a relief it is to discover that we too are oppressed. . . . I must question why radical, white women seldom, if ever, refer to black women when drawing analogies. Their problems, we say, are different. But we do draw analogies to the black movement which is infested with the same bourgeois, male supremicist [sic] ideology as our own radical white movement. . . . IF WE ARE TO BE TRUE TO OURSELVES WHEN WE THINK OF RELATING TO THE BLACK MOVEMENT, IT MUST BE IN TERMS OF RELATING TO BLACK WOMEN. (1968b:1–2)

In another example of explicit consciousness of choosing gender over race as a focus of organizing, white women's gender universalism was recognized and challenged by Black women activists at a panel entitled "The Black Woman in America," at the Cornell Conference on Women in January of 1969 (Cornell Conference on Women Report 1969). Rene Neblett, Minister of Culture with the Black Panther Party in Boston and a panel participant, said at the outset of discussion:

> It is my contention that there is no such thing as a universal feminist movement, because of the racist situation in this country. Historically and from a contemporary perspective we are in fact talking about two separate entities – the black woman and the white lady. (1969:1)

Neblett's formulation was challenged by a white feminist in the audience who countered that working-class white women – such as herself – were not ladies either, and that there were issues that both Black and white women could work together on. However, another conference attender – described by the author of the report as "a black girl" – countered that even if work on issues of mutual concern were to take place, it could not proceed without a discussion of differences between women; simple comparisons between white women's and Black women's place in the family and society were rejected by this attender and by the panel participants (1969:14).

In the wake of the Cornell panel, Alice Rossi (1970:541) wrote:

> In reading the transcript of [the Cornell] session, I felt anger and shame that the middle-class women in the audience had not appreciated the difference in the positions of the sexes among whites and blacks.... Nor do we sufficiently realize the continuing relevance of class differences in the ways a problem is perceived and experienced.... [R]ight now the middle-class women's rights movement can find a collaborative arrangement with black women only on such bread-and-butter issues as protecting and expanding economic and political rights.... [T]he white women's movement should try to deepen its understanding of the differences between their relations to men and those of black women.

Rossi recognized differences (chiefly those given by class) between groups of women, but only insofar as recognition of difference clarified the terms of white feminist political work, which appears to have been mainly to let Black women alone. But letting Black women alone and continuing a monist focus on gender oppression made white feminist organizations uncomfortable places for feminists of color (Blea 2000 interview; Blackwell interview with Nieto-Gómez 1991; davenport 1979; Redd 1983; Walker 1983).

There were differences in the ways in which Black and Chicana feminists were positioned vis-à-vis the universalist stance of white women's liberation on gender oppression. Chicana feminists emerged into a multimovement milieu that conceived of race in dualistic Black/white terms, and were thus spared hearing white women compare their situation to that of Mexican Americans; Chicanas did not hear white women's liberationists describe themselves as "brown." In contrast, the woman-as-Black analogy made Black feminists very angry and further alienated them from white feminist organizations proper. The use of the word "nigger" by white women was particularly offensive; Giddings (1984:308) wrote that Black women were "enraged" that white women would characterize themselves as "niggers," and quoted Toni Morrison on the matter, who saw it as "an effort to become Black without the responsibilities of being Black." And according to bell hooks, white feminists were blind to the implications of using the woman-as-Black analogy as a rhetorical strategy, as provocative rhetoric too quickly became a substitute for taking action: "All too frequently in the women's movement it was assumed one could be free of sexist thinking by simply adopting the appropriate feminist rhetoric; it was further assumed that identifying oneself as oppressed freed one from being an oppressor" (hooks 1981:8–9). Implicitly, the woman-as-Black analogy was a comparison of the status of white women to the status of Black men, so that the actual situation of Black women was erased from view (Spelman 1982). This erasure – noted only occasionally by white feminists like Allen – was not lost on Black feminists.

Lastly, white women's universalist view of gender oppression made it more difficult for Black and Chicana feminists to defend their feminist activism to the men in their respective movements. Black and Chicana feminists were not attracted to gender universalism, but white women's liberationist ideology had *negative* spillover effects for them, since activist men were familiar with it. Meyer and Whittier (1994:293) conceptualized "social movement spillover" as positive, as ways for previous movements to maintain influence and effectiveness over time: "[S]pillover effects are cause for greater optimism about movement survival and the scope of social movement influence." However, given competition among movements and the threat that feminist organizing represented to existing movements, gender universalism spilled over in a way that created problems for feminists of color. The monist perspective of white women's liberation was used by men in Black Liberation and the Chicano movement to argue that Black women and Chicanas could not even *be* feminists, since they suffered from race (and class) oppression as well. White women's liberation was used as a negative example, a specter hanging over Black and Chicana feminist heads, and both Black and Chicana feminists countered charges of being traitors to their communities in forming their feminist organizations. While it is surely the case that, as argued, the men in the Black and Chicano movements would have been threatened by any feminist organizing given their need for women's labor, white feminism's universalism and neglect of differences among women made it easier for these men to bash feminist efforts.

Taking a backseat role in the struggle for liberation was not acceptable to feminists of color; accepting a universalist concept of sisterhood was not possible either, as it was tantamount to the "acceptance of a concept of sisterhood that place[d] one's womanhood over and above

one's race" (Thorton Dill 1983:136). White women's universalist conception of gender oppression, developed to counter New Left accusations
of feminism's diversionary nature, both mobilized white women's liberationists and led to monism in large parts of their movement. Women's
liberation joined Black Liberation and, later, the Chicano movement
in insisting that female activists organize around one aspect of oppression only. Black and Chicana feminist activists were not attracted to
universalist feminism, and universalist feminism provided hostile activist men with a negative example to use against feminist activity by
women of color. Given the competitive intermovement politics of the
period, and this complex pattern of action and reaction, feminists from
different racial/ethnic communities established organizationally distinct
movements where they could be feminists without crossing racial/ethnic
lines. Furthermore, their separate organizing efforts were bolstered by the
1960s/1970s ethos of "organizing one's own."

Organizing One's Own: An Ethos and Its Origins

The emergence of a universalist white women's liberation movement –
another monist movement in an already crowded field – contributed to
the "either/or" choices available to feminists of color in the 1960s and
1970s. As feminists in all three communities organized, the possibilities for cross-racial/ethnic alliances were severely curtailed not just by
organizational allegiances, and monist movement competition, but also
by the idea that organizing outside one's community was not authentic, not truly radical politics. I therefore address the 1960s and 1970s
social movement ethos of "organizing one's own" in thinking about
the social movement sector/field within which feminists organized, and
how the ethos helped keep feminists working in distinct racial/ethnic
organizations.

I call organizing one's own an *ethos* because I wish to denote a char-
acteristic spirit of second-wave left political communities. The word
"ethos" is closely tied to the word "ethic," and thus carries with it a
moral imperative to do things in a particular way. The ethos of organizing
one's own constituted a generalized, consensual, and specific instruction
on how to organize as authentic leftists. As movements proliferated, it
directed/justified the way that leftists organized. As such, the ethos of
organizing one's own did not belong to the family of what social movement scholars call collective action "frames," that is, "action-oriented
sets of beliefs and meanings that inspire and legitimate the activities

and campaigns of social movement organizations" (Benford and Snow 2000:614); nor was it an elaborated "system of meaning" as might be expected of a full-blown ideology (Oliver and Johnston 2000:43). The ethos was a value judgment/directive about how to do radical action, and although they certainly had ideas about what constituted good politics, activists invoking the ethos did not actually establish *what* the politics of the groups organizing on their own should be. As the ethos of organizing one's own solidified, the key question for feminists and other activists became who or what gets defined as "one's own." In the racially/ethnically and class-stratified environment within which American leftists operated, and given a number of events in social movement organizing that I will outline, "one's own" came to be seen by feminists as one's own racial/ethnic community. Thus, the ethos of organizing one's own should be thought of as having force because it directed political practice, and not political program. It came to have the force of the unquestioned and the hegemonic.

Using the word "hegemony" to describe radical political ideas might seem strange; following Comaroff and Comaroff (1991:23), I use it to describe the way in which a political idea might become taken for granted:

> [W]e take hegemony to refer to that order of signs and practices, relations and distinctions, images and epistemologies – drawn from a historically situated cultural field – that come to be taken for granted as the natural and received shape of the world and everything that inhabits it.

Since feminists emerging from left movements were still leftists, and since they emerged into a particular intermovement political context, ideas that were hegemonic in the social movement milieu influenced them. Feminists in all three political communities were concerned about the consequences of doing feminist politics and wished to do politics in the right way; therefore, the ethos of organizing one's own came to have hegemonic appeal for them within an increasingly fragmented social movement sector/field in the 1960s and 1970s. The ethos helped to justify feminist organizing and keep feminisms distinct from one another organizationally.

As feminists organized in different racial/ethnic communities, the need for such separate organizing was assumed, and their organizing had the effect of further emphasizing the importance of creating boundaries based on the ethos itself. As social movement theorists have noted, the making of collective identity in contention rests on the establishment of difference (Gamson 1997; McAdam, Tarrow, and Tilly 2001; Taylor and Whittier 1992). But boundary demarcation is not just driven by internal discussion; the climate of communication environments (i.e., the audience) matters as well, and can influence who is included and excluded in groups (Gamson 1997). The ethos was one of the elements present in the "political field" within which feminists organized, a part of left-wing political culture, "the acceptable and legitimate ways of doing politics in a given field" (Ray 1999:7).[6] Interaction between movement entities in a fluid social movement milieu impacted the construction of feminist identities, and the ethos of organizing one's own as authentic politics represented a mandate for boundary making as much as the need for a workable collective identity did. Boundary making along racial/ethnic lines was a way of establishing credibility; having the proper boundary (and not just the proper enemy) was a political necessity.

The ethos of organizing around one's own oppression is commonly seen in retrospect as emanating from a series of events in the Black movement; in this view, its watershed moment is the decision by the Student Nonviolent Coordinating Committee (SNCC) to ask white activists to leave and go into their own communities to address racism there (Carson 1981; Evans 1979; Stoper 1989). SNCC's actions, the result of the influx of white volunteers into the organization during Freedom Summer, were (and still are) seen as sanctioning the idea that the most authentic and, therefore, most radical forms of activism involved fighting one's own oppression (Echols 1992). But the ethos of organizing one's own was not simply the result of growing Black militancy, or even of attempts by white activists to react to that militancy. Rather, the ethos was also clearly part and parcel of the organization Students for a Democratic Society (SDS), there at the group's inception and carried with it to activists within and beyond the university.

SDS started in the early 1960s as the student arm of the left-wing League for Industrial Democracy (LID). As Todd Gitlin (1987) recounted, the growing conflict between SDS and LID was essentially

---

[6] In Ray's terms, the milieu within which feminists organized was a "protest field," or "oppositional subfield" (1999:8). In her exploration of "political fields" as shaping women's organizing in Bombay and Calcutta, Ray includes the state as a principal participant in shaping the field. In the left movements of the 1960s and 1970s, the state recedes into the background somewhat, as more radical and revolutionary ideologies take hold among activists.

one of political approach and style recast as a generational conflict. Al Haber, who had regenerated SDS from the moribund
Student League for Industrial Democracy, had no interest in adopting
old LID forms of organization, that is, well-defined chapters with dues-
paying members as part of a hierarchical organization. Haber sought a
broader base for student activism; he was fired by LID, but helped to
organize a convention for SDS in 1961 with his friends in Ann Arbor,
Michigan. SDS's growing strength and developing ideological differences with its parent organization led to LID's clamping down on the
student group. LID fired many of the SDS staffers after the Ann Arbor
convention, although the fired staffers and their supporters came back
to challenge LID to reaccept them in a compromise. In June of 1962,
Tom Hayden and other activists drafted "The Port Huron Statement:
An Agenda for a Generation." Students were the focus of the call represented by the "Statement," students who were fighting for the redress
of racial injustice, the breaking of stalemate Cold War politics, and
the anti-intellectual, "business as usual" atmosphere of college life. In
short, the first "identity" created in the 1960s and 1970s era of "identity
politics" was that of "student."[7]

In the light of SDS's student-oriented efforts, those of the Free Speech
movement at Berkeley, and the growing student vanguard in the Civil
Rights movement, the "expulsion" of white volunteers from SNCC became an affirmation of a growing consensus about how authentic radicalism was accomplished, rather than its first moment. SNCC's actions
were important to white activists both because of the ties individual
activists had to the organization and because of SNCC's vanguard role
as a model for activism, as Evans (1979:173–174) argued:

Following the suggestion of black power advocates, who stated
that each oppressed group should organize itself first and flatly

[7] The creation of the activist identity of "student" in the early 1960s is, unfortunately, glossed over in Gitlin's (1995) lament regarding the 1960s legacy of
"identity politics." His argument concerns his view of the way in which identity
politics have fractured the Left, but as noted in Chapter Three, he has a condem-
natory definition of identity politics that neglects the way that feminists and others
used new collective identities to pursue political – i.e., not solely expressive – and
globally humanistic goals. I would suggest that failure to recognize the identity
constructions of white men as constructions, and the failure to recognize who
participated in the process of construction and who was excluded, both contribute
to Gitlin's sense that somehow a grand Left project was hijacked toward the end
of the 1960s by groups that manufactured themselves into existence.

rejected as paternalistic racism any wish of young whites to engage in civil rights work, the leaders of the new left turned
more and more to themselves and to their own environment: the
university.... [T]hey saw themselves as oppressed.[8]

SDS itself was split between activist projects that focused on the
university – such as the Peace Research and Education Project (PREP) –
and those that focused on poor communities, such as the Economic
Research and Action Project (ERAP) (Anderson 1995; Evans 1979;
Seese 1969). ERAP projects were run by many women who became
women's liberationists, but despite emerging from these cross-class/cross-
race projects, the idea of organizing one's own was still a powerful one.
ERAP project work was difficult, and New Left men within the activist
communities were unsupportive of women's efforts and women's power.
As white women's liberationists came to see themselves as oppressed
as women, their focus on their own oppression was sanctioned by the
widespread idea that "the most radical thing to do was to fight against
your own oppression" (Evans 1979:174, quoting Kathie Amatniek).

The ethos of organizing one's own was of clear importance for white
women's liberationists, and stemmed from multiple sources: SDS; a Civil
Rights movement that needed them less; and an antiwar movement
that defined draft resistance as the sine qua non of activism, thereby
excluding women from full participation (Evans 1979; Thorne 1975).
From the 1967 National Conference on New Politics on, emerging
white feminists would cast the need for their activism in terms of the
need for self-determination and self-organizing around women's own
oppression (Evans 1979; Seese 1969). Examples of the acceptance of
the ethos abound in the feminist writings of the time, and it is almost always accepted uncritically by the author. For example, Beverly
Jones, Judith Brown's writing partner in "Toward a Female Liberation
Movement," wrote that women had to learn that "[p]eople don't get

---

[8] The ethos of "organizing one's own" was even accepted by Pam Allen, who challenged the white women's liberation movement to pay greater attention to issues
of racism. In a 1968 radio interview with Julius Lester, Allen took for granted the
organizing of women in the "white movement," and she argued for white women
radicals to see their identity as women so as to be able to eventually "ally on certain
issues with black women and Puerto Rican women and then Third World women"
(Allen and Lester 1968:3). Lester agreed with Allen that her vision of a separate
white women's movement that would someday work together with racial/ethnic
women was good politics.

radicalized . . . fighting other people's battles," and she argued:

> No one thinks that poor whites can learn about their own lives by
> befriending black people. . . . No one even thinks that poor whites
> can help black people much. . . . [W]hite students in the early civil
> rights days [thought] that they were really helping, that they knew
> in what limited ways that society needed changing . . . and they
> were thoroughly shaken by Black Power, which said in effect: you
> don't understand anything. They also thought in those dim days
> of the past, that they as white students had no particular problems.
> (Jones 1968:2–3)

Jones went on to state that SNCC's expulsion of white students was
the "best thing that ever happened to potential white radicals," because
they "were forced to face their own oppression in their own worlds"
(1968:3). Women, especially, would "be forced to stop fighting for the
'movement' and start fighting primarily for the liberation and independence of women" (Jones 1968:3).

The idea that no one else could – or would – liberate women was
ubiquitous in the emerging white women's liberation movement, and
was often stated by feminist activists in just those terms. The uniden-
tified author of a position paper based on the conference of Berkeley
Women's Liberation in August of 1969 (no page given) bluntly stated
that "[o]nly women will struggle in our own self-interest." In the newspaper *Liberation*, Robin Morgan wrote that "[n]o matter how empathetic
you are to another's oppression, you can only become truly committed to radical change when you realize your own oppression – it has
to reach you on a gut level" (1968:34). And in an unsigned article
in San Francisco State College's newspaper, *The Daily Gater* ("Why
Liberation?" 1969a:1), the author makes clear that it is common knowledge that no one else can organize on another's behalf: "We know that
no one radicalizes around some one [sic] else's problems. We cannot hope
to fight for someone else's liberation when we ourselves are not free."

The ethos of organizing one's own thus went together with a kind of
flattening of privilege; in an unjust society, no one, not even those well-
off, were truly free. Carol McEldowney (1969a) emphatically made the
case that even middle-class white students were obligated to organize
around their own oppression. In a letter written over the period of July
and August of 1969, McEldowney, prompted by disillusionment with the
Black Panthers, wrote that "white middle-class students . . . must define

their needs, out of their own conditions and oppression to be genuine
participants in the revolution" (1969a:3; emphasis in the original). And
in a letter dated October 1, 1969 (that seems to be a draft for a position
paper), she stated that while feminists came to recognize their own
oppression while "fighting of others [sic] battles," it was unreasonable for
feminists to expect others to continue to come to their aid:

> People do not become revolutionaries as a result of intellec-
> tual reasoning. . . . People become revolutionaries when they are
> pushed so much up-against-the-wall that they have no breath-
> ing space, no chance for any decent form of survival. They be-
> come conscious of the nature of their oppression and begin to act.
> (1969b: no page given)

McEldowney's (and others') contradictory ideas about the impossibility of anyone else organizing on behalf of women surely developed from
the real day-to-day experiences of white women's liberationists being
subjected to a large amount of New Left male ridicule. But the absolute
certainty of these statements (and many others like them; see Ware 1970
and Weinfeld 1970) is especially puzzling given the fact that only a few
years earlier, "in the dim days of the past," many middle-class white
people – including white feminists – had been activists on behalf of
others, and had helped to accomplish real political change. SDS/New
Left ideas about student identity and the New Left's take on the "lessons"
to be learned from SNCC's actions came together to convince emerging
feminists that only in organizing on their own would they be acting as
authentic radicals.

The ethos of organizing one's own also had direct influence on the
way Black and Chicana feminists organized. As already mentioned,
organizing one's own became for some white feminists a legitimate
reason for leaving women of other racial and ethnic groups alone.
The idea that "radical black women don't want to work with radical
white women" (Radical Women, Chicago 1968) led to an acceptance
by white women's liberationists that a separation between feminists of
different colors was necessary; the argument was made, as by Rossi, that
only those with less sophisticated politics would expect women of different races/ethnicities to work together in the same organizations (see also
B. Stone 1970). But lest the blame be laid only at the doorstep of white
women's liberationists, it is important to understand that the ethos of
organizing one's own was accepted by feminists in each racial/ethnic

community, leading to a consensus whereby feminists agreed among themselves that it was impossible for them to organize across lines of race and ethnicity. When feminists did talk to one another across color lines, they frequently found common ground on just how impossible it would be for them to work closely together; instead, separate movements in some sort of vaguely defined future alliance was more often the preferred vision.

Certainly the evidence of organizing by Black and Chicana feminists recounted in Chapters Three and Four shows how the ethos shaped those movements. Black and Chicana feminists organized on their own away from white feminists, in part because of what they saw as white feminist privilege; Black and Chicana feminists were very concerned about being swallowed up by white feminism's agenda, given that different groups of women had very different amounts of power in the larger society. But also significant was the fact that a joint movement of women of color was not envisioned early in most of Black feminist organizing (the Third World Women's Alliance being a notable exception) or in Chicana feminist organizing. There was little discussion during the emergence of Chicana feminism about organizing with anyone else but Chicanas. Chicana feminists spent very little time trying to organize with either white or Black feminists. Instead, the major portion of Chicana feminist debate about autonomous organizing involved how Chicana feminists should relate to the rest of the Chicano movement. Joining up with Anglo women was not so much rejected as simply not seen as a real option, based on the conviction that appropriate politics involved working with and within the community.

Another expression of the ethos relevant to questions of joint Black/white feminist organizing took place in an exchange printed in June of 1970 in *The Christian Century*. Two Black female activists – Joan Brown and Helen Fannings – and one white one – Peggy Way – shared their ideas about the possibilities or, rather, lack of possibilities for such organizing. Way recounted that early on in the 1960s,

> probably more of us than would admit it were working <u>for</u> blacks
> rather than <u>with</u> blacks, though we didn't realize that until things
> became blacker and blacker, and what were we left with?...So I
> think that some of us in women's liberation are seeking a reification
> of who we are out of loss of the identity we thought we were
> developing in the movement. (M. Stone 1970:1; emphasis in the
> original)

The sin, as Way seemed to see it, was not working on one's own oppression, which caused white women activists to lose their way; white
feminism thus represented the path back to the proper ground of authentic activism. Joan Brown approved of this move by white women,
although for somewhat different reasons:

> I hope that white women are really trying to understand their
> own oppression, because if this country could ever unlock the
> riddle of why women, particularly white women are treated the way
> they are . . . that understanding might lead to other possibilities.
> (1970:1)

Both women continued to agree that each group of women – white and
Black – had to work separately. Way stated that "I think more people
now are realizing that the black woman has a thing she has to do. It's
not our thing" (1970:2). And Brown once again concurred that white
feminist issues were beyond the consideration of Black women: "As a
black woman I don't even feel that [white feminism] is my problem
or my responsibility. Under the circumstances, I wouldn't be a part of
a women's lib movement for anything in the world" (1970:6). Here,
Helen Fannings, the second Black activist at the discussion, supported
Brown: "That [liberating white women] is your problem, Peggy. We
just don't have time for it" (1970:6). It should be noted that neither
Brown nor Fannings negate white feminism as unnecessary, bourgeois,
or indulgent – quite the opposite is the case. But gender oppression is to
be handled within racial/ethnic communities, and not through work by
women across community boundaries.

The discussion summarized in this section was not the only place
where agreement on the impossibility of joint organizing was affirmed.
In an article in *Mademoiselle* magazine (of all places), editor Mary
Cantwell interviewed Dorothy Pitman, a Black feminist and social activist. Cantwell told Pitman that "[t]here was a point when some whites
were helping [Blacks] very much – and some of them died. Then we
came into a counter-trend where blacks said, 'We'd rather do it ourselves, thank you,' which is quite understandable, and a natural evolution" (Cantwell 1971:221). She then bemoaned the fact that there
seemed to be a move from the "natural evolution" to a sense that
Black women did not want white activists around at all, and stated
that she herself would shy away from cross-racial activism, so as not
to seem like "one more white do-gooder" (1971:221). Pitman agreed

with Cantwell that she would be seen in just this way:

> Well, I should have said that to you. . . . If you do something, you
> must do it from the point of view of being human. . . . The social
> worker should be working with white people who are producing
> the problem. Instead, the whole social-work situation . . . is put in
> the black community, to stick bandages on wounds. . . . If you look
> at Harlem, all of the white teachers who came out of college get
> their student-teaching on the backs of black children. Why don't
> they go into the white schools to teach? If they understand the
> situation, why don't they teach those white kids to understand it?
> (1971:221)

Pitman was relatively sympathetic to the white women's movement,
particularly to those feminists who prioritized class. Even so, she accepted
the necessity of separate political work and separate organizations for
women of different racial/ethnic groups.[9]

Eventually, the ethos of organizing one's own led to a proliferation
of campus groups organized along monist lines, and to a great deal of
time spent on symbolic politics, on the reiteration and reification of
difference. One example will stand in for what was surely the situation
at many college campuses and in many communities. At San Francisco
State College (SFSC), a group of seven campus activists (including at
least one man) wrote a letter protesting sexist comments made during an
appearance by Dick Gregory on April 16, 1970 (Independent Campus
Women 1970a: no page given). The letter's authors accused Gregory of
being degrading toward women, of being a "chauvinist" and "an oppressor." On May 15, 1970, the campus paper, *The Phoenix*, published the
response of the SDS Women's Liberation Committee, which slammed
Independent Campus Women (ICW) for writing the letter (SDS
Women's Liberation Committee 1970: no page given). The SDS group

---

[9] In her 1999 interview, Brenda Eichelberger of the Chicago National Black Femi-
nist Organization and founder of the National Alliance of Black Feminists echoed
Pitman's sympathy with white women's liberation and the necessity of separate
Black feminist organizing. When asked why she felt the need for a specifically
Black feminist organization, Eichelberger replied, "because so many Black women
felt that liberation was a white women's issue, not a Black women's issue." On the
West Coast, Frances Beal would drop out of the Bay Area chapter of the TWWA
by the early 1980s because of the group's work with white feminists interested in
multicultural issues (2000 interview).

recounted the controversy that erupted in the wake of the publication of the first letter, and the Committee's response:

> Independent Campus Women were confronted by about thirty black women students concerning a letter which appeared in the Phoenix . . . attacking Dick Gregory as a chauvinist. The black women saw this as a definite racist attack and demanded an apology. SDS Women's Liberation committee felt that the letter had racist implications, but that the letter was not written for the purpose of making a racist attack. [However] the argument put forth in the letter that 'sexism is the most basic for bigotry' is totally ignoring racism in the world.

The SDS group further accused Independent Campus Women of failing to note that their proposals for a women's studies department at SFSC were being put forward at the same time that the Black Studies Department was being "ripped off."

The next week, Independent Campus Women responded with two letters (1970b and 1970c: no page given). Acknowledging the importance of racial oppression, ICW members nonetheless invoked the ethos of organizing one's own to justify their criticism of Gregory: "[S]ince we are women we realize we are the only ones who will carry on the fight on our own behalf. The only true radicalization process comes from organizing around one's own oppression and not somebody else's" (1970b). And the ICW's second letter, essentially an apology to the Black women who had come to confront the group, showed the limits of activist cooperation based on the ethos:

> They [the Black women] considered the letter as an attack on the black struggle as a whole and felt that white women were in no position to judge whether or not the remarks of a black man were sexist or not. . . . We want to state clearly to the black students on this campus that ICW fully supports the Third World struggles against oppression. . . . We regret as an organization the bitterness the letter caused. We see the relationship between black lib and women's lib as one on which there must be continuing dialogue and pledge ourselves to make alliances whenever possible. (1970c)

From the eruption of bitterness over Gregory's visit, which provided a window onto wider, competitive campus politics, one may wonder just how or even if feminists "organizing their own" ever expected to make such alliances work.

Conclusion: The Legacy of Intermovement Politics and Possibilities for Feminist Organizing

In the course of this chapter, I have argued that we must understand the intermovement politics of the crowded social movement sector/field in order to explain the formation of organizationally distinct feminist movements. Feminist emergence from the New Left, the Black Liberation Movement, and the Chicano movement threatened the economy of social movement activism at a time when movements were actively competing with one another. White women's liberationists developed a universalist ideology of gender oppression aimed at pulling away from the New Left and legitimizing their feminist struggle. Gender universalism then spilled over, insofar as it made white feminism less appealing to feminists of color, and was used as a negative example by those hostile to feminism in racial/ethnic communities. Furthermore, also spilling over from movement to movement was the ethos of organizing one's own as being the only way to authentically radical politics. Left-wing feminists in all three communities considered themselves progressive for recognizing that cross-racial/ethnic politics was a long-term goal and not possible in the current political moment. Taken all together, these intermovement developments led to a consensual separation of emerging feminisms along racial/ethnic lines.

The picture of action and reaction in intermovement politics makes several things about second-wave feminist emergences clearer. First, as has been noted throughout this book, feminists in all three racial/ethnic communities needed to justify their activism to others and to themselves; in practical terms, they needed to manage competing demands on their time as activists. Their solutions to managing these demands were not designed to reach out to others – whatever the rhetoric of gender universalism – but were oriented toward creating group cohesion. Thus, despite rhetoric to the contrary, an ideology that would assist in actively recruiting large groups of women for coordinated activism across racial/ethnic lines was not prioritized. The ethos of organizing one's own, in fact, sanctioned efforts not to reach out across those lines; instead, it mobilized feminists into organizationally distinct movements. Arguably, decisions to stay within the racial/ethnic community maintained group coherence in the many small groups that made up feminisms in the second wave, since differences among women would have been magnified in such small groups.

Second, going back to the rejection by white women's liberationists of calls from the male Left to reintegrate themselves into mixed-gender groups, circa 1971, we can speculate that the "do for others" component that these radical white activists reintroduced into their activism was suspect precisely because white feminists were organizing their own. "Doing for others" on the part of radical white activists was particularly unattractive to Black and Chicana feminists, who by and large did not identify with what they saw as white adventurism, the romanticization of guerilla leaders in the Third World, and the forgiving of sexist masculinist nationalists at home on the part of sections of the white anti-imperialist movement. Thus, doing for others may have come to be seen as particularly unauthentic, if not ridiculous, especially when counterposed to the "real" job of organizing one's own that feminists had begun doing.

Finally, the dismissal of class-centered politics that accompanied SDS's severance of ties to the LID may have been as crucial a moment for subsequent feminist organizing as the much-mentioned "expulsion" of whites from SNCC. Once the potential of a class-based identity (even a middle-class one that would have the more fortunate doing for others) was dismissed from the menu, there were few identity options available that leftists could use to mobilize large groups; a universalist conception of gender oppression could easily be seen as stepping into the vacuum. In fact, white women's liberationists came to distrust the left sectarian groups that existed; nonfeminist socialist groups came to be seen as just another set of organizations competing for women's memberships (Freeman 1975). Due to the crisis ensuing from the Socialist Workers Party/Young Socialist Alliance attempts to infiltrate women's liberation groups, cross-class organizing was seen by some feminist activists as yet another challenge to their autonomy, despite the fact that a number of white feminist activists became socialist feminists, and despite the centrality of class to Black and Chicana feminist analysis.

In conclusion, one caveat the reader should keep in mind is that there were, from time to time, local and situational breaches of organizing one's own in the form of coalitional politics around specific local issues, but not until the late 1970s was such local work seen as more than provisional.[10]

---

[10] Women were sometimes able to build interracial links on the basis of nonfeminist identities; see Greene (1996) for a discussion of such an alliance between Black and white women from 1968 to 1975 in Durham, North Carolina.

In the conclusion that follows, the reader will find a more extensive discussion of the impact of feminisms' organizational distinctiveness on the possibilities for feminist coalition politics, but to close this chapter, I should note that as time has passed – as the second wave of feminisms has segued into the third, or maybe even a fourth – there has been much concern from feminists in all three racial/ethnic communities as well as others about the inadequacy of the ideological frameworks inherited from the late 1960s and early 1970s. As early as 1977, June Jordan wrote in the pages of Ms. that as a Black woman seeking to organize around issues that were important to her, she had "met with rigid formulations and stifling analyses . . . that membership in one movement must seem to discredit your support of any other" (1977:113–114). The competition within the social movement sector of the 1960s and early 1970s and the primary ideas within it led feminists to structure their activism in ways that had far-reaching consequences for the possibilities of feminist organizing across racial/ethnic boundaries throughout the second wave. Feminists lived with those consequences and confront them to this day.

Feminists on Their Own and for Their Own

Revisiting and "Re-Visioning" Second-Wave Feminisms

We ought to be able to find a few hours somewhere along the line to continue the revolution, because I think we are in a revolution and we need to do it.

Aileen C. Hernández
San Francisco, California
July 2000

Second-Wave Feminisms, Plural

The social divisions – the social inequities – of race/ethnicity, class, and gender that structured feminisms into organizationally distinct movements – Black, Chicana, and white – operated at several levels. The macrostructure of postwar American society created unequal sets of resources, privilege, and opportunity for feminists situated in different racial/ethnic communities, and these inequalities created obstacles to cross-racial/ethnic organizing. Feminists in oppositional movement communities organized in specific intramovement contexts that shaped their visions of what they could *and* should do. As they organized, they kept a sense of themselves as leftists who wished to do their politics the right way.

In previous chapters, I have shown that organizing within oppositional political milieus was never simply a question of feminists co-opting resources and splitting off from parent movements. Instead, the historical record gives us discussion, debate, and ambivalence about how to organize as feminists. White women's liberationists worked to separate themselves from a largely hostile, dismissive, and fragmenting white Left, but nonetheless saw themselves as leftists; Black feminists organized in a neotraditionalized, increasingly militant Black movement that battled white donor fatigue (see McAdam 1982) and U.S. government interference, but did not want to further enervate their movement; and Chicana feminists worked for changes to the Chicano movement as a whole even as they organized new Chicana-led groups. In a crowded and competitive social movement sector/field, feminists were faced with choices about liberation, as parent movements demanded that they not withdraw their energies from mixed-gender groups, and as the consensus regarding the ethos of organizing one's own became hegemonic. All of these factors combined structured second-wave feminisms on the left along racial/ethnic lines.

Why is it important to have a different vision of the second wave as composed of feminisms? For one thing – and I hope it is clear from this book and from other work done on second-wave feminisms – we need to understand just how broadly appealing the feminist project (writ large) was. Second-wave feminisms' appeal in the 1960s and 1970s was not limited to "bourgeois" white women, was *never* in fact practiced *only* by those women. When the second wave of feminism is seen as feminisms, the audacity of all feminists who challenged the status quo from wherever they were situated is recaptured and highlighted, and we are forced to recognize the power of feminist visions. Black women formed feminist groups despite a political climate that asked them to choose between fighting racism *or* sexism; Chicanas organized around their issues, with their efforts all but ignored by "mainstream" feminists and opposed by many in their own communities; white women's liberationists grew strong despite the ridicule of their activist brothers. This pluralistic reality of feminist organizing has been underexplored from the start; by ignoring it, we minimize the significance of feminisms as part of the cycle of postwar popular protest.

In the rest of this conclusion, I briefly consider what this different vision of 1960s and 1970s feminist movements brings to social movement theory. First, the linked emergences of Black, Chicana, and white feminisms suggest that the overall movement sector/field is important in thinking about what happens to specific movements. Second, the feminist intersectional perspective of considering the impact of interlocking oppressions is crucial for understanding how feminisms, and many other movements, formed. Third, the existence of feminisms in the postwar period should make us think further about how activists conceptualize questions of inclusion and exclusion in movements. Fourth, I argue that gender matters in considering social movement praxis, and not only when looking at feminist movements. I then turn to the question of what underlies this picture of divisions among feminists – about coalition making across racial/ethnic lines – before closing with a few very last words about the need for continued feminist activism.

Second-Wave Feminisms and Theoretical Considerations

There are several ways in which a new understanding of the linked emergences of Black, Chicana, and white feminisms can challenge social movement theory and our understanding of postwar American protest. First, an examination of the linked emergences of white, Black, and Chicana feminist movements shows the importance of the movement sector/field, especially insofar as we consider the cross-pollination of ideas from movement to movement (della Porta and Diani 1999; Marx Ferree and Roth 1998; Meyer and Whittier 1994; Ray 1999). In the specific historical case of the protest cycle of postwar America, the threat of feminist organizing was magnified by the proliferation of social movement organizations, of which feminisms were a part; in a sense, there was an "elective affinity" between the imperative of "organizing one's own" and the 1960s proliferating movement structure. As far as the linked emergences of feminisms is concerned, thinking about intermovement relationships that feminists emerged from and into subverts the idea that feminists of color reacted to personal racism on the part of white feminists. Instead, we see the emergence of movements within an overall leftist sector/field, movements that are on parallel tracks and whose edges sometimes come up against each other. Ironically, in considering different feminisms in the second wave, it becomes easier to see how much of a feminist agenda these parallel movements shared, and how their discourse, at least on some issues, overlapped. Feminists in all three communities had some basic agreements on a core set of issues regarding women's oppression, even if they argued about whether or not all women were oppressed in the same way; they had the same concerns with what could bring about revolution and liberation. Although I have emphasized movement-specific contexts in narrating the emergence of second-wave racial/ethnic feminisms, it is also clear that feminist politics cannot be understood without considering the overall oppositional movement sector/field.

Second, and related to the need to understand the influence of the overall movement sector/field in considering a specific movement's politics, I would argue that feminist intersectional analysis actually leads us closer to an appreciation of the way in which social movement actors move in nested boxes of constraint. Intersectionality itself can be expanded to include not only the categories of gender, class, and race/ethnicity, but also *any* salient social labels – achieved as well as ascribed, derived from meso- and microrelationships as well as macrostatuses – that position movement players in unequal positions relative to each other. To that end, while we analyze how movements interact with one another, as we examine how the existence of numerous movements at one time constructs the choices that participants make about organizing (Marx Ferree and Roth 1998; Ray 1999), we are by necessity engaging an intersectional perspective, as we assess the weights of constraints impacting one another.

As such, a feminist and intersectional approach to the study of social movements dictates a method that is congruent with social constructionism, since by using such a perspective, we of necessity explore how constraints on or opportunities for social movement actors are mutually constructed by the elements of unequal and systematic social divisions, and by movements-based relationships among activists whose interactions cannot help but be shaped by those divisions. That systematic oppressions and political inequality overlap and mutually constitute each other is an important insight for looking at activism because everyone has a social location. Since women (and men) start from social locations that are always constructed by gender plus some other kind of identity, the failure to attempt intersectional analysis means the failure to capture some aspect of what women activists face, and may lead to the reinforcement of monist interpretations of events that obscure actual aspects of real and lived lives (Crenshaw 1995). Taking an intersectional view does not mean that at some junctures, one or another axis of oppression may not become particularly salient in women's lives or in our analysis (D. H. King 1988); but not taking an intersectional perspective even militates against recognition of the possible shifts in the saliency of oppressions.

Third, the existence of organizationally distinct feminisms in the postwar period should make us think further about how activists on the ground conceptualize matters of collective identity, audience, and enemy. Take, for example, the matter of feminists' identity construction. The manufacturing of a particular collective identity about being a particular kind of feminist has underappreciated implications for our understanding of how activists develop categories of "us" versus "them." Key to the development of feminisms in postwar protest, as in the creation of any social movement, is a process of demarcating who is part of the movement and who is not, who is a friend and who is an enemy. The establishment of such boundaries is the first way in which activist identity is constituted, and typically, the making of boundaries "implies both a positive definition of those participating in a certain group, and a negative identification of those not only excluded but actively opposed" (della Porta and Diani 1999:87). More recently, McAdam, Tarrow, and Tilly (2001:143) have named this boundary-making process "category formation," and emphasized how important an element it is in social contention.

But if we consider how feminists engaged in category formation on the ground, we can see that the questions of who is excluded from the feminist community and whether being excluded meant becoming an enemy can be fairly complicated. For example, feminists of color drew around themselves organizational boundaries that excluded others who were to *various degrees* oppressed. Those on the other side of the categories formed by feminists of color were not necessarily the "enemy"; rather, those excluded were in part white feminists, who constituted a group with whom feminists of color were not going to work, rather than a group *against whom* they would fight. In combating intersecting oppressions, the establishment of boundaries is a provisional and shifting exercise (Sandoval 1991); exclusion does not automatically resolve into opposition. The paired identities of inclusion and exclusion that previous theorists have led us to see were less a part of feminists' thinking than was consideration of relevant position in an overall hierarchy. Boundaries were established and categories formed, but concerns lay with the assessment of who was close by in the hierarchy, and who was far away. Only those having the greatest social distance and social advantage – middle-class white men – were conceptualized as the best "enemy." Moreover, by virtue of sharing one axis of oppression – whether of color, class, gender, or sexual identity – relationships with those "nearby" were still more complicated, because they were still *not* included in Black and Chicana feminist organizing. The process through which feminists created new organizationally distinct movements in the second wave was one where categories were continually refined from within as much as from confrontation.

Fourth, the emergences of feminist movements in the postwar period show that we need to understand gender as a constitutive part of social life *in* social protest. Gender has often been assumed to be a subject of substantive interest, and thus relevant only in explaining activism that focuses on women protestors, be they feminist or otherwise. But looking at how women work within social protest movements – in a world where gender remains a fundamental cleavage in society and predictor of life chances – should always form an integral part of the exploration of social movement politics. Gender is an important issue to explore in social movements, not just because women's dissatisfactions with gendered restrictions occasionally give rise to feminist praxis, but because feminist praxis indicates how different the demands placed on women in extra-institutional political settings are. These different demands affect the ability of women to be political actors because women, both in doing activism and especially in working on their own issues, are systematically disadvantaged vis-à-vis men (Kuumba 1999; Roth 1998).

In the 1960s and 1970s, the centrality of women's daily reproductive labor to left social movement organizations meant that emerging feminisms threatened the economy of social movement activism at a time when movements were actively competing with one another. On the practical level, feminist emergences meant that mixed-gender groups might no longer have the "woman-power" to get things done. Moreover, the economy of social movement labor was the concern not just of male activists but of emerging feminists themselves, since they wished to further the cause of liberation through their organizing; loyalty to an organization becomes a different matter when experience tells one that the group will not function if one leaves, and that one's exit will jeopardize the cause. Black and Chicana feminists had even more acute concerns about feminist organizing, since explicit arguments were made by other activists that their rejection of the labor inherent in more restricted and supportive roles would jeopardize their entire communities' existence. Thus feminists, and especially feminists of color, juggled the knowledge of the centrality of their reproductive labor to their movements, their loyalties to their oppositional communities, and their needs to organize freely around their own issues. These were simply not the same dilemmas faced by male activists, who benefited not only from women's reproductive labor but also from a privileged ideological status that made them the ones who possessed an uninflected, "broad-spectrum" leftist politics. Given that gender hierarchy impacts interaction in all arenas of social life – whether or not the discussion at hand focuses on gender – women confront burdens on their ability to be political actors in social movement settings, and not just when they call for attention to women's issues.

Bridging Divisions: The Legacy of Second-Wave Feminisms and Coalition Making

One of my purposes in exploring the making of organizationally distinct racial/ethnic feminisms is to put front and center the question of what it means to organize women across social divides of race, ethnicity, and class. Transcending such barriers by forming coalitions is always difficult, inasmuch as it requires the recognition of inequality, the negotiation of real, experiential difference, *and* acknowledgment of common cause. Moreover, forming coalitions can come at the expense of internal resources of time and energy aimed at mobilizing one's own base (della Porta and Diani 1999:132); in short, coalitions can be risky for individual groups joining them. Clearly, feminists in the second wave were trying to mobilize their base from within the oppositional community. Given that, and given the ethos of organizing one's own, the making of coalitions across racial/ethnic divides was not a priority. Just as clearly, and despite the greater intersectionality of Black and Chicana feminist analyses, there was a fair amount of overlap as to the issues that feminists on the left saw as part of their agenda. Reproductive rights, economic parity and opportunity, freedom from rape and domestic violence, and day-care provision were just some of the issues that feminists in all three communities saw as necessary parts of a feminist agenda. But similar issues did not make for feminist partners as the movements emerged.

After a number of years – by the late 1970s and early 1980s – the space for the making of coalitions among feminists changed. Cross-racial/ethnic efforts among feminists, of the kind represented by Moraga and Anzaldúa's 1979 collection *This Bridge Called My Back*, began to appear (see also Albrecht and Brewer 1990). Prodded by feminists of color, some white feminists began engaging in antiracist activism, as Becky Thompson (2001) argued in *A Promise and a Way of Life: White Antiracist Activism*. According to Thompson, space for multiracial feminist organizing came as a result of two developments: the falling away, primarily as a result of government repression, of competing racial/ethnic nationalist groups, and the realization by white radical women that the theorizing of feminists of color could go a long way toward broadening and radicalizing feminist politics. I would only add that the waning of nationalist groups would be significant for the establishment of relationships between feminists of color, to the extent that nationalist movements represented an alternative site for the activism of feminists of color. In contrast, the space for the formation of multiracial organizations among feminists of color was a limited one; for example, and as noted in Chapter Three, when the Black Women's Alliance became a multiracial organization and changed its name to the Third World Women's Alliance, it lost some members who did not think the times were right for such a change (Beal 2000 interview; Springer 2001).

To take one local example of cross-racial/ethnic feminist organizing in the late 1970s and 1980s, Boston-area-based members of the Combahee River Collective were involved in the multiracial "Coalition for Women's Safety," a response to the 1978–1979 murders of Black women in Boston. White feminists from the adjacent cities of Cambridge and Somerville joined the coalition in explicitly supportive roles, according to former Combahee member Margo Okazawa-Rey (1999 interview). Okazawa-Rey felt that the way that the white feminists provided support, and not leadership, was "a pretty wonderful model" for joint racial/ethnic feminist organizing. She noted that there were other cross-racial/ethnic Boston-area feminist efforts in the late 1970s – in socialist feminist organizations, in groups formed to combat the sterilization abuse of Puerto Rican women, and in coalitions around Boston school deseg-regation struggles, among others. Okazawa-Rey felt that the best kind of cross-racial/ethnic organizing was situational, provisional, and issue-specific:

> I would say that the racial mix [of feminists] happened contex-tually, so when it was time to rally around a very specific thing, then we would get together, and then other times, there were the separations, there were the separate meetings . . . and I think the separations were initiated by the women of color, as you can imagine. . . . I think at the times that really mattered, people came together. (1999 interview)

Okazawa-Rey describes relationships between feminists that show how, at least in the Boston area, coalition making was seen as a way of working on issues while honoring already-established identities and political investments. The groups that participated in coalition poli-tics were given space as groups, such that organizational boundaries are recognized and maintained. The coalitions that she spoke of did not generally give rise to organizations, nor were they aimed at the creation of a long-standing multicultural feminist group. Instead – and congru-ent with the argument that coalitions tend to be instrumental entities, not primary venues for the establishment of collective identities (della Porta and Diani 1999) – the instrumentality of these issue-based coali-tions was acceptable to Boston-area feminists from different racial/ethnic communities because establishing new identities was not a goal.[1] Thus, as Okazawa-Rey's comments show, Boston-area feminists did not lack for common issues, but working together on issues was only acceptable if certain kinds of interaction between feminists – relationships free of dominance – could be established.

What Boston-area feminists sought in 1978, and what some Chicana and Black feminists earlier in the decade saw as *eventually* possible, was coalitions built on the basis of what Marx Ferree and Roth (1998:629) have called "inclusive solidarity." Inclusive solidarity represents attempts to organize in a manner in which no group becomes dominant, and where no "one movement, organization, or social group is in the position of defining the issues and identities that matter" (1998:629). The beauty of this kind of coalition making is the way that "diversity remains, and solidarity is temporary, specific, and strategic" (1998:643). Inclusive solidarity, therefore, will work to the extent that there are players willing to bet that no group will become dominant and that diversity would be respected. These were precisely the conditions that, in their initial organizing, feminists of color doubted could be maintained if they engaged white feminists. White feminists, though positioned at the top of the race/ethnicity hierarchy, were also initially fresh from intramovement struggles with men on the left, and therefore also concerned about the possibilities of diluting their political agenda.

These fears of coalition making by feminists in different racial/ethnic, class, and sexual communities were addressed by Bernice Johnson Reagon in a 1981 presentation to the West Coast Women's Music Festival, "Coalition Politics: Turning the Century" (a talk which first appeared in Barbara Smith's 1983 edited collection, *Home Girls: A Black Feminist Anthology*). Using her experiences as an activist and her sense of humor and metaphor, Johnson Reagon (1983:358) took a processional view of the necessity of gender/racial/ethnic separatism in organizing;

---

[1] Several years after the time that Okazawa-Rey refers to, in the early 1980s, I was part of a Boston-area cross-racial/ethnic feminist coalition called "Women's Alliance for Boston Elections," or WABE. The coalition came together in 1983 to raise awareness about women's issues in the upcoming Boston municipal elections. WABE consisted of something like twenty groups from different Boston-area communities; it sponsored candidates' nights and distributed literature publicizing candidates' positions on women's issues. Just like the coalitions that Okazawa-Rey describes, WABE was a provisional cross-racial/ethnic feminist project whose members did not prioritize building an organization that would exist past the elections.

she told her audience that while at times, it was necessary to "come to-gether to see what you can do about shouldering up all of your energies so that you and your kind can survive," that time had definitely passed. Coalitions should not be, and could not feel like, home; they were of ne-cessity both uncomfortable and indispensable places for feminists if they were to make progress. She even challenged the idea of "women-only" spaces (such as the Festival); from her standpoint, feminists had to give up the making of safe spaces for a fictional unity called "women," and move on to engagement with any number of human rights issues. For Johnson Reagon, then, the liberation of women and all human beings would only come with the risk, strain, discomfort, and inherent threat of being in coalitions.[2]

The century has turned, and in the current moment, there is contin-ued need for "inclusive solidarity" and coalition making between femi-nists situated in different parts of the social hierarchy. Though difficult to sustain, coalitions represent chances to go beyond social divides; the successful ones will rely on individuals and organizations who are willing to take the most risks and who will serve as bridge builders across di-vides of race/ethnicity, sexuality, and especially class (Christiansen 1997; Johnson Reagon 1983; Marx Ferree and Roth 1998; Poster 1995; see also Rose 2000, especially Chapter 9). To the extent that there is inequality between partners in coalition, bridge builders will have greater burdens as they attempt to get potential coalition partners to trust each other, and they will be seen with suspicion from both sides of the divide (Rose 2000:167). Continuing inequality between groups of feminists, then, makes coalition making both necessary and difficult; inclusive solidar-ity is only possible when partners at once take notice of inequality and strive not to reproduce dominance. That kind of process takes time and energy, and it is somewhat fragile, as it is hard to battle oppressions while fighting internal conflicts generated by those same injustices.[3]

[2] Crenshaw (1995) echoed Johnson Reagon's interrogation of the idea of the safe, homogeneous home from which progressives would make social change. Instead, like Johnson Reagon, she stressed the existence of intragroup difference, and ar-gued that an intersectional approach to conquering oppressions required seeing identity-based groups as coalitions themselves, only between individuals who share membership on one axis of identity/oppression. For further discussion about the ramifications of intragroup differences for social change, see Lugones (1994).

[3] The ramifications for coalition making of inequality between potential part-ners are curiously left unaddressed by Rose (2000:144–145) in his otherwise important study of relationships among the labor, peace, and environmental

But feminists already possess one thing necessary for making successful coalitions – an expansive vision of social change that links issues (Rose 2000). Within this broad feminist vision, narrowly focused, time-bound coalitions should form to work on specific issues, chiefly on local levels. One place feminists might look for specific issues is in community activism by women who may not necessarily identify with feminism (or with any kind of political movement). As Naples (1998a:125; see also 1991) has suggested through her study of community women activists in urban areas, political definitions are not always terribly important for people "acting to protect their communities." With the proliferation and institutionalization of feminist organizations (Marx Ferree and Hess 2000; Marx Ferree and Yancey Martin 1995), the time may be ripe for organizing those who do not, and may not even want to, think of themselves as feminists. And the needs of the most dispossessed women are ultimately all women's needs: All women need freedom from violence of all kinds; all women need freedom from poverty and the tyranny of the market; all women need the right to make decisions over the use of our own bodies; all women need the right to love/live with whomever we wish; all women need personal liberation and personal dignity. Experience has shown us that these rights do not "trickle-down" to those below from above (especially when they are only incompletely built above). Future feminist efforts should include new agendas brought in from outside feminist organizations and aimed at work on a transformed feminist politics that transcends social divides.

movements. While Rose addresses the working-class versus middle-class dynamics inherent in alliances between labor and the latter two movements, he assumes relative equality between coalition partners who "agree to disagree" and therefore manage conflict creatively. If equality is lacking, however, it becomes difficult for coalition partners coming from subordinate social locations to feel very much at ease with disagreements. A similar complaint regarding the neglect of the experiential legacy of inequalities may be made of the call by Gitlin (1995) for the creation of a left political community based on common identity. As Gitlin himself recognizes, common identities really matter rather less than common agendas in the making of political coalitions. In any case, successful organizing across divides created by inequalities would mean engaging the lived experiences of activists who suffer structural disadvantage; it seems to me that the failure to acknowledge disadvantage can never contribute to the stability of any sort of coalition that activists attempt to build across lines of class, race, or gender.

Last Words

My exploration of the linked cases of Black, Chicana, and white women's liberation in the second wave has hopefully shown that second-wave feminisms were not automatic responses by activist women to gender oppression. They were linked to other movements for social change, and consequently other movements for social change were linked to them. One might easily suggest different and even more successful outcomes for the New Left and the Black and Chicano movements had they taken feminism seriously, and incorporated a feminist agenda into their activism. Instead, arguably, the hostility shown to feminists' extension of liberationist ideologies to their own situation played a role in making those movements less effective, as they lost "woman power" and faced a social movement sector where feminism began to compete for the hearts and minds of potential recruits.

It has been fashionable for a number of years (or so it seems to me) to decry the role that so-called identity politics – whose development is frequently laid at the doorstep of feminists and people of color – has had in painting progressives into corners. There is some merit to this stand, as making exclusion from activism programmatic on ascriptive grounds seems to have limited the possibilities for unity on the left, including feminist unity. But, however much some may rue the rise of identity politics, my work shows that feminists (and the rest of the Left) did not get there overnight, or as a result of forces beyond our understanding. Nor is the formation of identity-based groups necessarily the end of the road for progressives, as Johnson Reagon and other feminists remind us. By examining the different choices available to feminists in the second wave, and by thinking about what their activism shows us, I hope that I have added to our understanding about how to build bridges between feminists and progressives on all sides of racial, ethnic, class, and sexual divides. Understanding how feminists have worked in the past in different racial/ethnic communities – indeed, that women *have* worked as feminists in different racial/ethnic communities – should be of interest to all those concerned with progressive social change. After all, in the words of Aileen C. Hernández that opened this chapter, the revolution is still on, and "we need to do it."

The Interviews/Living After the Second Wave

Feminist scholars have made fruitful use of oral histories by second-wave white feminists, although gathering the histories of feminists of color has been a relatively recent pursuit, and is by no means complete (Gluck et al. 1998). Although this book is not centered on oral history data, the insights of the Black and Chicana/Latina feminists I interviewed have added immensely to it. I am grateful to them for their time and generosity, and to Kimberly Springer for providing me with contact information for a number of them. In all, I conducted nine interviews and used material from two oral histories, as listed below:

- Frances M. Beal, San Francisco, California, July 2000
- Irene Blea, Albuquerque, New Mexico, March 2000
- Brenda Eichelberger, Chicago, Illinois, August 1999
- Jane Galvin-Lewis, Brooklyn, New York, February 2000
- Aileen C. Hernández, San Francisco, California, July 2000
- Dorothy King, Harrisburg, Pennsylvania, February 2000
- Dorinda Moreno, Concord, California, July 2000
- Margo Okazawa-Rey, San Francisco, California, July 1999
- Mirta Vidal, Brooklyn, New York, May 2000

I drew on two oral histories in writing this book; these were conducted by Maylei Blackwell with Ana Nieto-Gómez in 1991 and Leticia Hernández in 1992, and archived at the Special Collections/University Archives Oral History Collection. I wish to thank Sherna Gluck, director of the Oral History Program at California State University at Long Beach, and Maylei Blackwell for access to these very rich interviews.

The sample of interviews listed here is, of course, small and decidedly nonrandom. Nonetheless, I think that the small gathering of the voices of second-wave feminists of color adds to our understanding of the experience of activism, particularly when combined with archival research designed to complement partial and partisan memories. That is why I interviewed only after doing archival research (see Morris 1984, "Appendix A: Data and Methods" on this point). The interviews themselves ranged from not quite an hour to over three hours. Although both the interviewees and I approached the encounters as formal interviews, they tended to become conversations rather quickly. Like Ruth Frankenberg (1993:30), I took a "dialogical" approach to the process, and made no attempt to portray myself to the interviewees as disinterested or otherwise neutral. I cannot stress enough how much I learned from conducting these interviews, if indeed I was the only conductor present. Whether in homes or in restaurants, intruding upon schedules that were packed, in the middle of lives that were being lived, the women I talked with were unfailingly gracious and generous to me.

The stories told to me by second-wave feminists also confirmed a pattern present in previous work on 1960s/1970s activists: that most activists stay true to their commitments in the face of changes around them (McAdam 1988, 1989; Whalen and Flacks 1987). All of the women I talked with or whose histories I used continued to live their politics in one way or another. Margo Okazawa-Rey is a professor of social work at San Francisco State University, and has continued her feminist work within the academy and without. Beyond starting the NABF when the NBFO faltered, Brenda Eichelberger kept working as a counselor in a predominantly Black Chicago public high school. After her work with the NBFO, Jane Galvin-Lewis formed a business with a partner called "Social Change Advocates" that consulted on issues of workplace diversity for businesses. Aileen C. Hernández remains, after more than forty years, a feminist activist, a consultant on urban affairs, and part of several networks of Black and non-Black women activists nationally and in the San Francisco area. Dorothy King teaches women's studies in the Harrisburg area, and is the founder/director of PennOwl, a theater group that stages plays that celebrate the African American experience. Irene Blea fashioned a successful career in academia that included being the chair of the California State University at Los Angeles Chicano Studies Department, where a workplace accident forced her retirement; she still writes and speaks on Chicana feminism and issues of spirituality, and she considers herself to be doing "beautiful work." After the early 1970s, Mirta Vidal remained closely tied to the Socialist Workers Party for many years, only resigning out of health; she sees herself as a socialist still, and does translation work for political causes when able. Dorinda Moreno is active in a variety of causes focused on the environment and indigenous peoples' struggles, and is part of an organized support network of Bay Area Latinas called "The Comadres." Frances Beal works as a research associate for the American Civil Liberties Union Racial Justice Department in San Francisco. In 1991, Ana Nieto-Gómez, despite having encountered obstacles, had kept an affiliation with the Civil Rights movement by working as an affirmative action officer for San Bernardino County. As of 1992, Leticia Hernández had left behind electoral politics proper, having worked as a field deputy for Congressman Esteban Torres for a number of years before leaving to take a job in the California State University system.

It is the case for these women that their activism in second-wave feminisms was part and parcel of a lifetime of commitments, indeed of a lifestyle of commitment. The feminists I talked with were mindful of the fact that the battle has not been won, but they expressed positive feelings regarding their activism. Irene Blea, for example, noted that she had given "a lot" of her energy away in her feminist work with young women students, and that although she loved her work fiercely, being an activist teacher in some ways meant that "you give yourself away." But Blea and the others echoed in their own words the kinds of sentiments that Mirta Vidal expressed to me about the ability to be "consistent" in political ideas and political action:

> To be able to work for the common good and for a common cause, I think, in a society where we are taught to be so fiercely individualistic and self-centered, that takes a certain amount of courage and conviction. And so I'm glad that I've been able to contribute.

I would like Mirta, and the reader, to know that the feminists that I met during the course of this project have lived activist lives that have inspired me. In the words of Aileen Hernández,

> I think it's very energizing to be involved with people whose visions are larger than they would be if you were plodding along day to day. . . . I've never had the feeling that I was working at a job that I needed just to earn a living. . . . I think I've gained a whole lot more than I have lost in the process.

And I have gained a whole lot in talking to them.

References

"A Year Ago . . . A Sister Remembers." 1971. Unsigned article. *RAT* (January).

Aberbach, Joel D., and Jack L. Walker. 1971. "The Meanings of Black Power: A Comparison of White and Black Interpretations of a Political Slogan." In *Conflict and Competitions: Studies in the Recent Black Protest Movement*, edited by John H. Bracey, Jr., August Meier, and Elliot Rudwick. Belmont, CA: Wadsworth Publishing Company.

Adams, Milton. 1973. "Blacks Start a Women's Lib Group." *New York Post* (August 16).

Addams, Jane. 1968. "Notes After Reading 'Toward a Female Liberation Movement.'" Unpublished position paper. Women's Liberation Ephemera Files, Special Collections, Northwestern University.

  1969. "Factionalism Lives." *Voice of the Women's Liberation Movement* (February).

Adler, Karen S. 1992. "'Always Leading Our Men in Service and Sacrifice': Amy Jacques Garvey, Feminist Black Nationalist." *Gender & Society* 6 (September):346–375.

Aguilar, Amparo. 1975. "International Women's Conference in Mexico City." *Caracol* (September):10–11, 16.

Aguirre, Lydia R. 1971. "The Meaning of the Chicano Movement." In *La Causa Chicana: The Movement for Justice*, edited by Margaret M. Mangold. New York: Family Service Association of America.

Alafia. c. 1969. "Black Woman's Role in the Revolution." Unpublished pamphlet issued by "Mother of African Unity" (MAU MAU). Women's Liberation Ephemera Files, Special Collections, Northwestern University.

Alarcón, Norma. 1991. "The Theoretical Subject(s) of *This Bridge Called My Back* and Anglo-American Feminism." In *Criticism in the Borderlands*, edited by Hector Calderón and José David Saldívar. Durham, NC: Duke University Press.

Alarcón, Norma, Ana Castillo, and Cherríe Moraga. 1993. "Introduction." In *The Sexuality of Latinas,* edited by Norma Alarcón, Ana Castillo, and Cherríe Moraga. Berkeley: Third Woman Press.

Albrecht, Lisa, and Rose M. Brewer. 1990. *Bridges of Power: Women's Multicultural Alliances.* Philadelphia: New Society Publishers.

Ali, Moiram. 1987. "The Coal War: Women's Struggle During the British Miner's Strike." In *Women and Political Conflict: Portraits of Struggle in Times of Crisis,* edited by Rosemary Ridd and Helen Callaway. New York: New York University Press.

Allen, Pam. 1968a. "What Strategy for Movement Women?" *Guardian* (October 5):9.

1968b. "Memo to My White Sisters in Our Struggle to Realize Our Full Humanity." Draft of position paper sent in letter from Pat Robinson to Joan Jordan (Vilma Sanchez), April 21. Joan Jordan Papers, State Historical Society, Madison, WI.

Allen, Pam, and Julius Lester. 1968. "Interview with Pam Allen and Julius Lester." Transcript of May 5, 1968, interview with Allen conducted by Lester, for WBAI radio program *Conversation.* Leni Wildflower Collection, Southern California Library for Social Science and Research.

Allen Shockley, Ann. 1983. "The Black Lesbian in American Literature: An Overview." In *Home Girls: A Black Feminist Anthology,* edited by Barbara Smith. New York: Kitchen Table/Women of Color Press.

Almott, Teresa L., and Julie A. Matthaei. 1991. *Race, Gender and Work: A Multicultural History of Women in the United States.* Boston: South End Press.

"Alternate U." 1971. Unsigned article. *RAT* (January).

Alvarez, Sonia E. 2000. "Translating the Global Effects of Transnational Organizing on Local Feminist Discourses and Practices in Latin America." *Meridians: feminism, race, transnationalism* 1:1 (Autumn):29–67.

Anderson, Terry H. 1995. *The Movement and the Sixties: Protest in America from Greensboro to Wounded Knee.* New York and Oxford: Oxford University Press.

Anderson-Bricker, Kristin. 1999. "'Triple Jeopardy': Black Women and the Growth of Feminist Consciousness in SNCC, 1964–1975." In *Still Lifting, Still Climbing: Contemporary African American Women's Activism,* edited by Kimberly Springer. New York: New York University Press.

"Ann." 1970. "Women and Anti-war Work." *It Ain't Me Babe* 1:8 (June 11–July 1).

Anna Louise Strong Brigade. 1970. "Women Inspired to Commit Herstory." *Ain't I a Woman* (October).

Anzaldúa, Gloria. 1981. "O.K. Momma, Who the Hell Am I? An Interview with Luisah Teish." In *This Bridge Called My Back: Writings by Radical*

Women of Color, edited by Cherríe Moraga and Gloria Anzaldúa. Watertown, MA: Persephone Press.

1999 [1987]. *Borderlands/La Frontera: The New Mestiza*. San Francisco: Aunt Lute Books.

Aulette, Judy, and Trudy Mills. 1988. "Something Old, Something New: Auxiliary Work in the 1983–1986 Copper Strike." *Feminist Studies* 14:2 (Summer).

Baca Zinn, Maxine. 1975. "Political Familialism: Toward Sex Role Equality in Chicano Families." *Aztlán* 6:13–26.

Baker, Sue. 1970. "Venceremos Part 2." *off our backs* (March).

Banks, Olive. 1981. *Faces of Feminism: A Study of Feminism as a Social Movement*. Oxford: Basil Blackwell.

Barrera, Mario. 1979. *Race and Class in the Southwest: A Theory of Racial Inequality*. Notre Dame and London: University of Notre Dame Press.

Basso, Sister Teresita. 1971. "The Emerging Chicana Woman Religious." In *The Third Annual El Alma Chicana Symposium, California State University, San Jose*. (Subsequently published as "The Emerging 'Chicana' Sister." *Review for Religious* (November 1971):1019–1028.)

Batten, Jack. 1969. "After Black Power, Woman Power." *Chatelaine* (September).

Baxandall, Ros. 1968. Letter to Pam Allen (September 20). Pam Allen Papers. State Historical Society, Madison, WI.

2001. "Re-visioning the Women's Liberation Movement's Narrative: Early Second Wave African American Feminists." *Feminist Studies* 27:1 (Spring).

Baxandall, Rosalyn, and Linda Gordon, eds. 2000. *Dear Sisters: Dispatches from the Women's Liberation Movement*. New York: Basic Books.

Beal, Frances. 1970. "Double Jeopardy: To Be Black and Female." In *The Black Woman: An Anthology*, edited by Toni Cade (Bambara). New York: New American Library.

c. 1971. "Third World Women's Struggle." Letter (July). Women's Liberation Ephemera Files, Special Collections, Northwestern University.

2000. Interview with author.

Bender, Marilyn. 1969. "Black Women in Civil Rights: Is She a Second-Class Citizen?" *New York Times* (September 2).

Benford, Robert D., and David Snow. 2000. "Framing Processes and Social Movements: An Overview and Assessment." *Annual Review of Sociology* 26:611–639.

Bennett, Elizabeth. 1971. "Chicana Conference May Change Image." *Houston Post* (May 25).

Berger, Leslie. 2000. "'Our Bodies' Is Recast for Latina Culture." *New York Times* (June 13):F8.

Berkeley Women's Liberation. 1969. "Why the Women's Liberation Movement Must Be Autonomous." Unpublished position paper from Berkeley

Women's Liberation Conference, August 15–17. Schlesinger Library, Harvard University.

Bernstein, Anne, et al. 1968. "The Nitty Gritty on the Woman Question." *Voice of the Women's Liberation Movement* (October). Reprinted from the *San Francisco Express Times*, August 28, 1968.

"Black Women and Liberation Fad." 1970. *Daily Defender*. Unsigned editorial (December 5).

Black Women Stirring the Waters. 1997. *Black Women Stirring the Waters*. Oakland, CA: Marcus Books Printing.

Black Women's Liberation Group of Mt. Vernon/New Rochelle. 1970. "Statement on Birth Control." In *Sisterhood Is Powerful*, edited by Robin Morgan. New York: Vintage Books.

"Black Women's Liberation Is a Component Part of Black People's Liberation." 1975. Unsigned pamphlet, issued by October League, Detroit. Women's Liberation Ephemera Files, Special Collections, Northwestern University.

"Blacks v. Feminists." 1973. *Time* (March 26).

Blackwell, Maylei. 2000a. "The Hijas de Cuauhtémoc: Chicana Feminist Historical Subjects Between and Beyond Nationalist Imaginaries." In *Las Nuevas Fronteras del Siglo XXI/New Frontiers of the 21st Century*, edited by Norma Klahn, Pedro Castillo, Alejandro Álvarez, and Federico Manchón. Mexico City: La Jornada Ediciones (in conjunction with DEMOS, UNAM, UAM, and the Chicano/Latino Research Center of the University of California, Santa Cruz).

2000b. "Geographies of Difference: Mapping Multiple Feminist Insurgencies and Transnational Public Cultures in the Americas (Mexico)." Ph.D. diss., University of California, Santa Cruz.

Forthcoming. "Contested Histories: *Las Hijas de Cuauhtémoc*/Chicana Feminisms and Print Culture in the Chicano Movement, 1968–1973." In *Chicana Feminisms: Disruptions in Dialogue*, edited by Gabriella Arredondo, Aida Hurtado, Norma Klahn, Olga Nájera-Ramirez, and Patricia Zavella. Durham, NC: Duke University Press.

Blea, Irene I. 1992. *La Chicana and the Intersection of Race, Class, and Gender*. Westport and London: Praeger Publishers.

2000. Interview with author.

Bookman, Ann, and Sandra Morgen, eds. 1988. *Women and the Politics of Empowerment*. Philadelphia: Temple University Press.

Bouchier, David. 1983. *The Feminist Challenge: The Movement for Women's Liberation in Britain and the United States*. New York: Schocken Books.

Breines, Wini. 1982. *The Great Refusal: Community and Organization in the New Left: 1962–1968*. South Hadley, MA: Praeger Publishers.

Brock, Annette K. 1990. "Gloria Richardson and the Cambridge Movement." In *Women in the Civil Rights Movement: Trailblazers and Torchbearers 1941–1965*, edited by Vicki L. Crawford, Jacqueline Anne Rouse, and Barbara Woods. Bloomington and Indianapolis: Indiana University Press.

Brown, Elaine. 1992. *A Taste of Power: A Black Woman's Story*. New York: Pantheon Books.

Brown, Judith. 1968. "Part II." In Beverly Jones and Judith Brown, *Toward a Female Liberation Movement*. Pamphlet published by the authors. Women's Liberation Ephemera Files, Special Collections, Northwestern University.

Brownmiller, Susan. 1999. *In Our Time: Memoir of a Revolution*. New York: Delta Trade Paperbacks.

Buechler, Steven M. 1990. *Women's Movements in the United States: Woman Suffrage, Equal Rights and Beyond*. New Brunswick and London: Rutgers University Press.

Burris, Barbara. 1971. "The Fourth World Manifesto." *Notes from the Third Year*. New York: Notes from the Second Year, Inc.

Cade (Bambara), Toni, ed. 1970. *The Black Woman: An Anthology*. York and Scarborough, Ontario: Mentor Books.

1970a. "On the Issue of Roles." Ibid.

1970b. "Preface." Ibid.

1970c. "The Pill: Genocide or Liberation." Ibid.

Cagan, Beth. 1971. "Why Should Women Join the NUC?" *New University Conference Women's Caucus Newsletter* (March). Schlesinger Library, Harvard University.

California Women's Caucus, La Raza Unida Party. 1972. "National Chicano Political Conference, San Jose California." Unpublished (April) draft document for presentation to the statewide convention of the RUP in July of 1972. Women's Liberation Ephemera Files, Special Collections, Northwestern University.

Cameron, Ardis. 1985. "Bread and Roses Revisited: Women's Culture and Working Class Activism in the Lawrence Strike of 1912." In *Women, Work, and Protest: A Century of U.S. Women's Labor History*, edited by Ruth Milkman. Boston: Routledge and Kegan Paul.

Campbell, Barbara. 1973. "Black Feminists Form Group Here." *New York Times* (August 8).

Cantwell, Mary. 1971. "'I Can't Call You My Sister Yet': A Black Woman Looks at Women's Lib." *Mademoiselle* (May).

Carden, Maren Lockwood. 1974. *The New Feminist Movement*. New York: Russell Sage Foundation.

Cárdenas, Reyes. 1976. "The Machismo Manifesto (humourous article)." *Caracol* (April):7.

Carey Bond, Jean, and Patricia Perry. 1970. "Is the Black Male Castrated?" In *The Black Woman: An Anthology*, edited by Toni Cade (Bambara). York and Scarborough, Ontario: Mentor Books.

Carmichael, Stokely, and Charles V. Hamilton. 1967. *Black Power: The Politics of Liberation in America*. New York: Vintage Books.

Carson, Clayborne. 1981. *In Struggle: SNCC and the Black Awakening of the 1960s*. Cambridge, MA: Harvard University Press.

Castillo, Ana. 1994. *Massacre of the Dreamers: Essays on Xicanisma*. New York: Plume/Penguin Books.

Chafetz, Janet, and Anthony Dworkin. 1986. *Female Revolt: Women's Movements in World and Historical Perspective*. Totowa, NJ: Rowman and Allanheld.

Chancer, Lynn S. 1998. *Reconcilable Differences: Confronting Beauty, Pornography and the Future of Feminism*. Berkeley, Los Angeles, London: University of California Press.

Cherot, Lorna. 1970. "I Am What I Am." *Liberation News Service*: 294 (October 29):16.

"Chicana Regional Conference." 1971. Unsigned article. *La Raza* 1:6:43–44.

"Chicago Women Form Liberation Group/Preliminary Statement of Principles." 1967. *New Left Notes* (November 13).

Christiansen, Kimberly. 1997. "'With Whom Do You Believe Your Lot Is Cast': White Feminists and Racism." *Signs: Journal of Women in Culture and Society* 22:3:617–648.

Clarke, Cheryl. 1983. "The Failure to Transform: Homophobia and the Black Community." In *Home Girls: A Black Feminist Anthology*, edited by Barbara Smith. New York: Kitchen Table/Women of Color Press.

Cohen, Jean L. 1985. "Strategy or Identity: New Theoretical Paradigms and Contemporary Social Movements. *Social Research* 52:663–716.

Cohen, Philip N. 1996. "Nationalism and Suffrage: Gender Struggle in Nation-Building America." *Signs* 21:3:707–727.

Comaroff, Jean, and John Comaroff. 1991. *Of Revelation and Revolution: Christianity, Colonialism and Consciousness in South Africa*. Vol. 1. Chicago and London: The University of Chicago Press.

Combahee River Collective (CRC). 1979. "Why Did They Die? A Document of Black Feminism." *Radical America* 13:6 (November–December):40–47.

——— 1981. "A Black Feminist Statement." In *This Bridge Called My Back: Writings by Radical Women of Color*, edited by Cherríe Moraga and Gloria Anzaldúa. Watertown, MA: Persephone Press.

Comision Femenil Mexicana (CFM). 1971a. "Resolution." *Regeneración* 1:10 (Reprint of October 1970 resolution made at National Mexican American Issues Conference, Sacramento, CA).

——— 1971b. "Resolution on Mrs. Romana A Banuelos." Unpublished internal document, October 15. Women's Liberation Ephemera Files, Special Collections, Northwestern University.

——— 1973. "First Convention, Comision Femenil Mexicana, Inc." Unpublished pamphlet, April. Women's Liberation Ephemera Files, Special Collections, Northwestern University.

Concilio Mujeres (CM). n.d. "Biography: Concilio Mujeres Records 1970–1975." Concilio Mujeres Papers: State Historical Society, Madison, WI.

n.d. *La Mujer en Pie de Lucha*. Flyer. Ibid.

c. 1973. "Hermanas y Amigos." Letter, Women's Liberation Ephemera Files, Special Collections, Northwestern University.

c. 1974. "Friends of La Raza Women." Letter. Ibid.

1974. "Fifth Festival de Los Teatros Chicanos." Flyer, Concilio Mujeres Papers, State Historical Society, Madison, WI.

1975a. "Body Language – A Cultural Ms.understanding." *La Razon Mestiza II* (Summer). Ibid.

1975b. "TENAZ meeting." Flyer (May). Ibid.

1975c. "Estimadas Hermanas." September letter. Ibid.

c. 1975a. "Chicana Collection Project." Flyer and Letter/Solicitation. Women's Liberation Ephemera Files, Special Collections, Northwestern University.

c. 1975b. "Las Cucarachas." Flyer, Concilio Mujeres Papers, State Historical Society, Madison, WI.

c. 1975c. "Friends of Peace, Unity and La Mujer." Letter, Women's Liberation Ephemera Files, Special Collections, Northwestern University.

Conley, Madelyn. 1970. "Do Black Women Need the Women's Lib?" *Essence* 1:4 (August):29–34.

Cooney, Rosemary Santana. 1975. "Changing Labor Force Participation of Mexican American Wives: A Comparison with Anglos and Blacks." *Social Science Quarterly* 56:2 (September):252–261.

"Cornell Conference on Women Report." 1969. Unpublished January 25 report on "Panel 7: THE BLACK WOMEN IN AMERICA." Sophia Smith Collection, Smith College.

Cortera, Marta. 1976a. *Diosa y Hembra: The History and Heritage of Chicanas in the U.S.* Austin, TX: Information Systems Development.

1976b. "Chicana Identity (platica de Marta Cortera)." *Caracol* 2:6 (February):14–15, 17.

1977. *The Chicana Feminist*. Austin, TX: Information Systems Development.

1980. "Feminism: The Chicano and Anglo Versions." *Twice a Minority: Mexican American Women*, edited by Margarita Melville. St. Louis: C. V. Mosby Company.

Cott, Nancy. 1989. "Comment on Karen Offen's 'Defining Feminism: A Comparative Historical Approach.'" *Signs* 15:1 (Autumn):203–205.

Crawford, Vicki L., et al. 1993. *Women in the Civil Rights Movement: Trailblazers and Torchbearers 1941–1965*. Bloomington and Indianapolis: Indiana University Press.

Crawford, Vicki L., Jacqueline Anne Rouse, and Barbara Woods. 1990. *Women in the Civil Rights Movement: Trailblazers and Torchbearers*. Brooklyn, NY: Carlson Publishing.

Crenshaw, Kimberlé. 1989. "Demarginalizing the Intersection of Race and Sex: A Black Feminist Critique of Antidiscrimination Doctrine, Feminist Theory and Antiracist Politics." *The University of Chicago Legal Forum*:139–167.

———. 1995. "Mapping the Margins: Intersectionality, Identity Politics and Violence Against Women." In *Critical Race Theory: The Key Writings That Formed the Movement,* edited by Kimberlé Crenshaw, Neil Gotanda, Gary Peller, and Kendall Thomas. New York: The New Press (357–383).

Curtis, Russell L., and Louis A. Zurcher. 1973. "Stable Resources of Protest Movements: The Multi-organizational Field." *Social Forces* 52:53–61.

Damned, The. 1990 [1973]. *Lessons From the Damned: Class Struggle in the Black Community.* Ojai, CA: Times Change Press.

davenport, doris. 1979. "The Pathology of Racism: A Conversation with Third World Women." In *This Bridge Called My Back: Writings by Radical Women of Color,* edited by Cherríe Moraga and Gloria Anzaldúa. Watertown, MA: Persephone Press (85–86).

Davidica, Maureen. 1968. "Women and the Radical Movement." *No More Fun and Games*:1.

Davies, James C. 1971. "Toward a Theory of Revolution." In *When Men Revolt and Why: A Reader in Political Violence.* New York: Free Press.

Davis, Beverly. 1988. "To Seize the Moment: A Retrospective on the National Black Feminist Organization." *Sage* 5:2 (Fall).

Dean, Heather. 1966. "The Sexual Caste System." Pamphlet published by Research, Information and Publications Project of Student Union for Peace Action, and distributed by Women's Liberation, Washington, DC. Originally appeared in University of Toronto student magazine, *Random.* Leni Wildflower Collection, Southern California Library for Social Science and Research.

de la Garza, Rudolph O. 1979. "The Politics of Mexican Americans." In *The Chicanos: As We See Ourselves,* edited by Arnulfo D. Trejo. Tucson: The University of Arizona Press.

del Castillo, Adelaida R. 1980. "Mexican Women in Organization." In *Mexican Women in the United States: Struggles Past and Present,* edited by Magdelena Mora and Adelaida R. del Castillo. Los Angeles: Chicano Studies Research Center Publications, University of California.

della Porta, Donatella, and Mario Diani. 1999. *Social Movements: An Introduction.* Oxford: Blackwell Publishers.

Densmore, Dana. 1971. "On Unity." *No More Fun and Games* 5 (July). Reprint of speech delivered at the Conference to Unite Women in Washington, DC, October 1970.

de Tocqueville, Alexis. 1978. *The Old Regime and the French Revolution.* Translated by Stuart Gilbert. Gloucester, MA: Peter Smith.

Dixon, Marlene. 1968. "Reply to 'One Editor's View of the Women's Caucus.'" *New University Conference Newsletter* (September). Women's Liberation Ephemera Files, Special Collections, Northwestern University.

1970a. "On Women's Liberation." *Radical America* (February). Reprinted in *Ain't I a Woman* (November):10–11 as "Where Are We Going?"

1970b. "The Restless Eagles: Women's Liberation 1970." *The Daily Gater* (March 5–6):4. Originally appeared in *Motive* magazine, 29:6–7 (March–April 1969).

Dowd Hall, Jacqueline. 1990. "Disorderly Women: Gender and Labor Militancy in the Appalachian South." In *Unequal Sisters: A Multicultural Reader in U.S. Women's History*, edited by Ellen Carol DuBois and Vicki L. Ruiz. New York and London: Routledge.

Dubey, Madhu. 1994. *Black Women Novelists and the Nationalist Aesthetic.* Bloomington and Indianapolis: Indiana University Press.

DuBois, Ellen Carol. 1978. *Feminism and Suffrage: The Emergence of an Independent Women's Movement in America 1848–1869.* Ithaca and London: Cornell University Press.

1989. "Comment on Karen Offen's 'Defining Feminism: A Comparative Historical Approach.'" *Signs* 15:1 (Autumn):195–197.

Dunbar, Roxanne. 1968. "Slavery." *No More Fun and Games*:1.

1969. "Sexual Liberation: More of the Same." *No More Fun and Games* (November):3.

1970. "Female Liberation as the Basis for Social Revolution." In *Sisterhood is Powerful*, edited by Robin Morgan. New York: Vintage Books.

Echols, Alice. 1989. *Daring to Be Bad: Radical Feminism in America 1967–1975.* Minneapolis: University of Minnesota Press.

1992. "'We Gotta Get Out of This Place': Notes Toward a Remapping of the Sixties." *Socialist Review* 22:2 (April/June):9–33.

Eichelberger, Brenda D. 1974. "Black Feminism – A New Directive: Consciousness Raising Guidelines for Black Men and Women." Unpublished paper delivered to the Association of Black Psychologists' Seventh Annual Convention, August 26–28. Women's Liberation Ephemera Files, Special Collections, Northwestern University.

1974–1975. Letters. National Black Feminist Organization Papers, Special Collections, University of Illinois, Chicago.

1975. "Dear Concerned Academician." Letter from National Black Feminist Organization's Chicago Chapter to area academics, February 25. Women's Liberation Ephemera Files, Special Collections, Northwestern University.

1999a. Interview with author.

1999b. Phone conversation with author.

"El Movimiento and the Chicana: What Else Could Breakdown [sic] a Revolution but Women Who Do Not Understand True Equality." 1971. Unsigned article. *La Raza* 1:6:40–42.

Elkins, Marlene. 1970. "Women-Identified Women: On the Man's Convention." *RAT* (October).

Encuentro Feminil Editors. 1997. "Introduction to *Encuentro Feminil*." In *Chicana Feminist Thought: The Basic Historical Writings*, edited by Alma García. New York and London: Routledge. Originally appeared in *Encuentro Feminil* 1:2:3–7 (1973).

Enríquez, Evangelina, and Alfredo Mirandé. 1978. "Liberation Chicana Style: Colonial Roots of Feministas Chicanas." *De Colores* 4:3.

Escobar, Edward J. 1993. "The Dialectics of Repression: The Los Angeles Police Department and the Chicano Movement, 1968–1971." *Journal of American History* 79:4 (March):1483–1514.

Estellachild, Vivian. 1971. "Hippie Communes." *Women: A Journal of Liberation* 2:2 (Winter).

Evans, Sara. 1979. *Personal Politics: The Roots of Women's Liberation in the Civil Rights Movement and the New Left*. New York: Vintage Books.

Fair Burks, Mary. 1990. "Trailblazers: Women in the Montgomery Bus Boycott." In *Women in the Civil Rights Movement: Trailblazers and Torchbearers 1941–1965*, edited by Vicki L. Crawford, Jacqueline Anne Rouse, and Barbara Woods. Bloomington and Indianapolis: Indiana University Press.

"Feminist Women March Against the War." 1969. Unsigned article. *The Militant* (November 7).

Ferguson, Renee. 1970. "Women's Liberation Has a Different Meaning for Blacks." *The Washington Post* (October 3).

Fireman, Bruce, and William Gamson. 1979. "Utilitarian Logic in the Resource Mobilization Perspective." In *The Dynamics of Social Movements*, edited by Mayer Zald and John D. McCarthy. Cambridge, MA: Winthrop Publishers, Inc.

Firestone, Shulamith. 1969. "D.C. Speech." *Voice of the Women's Liberation Movement* (February).

Flores, Francisca. 1971a. "Conference of Mexican Women: Un Remolino." *Regeneracíon* 1:10.

———. 1971b. "Editorial." *Regeneracíon* 1:10.

Frankenberg, Ruth. 1993. *White Women, Race Matters: The Social Construction of Whiteness*. Minneapolis: University of Minnesota Press.

Fraser, Clara. 1970. "Which Road Towards Women's Liberation?" *Women: A Journal of Liberation* 2:1 (Fall).

Freeman, Jo ["Joreen"]. 1968. "What in the Hell Is Women's Liberation Anyway?" *Voice of the Women's Liberation Movement* (March).

———. 1973. "The Origins of the Women's Liberation Movement." *American Journal of Sociology* 78:792–811.

———. 1975. *The Politics of Women's Liberation*. New York and London: Longman.

———. 1979. "Resource Mobilization and Strategy: A Model for Analyzing Social Movement Organization Actions." In *The Dynamics of Social Movements:*

Resource Mobilization, Social Control, and Tactics, edited by Mayer N. Zald and John D. McCarthy. Cambridge, MA: Winthrop Publishers.

Fulman, Ricki. 1973. "Black Feminist Group Launched." *New York Daily News* (August 16).

Galvin-Lewis, Jane. 2000. Interview with author.

Gamson, Joshua. 1997. "Messages of Exclusion: Gender, Movements, and Symbolic Boundaries." *Gender & Society* 11:2.

García, Alma. 1990. "The Development of Chicana Feminist Discourse, 1970–1980." In *Unequal Sisters: A Multicultural Reader in U.S. Women's History*, edited by Ellen Carol DuBois and Vicki L. Ruiz. New York and London: Routledge.

——— 1997. *Chicana Feminist Thought: The Basic Historical Writings*. New York and London: Routledge.

Garcia, Patti. 1975. "Pa' Delante Mujer." *La Razon Mestiza II* (Summer). Concilio Mujeres Papers, State Historical Society, Madison, WI.

García-Camarillo, Mia. 1976. "Equal Rights Amendment: Report by Mia García-Camarillo." *Caracol* (November):8.

García-Camarillo, Mia, and Susan de la Torre. 1976. "Mujeres En El Movimiento: Platica de Las Mujeres de Caracol" [Women in the Movement: A Conversation with the Women of Caracol]. *Caracol* (August).

Gerlach, Luther P., and Virginia H. Hine. 1970. *People, Power, Change: Movements of Social Transformation*. Indianapolis: Bobbs-Merrill.

Geschwender, James A. 1968. "Explorations in the Theory of Social Movements and Revolutions." *Social Forces* 47:2 (December).

Giddings, Paula. 1984. *When and Where I Enter: The Impact of Black Women on Race and Sex in America*. New York: Bantam Books.

Gitlin, Todd. 1987. *The Sixties: Years of Hope, Days of Rage*. Toronto: Bantam Books.

——— 1995. *The Twilight of Common Dreams: Why America is Wracked by Culture Wars*. New York: Metropolitan Books.

Gluck, Sherna, with Maylei Blackwell, Sharon Cotrell, and Karen S. Harper. 1998. "Whose Feminism, Whose History? Reflections on Excavating the History of (the) US Women's Movement(s)." In *Community Activism and Feminist Politics: Organizing Across Race, Class, and Gender*, edited by Nancy A. Naples. Philadelphia: Temple University Press.

Goldfield, Evelyn, Sue Munaker, and Naomi Weisstein. c. 1968. "A Woman Is a Sometime Thing." Pamphlet published by the Literature Committee, Toronto's Women's Liberation, and the Hogtown Press. Women's Liberation Ephemera Files, Special Collections, Northwestern University.

Gómez-Quiñones, Juan. 1990. *Chicano Politics: Reality and Promise 1940–1990*. Albuquerque: University of New Mexico Press.

Gonzales, Sylvia Alicia. 1975. "White Women's Liberation: The Oppressive Revolution." *La Razon Mestiza* II (Summer).
——— 1979. "The Chicana Perspective: A Design for Self-Awareness." In *The Chicanos: As We See Ourselves*, edited by Arnulfo D. Trejo. Tucson: The University of Arizona Press.
Gray White, Deborah. 1999. *Too Heavy a Load: Black Women in Defense of Themselves, 1894–1994*. New York and London: W. W. Norton.
Greene, Christina. 1996. "'In the Best Interests of the Total Community?': Women-in-Action and the Problems of Building Interracial, Cross-class Alliances in Durham, North Carolina, 1968–1975." *Frontiers* 16:2–3 (March):190–228.
"*Guardian*: Strike and Split." 1970. Unsigned article. *off our backs* (April).
Gurr, Ted R. 1970. *Why Men Rebel*. Princeton, NJ: Princeton University Press.
Hanisch, Carol. 1970. "Hard Knocks." *Notes From the Second Year*. New York: Shulamith Firestone and Anne Koedt (self-published).
Harding, Nina. 1970. "The Interconnections Between the Black Struggle and the Woman Question." Reprint, published by Seattle Radical Women. Women's Liberation Ephemera Files, Special Collections, Northwestern University.
Harris, Duchess. 1999. "'All of Who I Am in the Same Place': The Combahee River Collective." *Womanist Theory and Research* 2:1 (Fall).
Hartmann, Susan M. 1998. *The Other Feminists: Activists in the Liberal Establishment*. New Haven and London: Yale University Press.
Hernández, Aileen C. 2000. Interview with author.
Hernández, Leticia. 1992. Oral History Interview. Conducted and tape recorded by Maylei Blackwell. California State University at Long Beach, Oral History Collection in Women's History.
Hernandez, Patricia. 1980. "Lives of Chicana Activists: The Chicano Student Movement (A Case Study)." In *Mexican Women in the United States: Struggles Past and Present*, edited by Magdelena Mora and Adelaida R. del Castillo. Los Angeles: Chicano Studies Research Center Publications, University of California.
Herrera, Albert. 1971. "The National Chicano Moratorium and the Death of Ruben Salazar." In *The Chicanos: Mexican American Voices*, edited by Ed Ludwig and James Santibanez. Baltimore: Penguin Books.
Heywood, Leslie, and Jennifer Drake, eds. 1997. *Third Wave Agenda: Being Feminist, Doing Feminism*. Minneapolis and London: University of Minnesota Press.
Higginbotham, Elizabeth. 1994. "Black Professional Women: Job Ceilings and Employment Sectors." In *Women of Color in U.S. Society*, edited by Maxine Baca Zinn and Bonnie Thorton Dill. Philadelphia: Temple University Press.

Hill Collins, Patricia. 1990. *Black Feminist Thought: Knowledge, Consciousness, and the Politics of Empowerment*. Boston: Unwin Hyman.

Hole, Judith, and Ellen Levine. 1971. *Rebirth of Feminism*. New York: Quadrangle Books.

Hollins Flowers, Sandra. 1974a. Letter to Brenda Eichelberger (August 15). National Black Feminist Organization Papers, Special Collections, University of Illinois, Chicago.

1974b. Letter to Jane Galvin-Lewis (September 9). Ibid.

1974c. "Feedback on Press Conference." (October 6). Ibid.

1974d. "Proposal for The Black Woman's Self Image Task Force, Atlanta." Ibid.

Holmes Norton, Eleanor. 1970. "For Sadie and Maude." In *Sisterhood Is Powerful*, edited by Robin Morgan. New York: Vintage Books.

hooks, bell. 1981. *Ain't I a Woman: Black Women and Feminism*. Boston: South End Press.

1984. *Feminist Theory: From Margin to Center*. Boston: South End Press.

Horowitz, Daniel. 1996. "Rethinking Betty Friedan and *The Feminine Mystique*: Labor Union Radicalism and Feminism in Cold War America." *American Quarterly* 48:1 (March).

Huerta, Dolores. 1975. "Dolores Huerta Talks." *Regeneración* 2:4:20–24.

Hull, Gloria T., Patrica Bell Scott, and Barbara Smith, eds. 1982. *All the Women Are White, All the Men Are Black, but Some of Us Are Brave: Black Women's Studies*. Old Westbury, NY: Feminist Press.

Hunter, Charlayne. 1970. "Many Blacks Wary of 'Women's Liberation' Movement in the U.S." *New York Times* (November 17):B1.

Independent Campus Women. 1970a. Letter published in *The Phoenix* 5:10 (April). Joan Jordan Papers, State Historical Society, Madison, WI.

1970b, 1970c. Letters to *The Phoenix* (May 21). Ibid.

Jefferson, Margo, and Margaret Sloan. 1974. "In Defense of Black Feminism." *Encore* (July):46.

Johnson, Linda Asantenwaa. 1980. "Women of Color: Organizing on Our Own." *Upfront: A Black Woman's Newspaper* 2:1 (Fall/Winter):9.

Johnson Reagon, Bernice. 1978. "The Borning Struggle: The Civil Rights Movement." *Radical America* 12:6 (November/December):9–25.

1983. "Coalition Politics: Turning the Century." In *Home Girls: A Black Feminist Anthology*, edited by Barbara Smith. New York: Kitchen Table/Women of Color Press.

Jones, Beverly. 1968. "Part I." In Beverly Jones and Judith Brown, *Toward a Female Liberation Movement*. Pamphlet published by the authors. Women's Liberation Ephemera Files, Special Collections, Northwestern University.

Jones, Beverly, and Judith Brown. 1968. *Toward a Female Liberation Movement*. Pamphlet published by the authors. Women's Liberation Ephemera Files, Special Collections, Northwestern University.

Jordan, Joan (aka Vilma Sanchez). 1968. "Black Women as Leaders in the Coming Crisis: A Psycho-Dynamic Approach." Unpublished paper. Joan Jordan Papers, State Historical Society, Madison, WI.

1969. "Proposal for San Francisco Women's Center." Unpublished paper. Ibid.

1965–1970. Letters. Ibid.

Jordan, June. 1977. "Second Thoughts of a Black Feminist." Ms. (February):113–115.

Joseph, Gloria. 1981. "The Incompatible Menage a Trois: Marxism, Feminism and Racism." In Women and Revolutions: A Discussion of the Unhappy Marriage Between Marxism and Feminism, edited by Lydia Sargent. Boston: South End Press.

Joseph, Gloria I., and Jill Lewis. 1981. Common Differences: Conflicts in Black and White Feminist Perspectives. Garden City, NY: Anchor Books.

Kaplan, Temma. 1982. "Female Consciousness and Collective Action: The Case of Barcelona, 1910–1918." Signs 7:3 (Spring):545–566.

Kashif, Lonnie. 1970. "Color, Class Status Big Factors in Women's Liberation." Muhammed Speaks (September 4):22.

Katzenstein, Mary F. 1998. Faithful and Fearless: Moving Feminist Protest Inside the Church and Military. Princeton, NJ: Princeton University Press.

Kearns, Karen. 1970. "Grove Press: Crimes Against Women." off our backs (April).

King, Deborah H. 1988. "Multiple Jeopardy, Multiple Consciousness: The Context of a Black Feminist Ideology." Signs 14:1 (Autumn).

King, Dorothy. 2000. Interview with author.

King, Mae C. 1975. "Oppression and Power: The Unique Status of the Black Woman in the American Political System." Social Science Quarterly 56:1 (June):116–128.

Kingsolver, Barbara. 1996 [1983]. Holding the Line: Women in the Great Arizona Mine Strike of 1983. Ithaca and London: ILR Press.

Kitschelt, Herbert. 1985. "New Social Movements in West Germany and the US." Political Power and Social Theory 5:273–324.

Klandermans, Bert, and Sidney Tarrow. 1988. "Mobilization into Social Movements: Synthesizing European and American Approaches." In International Social Movement Research. Vol. 1. Greenwich, CT: JAI Press, Inc.

Klein, Ethel. 1987. "The Diffusion of Consciousness in the United States and Europe." In The Women's Movements of the United States and Western Europe: Consciousness, Political Opportunity, and Public Policy, edited by Mary Fainsod Katzenstein and Carol McClurg Mueller. Philadelphia: Temple University Press.

Koedt, Anne. 1968. "Women and the Radical Movement." Notes from the First Year. New York: New York Radical Women.

Kuumba, M. Bahati. 1999. "Engendering the Pan African Movement: Field Notes from the All-African Women's Revolutionary Union." In *Still Lifting, Still Climbing: Contemporary African American Women's Activism*, edited by Kimberly Springer. New York: New York University Press.

La Raza Unida Party. 1972. "Mujeres Find Excellent Expression in La Raza Unida Party." Unpublished convention report (El Paso, Texas, September 1–5). Women's Liberation Ephemera Files, Special Collections, Northwestern University.

La Rue, Linda. 1970. "The Black Movement and Women's Liberation." Reprint c. 1970; originally printed in May 1970 issue of *The Black Scholar*. Women's Liberation Ephemera Files, Special Collections, Northwestern University.

"L.D., black student." 1970. "Black Working Women Will Rebel." *Notes on Women's Liberation: We Speak in Many Voices*. Detroit: Issued by News & Letters (January).

Lewis, Diane K. 1977. "A Response to Inequality: Black Women, Racism, and Sexism." *Signs* 3:2 (Winter).

Lewis, Ida, and Aileen C. Hernández. 1971. "Conversation." *Essence* (February).

Liberation News Service. 1970. Advertisement.

Liddick, Betty. 1973. "Black Lib: Sisters Going Their Own Way." *Los Angeles Times* (July 8).

Lincoln, Abbey. 1970. "Who Will Revere the Black Woman?" In *The Black Woman: An Anthology*, edited by Toni Cade (Bambara). York and Scarborough, Ontario: Mentor Books.

Lindsey, Kay. 1970. "The Black Woman as a Woman." In *The Black Woman: An Anthology*, edited by Toni Cade (Bambara). York and Scarborough, Ontario: Mentor Books.

Locke, Mamie E. 1990. "Is This America? Fannie Lou Hamer and the Mississippi Freedom Democratic Party." In *Women in the Civil Rights Movement: Trailblazers and Torchbearers 1941–1965*, edited by Vicki L. Crawford, Jacqueline Anne Rouse, and Barbara Woods. Bloomington and Indianapolis: Indiana University Press.

Longauex y Vasquez, Enriqueta. 1970. "The Mexican-American Woman." In *Sisterhood Is Powerful*, edited by Robin Morgan. New York: Vintage Books.

Lopez, Ronald, and Darryl D. Enos. 1972. *Chicanos and Public Higher Education in California*. Report prepared for the Joint Committee on the Master Plan for Higher Education, California State Legislature.

López, Sonia A. 1977. "The Role of the Chicana Within the Student Movement." In *Essays on La Mujer*, edited by Rosaura Sánchez. Los Angeles: Chicano Studies Center Publications, University of California, Los Angeles.

Lorde, Audre. 1982. *Zami: A New Spelling of My Name*. Freedom, CA: Crossing Press.

———. 1984. *Sister Outsider: Essays and Speeches*. Freedom, CA: Crossing Press.

Ludwig, Ed. 1971. "Introduction." In *The Chicanos: Mexican American Voices*, edited by Ed Ludwig and James Santibanez. Baltimore: Penguin Books.

Lugones, María. 1994. "Purity, Impurity and Separation." *Signs* 19:2 (Winter).

Lund, Caroline. 1970. "Female Liberation and Socialism." Interview with Pat Galligan. *The Militant* (November 27):9–12.

Mansbridge, Jane, and Aldon Morris. 2001. *Oppositional Consciousness: The Subjective Roots of Social Protest*. Chicago and London: University of Chicago Press.

Marable, Manning. 1978. "Reaction: Thoughts on the Political Economy of the New South Since the Civil Rights Movement." *Radical America* 12:5 (September/October):9–21.

    1983. "Groundings with My Sisters: Patriarchy and the Exploitation of Black Women." *Journal of Ethnic Studies* 11:2 (Summer).

Martínez, Elizabeth. 1997 [1971]. "Viva La Chicana and All Brave Women of La Causa." In *Chicana Feminist Thought: The Basic Historical Writings*, edited by Alma García. New York and London: Routledge (80–81). Originally appeared in *El Grito del Norte*: 4:4–5 (June 5):a–b.

    1998. *De Colores Means All of Us: Latina Views for a Multi-colored Century*. Cambridge, MA: South End Press.

Martinez, Jeannette. 1971. "The Melting Pot of Greed – ya basta." *Fourth World* 1:2:12, 17–18.

Marx Ferree, Myra, and Beth B. Hess. 1985. *Controversy and Coalition: The New Feminist Movement*. Twayne Publishers: New York.

    1994. *Controversy and Coalition: The New Feminist Movement Across Three Decades of Change*. Twayne Publishers: New York.

    2000. *Controversy and Coalition: The New Feminist Movement Across Four Decades of Change* (3d ed.). New York and London: Routledge.

Marx Ferree, Myra, and Silke Roth. 1998. "Gender, Class, and the Interaction Between Social Movements: A Strike of West Berlin Day Care Workers." *Gender & Society* 12:6 (December):626–648.

Marx Ferree, Myra, and Patricia Yancey Martin, eds. 1995. *Feminist Organizations: Harvest of the New Women's Movement*. Philadelphia: Temple University Press.

Matthews, Tracye. 1998. "'No One Ever Asks, What a Man's Place in the Revolution Is': Gender and the Politics of the Black Panther Party, 1966–1971." In *The Black Panther Party Reconsidered*, edited by Charles P. Jones. Baltimore: Black Classic Press, 1998.

Matusow, Allen J. 1971. "From Civil Rights to Black Power: The Case of SNCC, 1960–1966." In *Conflict and Competitions: Studies in the Recent Black Protest Movement*, edited by John H. Bracey, Jr., August Meier, and Elliot Rudwick. Belmont, CA: Wadsworth Publishing Company.

McAdam, Doug. 1982. *Political Process and the Development of Black Insurgency 1930–1970*. Chicago: University of Chicago Press.

    1988. *Freedom Summer*. Oxford: Oxford University Press.

1989. "The Biographical Consequences of Activism." *American Sociological Review* 54:744–60.

McAdam, Doug, Sidney Tarrow, and Charles Tilly. 2001. *Dynamics of Contention.* New York and Cambridge: Cambridge University Press.

McCarthy, John D., and Mayer Zald. 1977. "Resource Mobilization and Social Movements: A Partial Theory." *American Journal of Sociology* 82:1212–1241.

McEldowney, Carol. 1969a. Letter (July/August). Carol McEldowney Papers. State Historical Society, Madison, WI.

1969b. Letter/position paper draft (October 1). Ibid.

McNair Barnett, Bernice. 1993. "Invisible Southern Black Women Leaders in the Civil Rights Movement: The Triple Constraints of Gender, Race and Class." *Gender & Society* 7:2:162–182.

Medal, Tomasin. 1971. "Chicana Conference." *El Tecolote* 1:20 (June 16).

Mellor, Catha, and Judy Miller. 1970. "What We Think is Happening..." *Women: A Journal of Liberation* 1:2.

Melucci, Alberto. 1980. "The New Social Movements: A Theoretical Approach." *Social Science Information* 19:199–226.

1989. *Nomads of the Present: Social Movements and Individual Needs in Contemporary Society.* London: Hutchinson Radius.

Mexican American Legal Defense and Education Fund (MALDEF). 1974. "The Chicana Rights Project." Excerpt from 1974 MALDEF Report. Women's Liberation Ephemera Files, Special Collections, Northwestern University.

Meyer, David S., and Nancy Whittier. 1994. "Social Movement Spillover." *Social Problems* 41:2 (May):277–298.

Milkman, Ruth. 1985. "Women Workers, Feminism and the Labor Movements Since the 1960s." In *Women, Work, and Protest: A Century of U.S. Women's Labor History.* Boston: Routledge and Kegan Paul.

1990. Appendix I. In *Women, Families, and Communities: Readings in American History,* edited by Nancy A. Hewitt. New York: Scott Foresman.

Minkoff, Debra C. 1995. *Organizing for Equality: The Evolution of Women's and Racial-Ethnic Organizations in America, 1955–1985.* New Brunswick, NJ: Rutgers University Press.

Mirandé, Alfredo, and Evangelina Enríquez. 1979. *La Chicana: The Mexican American Woman.* Chicago and London: The University of Chicago Press.

Mohanty, Chandra, Ann Russo, and Lourdes Torres, eds. 1991. *Third World Women and the Politics of Feminism.* Bloomington and Indianapolis: Indiana University Press.

Moraga Cherríe. 1983. *Loving in the War Years: Lo que nunca pasó por sus labias.* Boston: South End Press.

Moraga, Cherríe, and Gloria Anzaldúa. 1979. "Introduction." In *This Bridge Called My Back: Writings by Radical Women of Color,* edited by Cherríe Moraga and Gloria Anzaldúa. Watertown, MA: Persephone Press.

Moreno, Dorinda. c. 1975. Letter/advertisement for *La Mujer en Pie de Lucha*. Concilio Mujeres Papers, State Historical Society, Madison, WI.

——— 1975. "Colonization and the Mestiza, a Framework for Discrimination and the Chicana." Unpublished document. Women's Liberation Ephemera Files, Special Collections, Northwestern University.

——— 2000. Interview with author.

Morgan, Robin. 1968. "The Oldest Front: On Freedom for Women." *Liberation* 8:5 (October):34–37.

——— 1970a. "Goodbye to All That." *RAT* (February takeover issue).

——— 1970b. Editor, *Sisterhood Is Powerful*. New York: Vintage Books.

Morris, Aldon D. 1984. *The Origins of the Civil Rights Movement: Black Communities Organizing for Change*. New York: Free Press.

——— 1992. "Political Consciousness and Collective Action." In *Frontiers in Social Movement Theory*, edited by Aldon D. Morris and Carol McClurg Mueller. New Haven and London: Yale University Press.

Morris, Aldon D., and Carol McClurg Mueller, eds. 1992. *Frontiers in Social Movement Theory*. New Haven and London: Yale University Press.

Morrison, Toni. 1971. "What the Black Woman Thinks About Women's Lib." *New York Times Magazine* (August 22).

Morton, Carlos. 1975. "La Virgen [The Virgin] Goes Through Changes." *Caracol* (July).

Moya, Paula M. L. 2001. "Chicana Feminism and Postmodernist Theory." *Signs: Journal of Women in Culture and Society* 26:2:441–483.

Moynihan, Daniel Patrick. 1967. *The Negro Family: The Case for National Action*. Washington, DC: U.S. Government Printing Office.

Mueller, Carol. 1997. "Conflict Networks and the Origins of Women's Liberation." In *Social Movements: Readings on Their Emergence, Mobilization, and Dynamics*, edited by Doug McAdam and David A. Snow. Los Angeles: Roxbury Publishing Company.

Murphy, Jean. 1971. "Unsung Heroine of La Causa." *Regeneracíon* 1:10:20.

Murray, Pauli. 1975. "The Liberation of Black Women." In *Women: A Feminist Perspective*, edited by Jo Freeman. Palo Alto, CA: Mayfield Publishing Company.

Myers, Kristin. 1999. "Racial Unity in the Grass Roots? A Case Study of a Women's Social Service Organization." In *Still Lifting, Still Climbing: Contemporary African American Women's Activism*, edited by Kimberly Springer. New York: New York University Press (107–130).

Myrdal, Gunnar. 1944. *An American Dilemma: The Negro Problem and Modern Democracy*. New York: Harper Brothers.

Naples, Nancy. 1991. "Just What Needed to Be Done: The Political Practice of Women Community Workers in Low-Income Neighborhoods." *Gender & Society* 5:4 (December):478–494.

1998a. *Grassroots Warriors: Activist Mothering, Community Work, and the War on Poverty*. New York and London: Routledge.

1998b. Editor, *Community Activism and Feminist Politics: Organizing Across Race, Class, and Gender*. Philadelphia: Temple University Press.

National Alliance of Black Feminists (NABF). 1976. "Black Women's Bill of Rights." Position paper. Women's Liberation Ephemera Files, Special Collections, Northwestern University.

1977a. "National Alliance of Black Feminists." Flyer. Ibid.

1977b. "A Meeting of the Minds: A National Conference for, by and About Black Women." Conference announcement. National Alliance of Black Feminists Papers, Special Collections, University of Illinois, Chicago.

c. 1977. "Resolutions." Unpublished internal document. Ibid.

1978. "March/April 1978 Calendar of Events." Unpublished flyer. Ibid.

1979. "Alternative Education School Program." Unpublished pamphlet. Ibid.

National Black Feminist Organization (NBFO). 1973a. "Statements." Women's Liberation Ephemera Files, Special Collections, Northwestern University.

1973b. "National Black Feminist Organization: Would You Like to Join Us." Flyer. Ibid.

1973c. "Workshops, Eastern Regional Conference." Unpublished internal document. Ibid.

c. 1973. "Statement of National Black Feminist Organization." Unpublished document. Ibid.

1974a. Letter to NBFO chapters from Executive Board (September 18). NBFO Papers, Special Collections, University of Illinois, Chicago.

1974b. Ballot for Coordinating Council (October). Unpublished internal document. Ibid.

c. 1974a. "Chapters." Unpublished internal document. Ibid.

c. 1974b. "Statement of Purpose." Unpublished document. Ibid.

1975a. "Standard Questions You Might Be Asked – Suggested Answers That Might Work." Unpublished internal document. Women's Liberation Ephemera Files, Special Collections, Northwestern University.

1975b. Newsletter (January).

1975c. Newsletter (March).

1975d. Newsletter (September).

1975e. "Points Taken from the Platform of the National Black Feminist Organization." Unpublished internal document. Ibid.

1973–1975. Minutes. NBFO Papers, Special Collections, University of Illinois, Chicago.

National Chicana Political Caucus. 1973. "Newsletter August–Sept. 1973." Schlesinger Library, Harvard University.

Nellhaus, Arlynn. 1971. "Family Tops List of Efforts as Chicanas Join Lib (Conference Story in Houston)." *Denver Post* (June 3).

Neumaier, Diane. 1990. "Judy Baca: Our People Are the Internal Exiles." In *Making Face, Making Soul/Haciendo Caras: Creative and Critical Perspectives by Women of Color,* edited by Gloria Anzaldúa. San Francisco: Aunt Lute Foundation Books.

New University Conference, Women's Caucus (NUC). c. 1970a. "History of the Women's Caucus." Unpublished, unsigned position paper. Sophia Smith Collection, Smith College, Northampton, MA.

c. 1970b. "Whither the Women's Caucus?" Unsigned, unpublished position paper. Ibid.

Newman, Pamela. 1970. "Black Women's Liberation." *The Militant* (October 30). Reprinted 1970, 1971, and 1972 as *Black Women's Liberation.* New York: Pathfinder Press.

Newton, Huey P. 1970. "A Letter from Huey to the Revolutionary Brothers and Sisters About the Women's Liberation and Gay Liberation Movement." Reprint from *Black Panther* 5:8 (August 21). Women's Liberation Ephemera Files, Special Collections, Northwestern University.

Nieto-Gómez, Ana. 1970. "A Chicano Student's Perspective of the White Campus." *The Minority Student on the Campus: Expectations and Possibilities,* edited by Robert A. Altman and Patricia O. Snyder. Boulder, CO: Western Interstate Commission on Higher Education.

1971. "Chicanas Identify." *Regeneración* 1:10:9.

1976. "Chicana Feminism." *Caracol* 2:5 (January):3–5.

1991. Oral History Interview. Conducted and tape recorded by Maylei Blackwell. California State University at Long Beach, Oral History Collection in Women's History.

Offen, Karen. 1988. "Defining Feminism: A Comparative Historical Approach." *Signs* 14:1 (Autumn):119–157.

Okazawa-Rey, Margo. 1999. Interview with author.

Oliver, Pamela E., and Hank Johnston. 2000. "What a Good Idea! Ideologies and Frames in Social Movement Research." *Mobilization: An International Journal.* 4:1:37–53.

Omolade, Barbara. 1994. *The Rising Song of African American Women.* New York and London: Routledge.

Orozco, Yolanda. 1976. "La Chicana and 'Women's Liberation.'" *Voz Fronteriza* (January 5):6.

Ortego, Philip D. 1971. "The Education of Mexican-Americans." In *The Chicanos: Mexican American Voices,* edited by Ed Ludwig and James Santibanez. Baltimore: Penguin Books.

Orum, Anthony. 1970. *Black Students in Protest: A Study of the Origins of the Black Student Movement.* Washington, DC: Rose Monograph Series, American Sociological Association.

Overton, Betty Jean. 1970. "Black Women in Women's Liberation." *Race Relations Reporter* (July 1). Newsletter published by Race Relations Information Center, Nashville, TN.

"Panther Constitutional Convention." 1970. *Ain't I a Woman* (October). Unsigned report.

"Panther Sisters on Women's Liberation." 1969. Unsigned article. *The Movement* (September):9–10.

Patton, Gwen. 1970. "Black People and the Victorian Ethos." In *The Black Woman: An Anthology,* edited by Toni Cade (Bambara). York and Scarborough, Ontario: Mentor Books.

Payne, Charles. 1989. "Ella Baker and Models of Social Change." *Signs* (Summer):885–899.

———. 1990. "Men Led, but Women Organized: Movement Participation of Women in the Mississippi Delta." In *Women in the Civil Rights Movement: Trailblazers and Torchbearers 1941–1965,* edited by Vicki L. Crawford, Jacqueline Anne Rouse, and Barbara Woods. Bloomington and Indianapolis: Indiana University Press.

Pérez, Emma. 1991. "Sexuality and Discourse: Notes from a Chicana Survivor." In *Chicana Lesbians: The Girls Our Mothers Warned Us About,* edited by Carla Trujillo. Berkeley: Third Woman Press (159–184).

Philadelphia Area Women's Liberation. 1970. "Abortion = Genocide? Letters from *Plain-Dealer* Women"; "Control of Our Bodies and Lives for White Women Only?"; "Abortion or Genocide?" *Women* 1:3 (June).

Piartney, Lynn. 1968. "A Letter to the Editor of *Ramparts* Magazine." *Notes From the First Year.* New York: New York Radical Women.

Piercy, Marge. 1970. "The Grand Coolie Damn." In *Sisterhood Is Powerful,* edited by Robin Morgan. New York: Vintage Books.

Piven, Frances Fox, and Richard A. Cloward. 1977. *Poor People's Movements: Why They Succeed and How They Fail.* New York: Vintage Books.

Polatnik, M. Rivka. 1996. "Diversity in Women's Liberation Ideology: How a Black and a White Group of the 1960s Viewed Motherhood." *Signs* 21:3:679–706.

Popkin, Annie. 1988. "An Early Moment in Women's Liberation: The Social Experience Within *Bread and Roses.*" *Radical America* 22:1 (January–February):19–34.

Poster, Winifred R. 1995. "The Challenges and Promises of Class and Racial Diversity in the Women's Movement: A Study of Two Women's Organizations." *Gender & Society* 9:6 (December):659–679.

Prestage, Jewel L. 1980. "Political Behavior of American Black Women: An Overview." In *The Black Woman,* edited by La Frances Rodgers-Rose. Newbury Park, CA: Sage Publications.

Radical Women, Chicago. 1968. "Meeting of Radical Women, Chicago, March 24–25, 1968." Unsigned report. Women's Liberation Ephemera Files, Special Collections, Northwestern University.

RAT. 1970. Unsigned advertisement (October).

 1971. Unsigned editorial (August).

Ray, Raka. 1999. *Fields of Protest: Women's Movements in India.* Minneapolis and London: University of Minnesota Press.

Redd, Spring. 1983. "Something Latino Was Up with Us." In *Home Girls: A Black Feminist Anthology,* edited by Barbara Smith. New York: Kitchen Table/Women of Color Press.

Redstockings. 1970. "Redstockings Manifesto." In *Sisterhood Is Powerful,* edited by Robin Morgan. New York: Vintage Books.

Rincon, Bernice. 1971. "La Chicana: 'Her Role in the Past and Her Search for a New Role in the Future.'" *Regeneracíon* 1:10:15–18.

Risco-Lozada, Eliezer. 1970. "The Communication Gap." In *The Minority Student on the Campus: Expectations and Possibilities,* edited by Robert A. Altman and Patricia O. Snyder. Boulder, CO: Western Interstate Commission on Higher Education.

Rivero, Eliana. 1977. "La Mujer y La Raza: Latinas y Chicanas" [Woman and Race: Latinas and Chicanas]. *Caracol* 4:3 (November):6–7, 17.

Robinson, Jo Anne. c. 1970. "Sex Discrimination and the Beloved Community." Pamphlet reprinted from *Fellowship* magazine. Women's Liberation Ephemera Files, Special Collections, Northwestern University.

Robinson, Patricia, and the Mount Vernon/New Rochelle Group. 1970a. "Poor Black Women's Study Papers by Poor Black Women of Mount Vernon, New York." In *The Black Woman: An Anthology,* edited by Toni Cade (Bambara). York and Scarborough, Ontario: Mentor Books.

 1970b. "Statement on Birth Control." In *Sisterhood Is Powerful,* edited by Robin Morgan. New York: Vintage Books (360–361).

 c. 1970. "Poor Black Women." Reprint published by New England Free Press. Women's Liberation Ephemera Files, Special Collections, Northwestern University.

 1966–1971. Letters from Robinson to Joan Jordan (aka Vilma Sanchez). Joan Jordan Papers, State Historical Society, Madison, WI.

Robnett, Belinda. 1997. *How Long? How Long? African American Women in the Struggle for Civil Rights.* New York: Oxford University Press.

Rominski, Fran. 1968. "Sexual Service System." *Voice of the Women's Liberation Movement* (June).

Rose, Fred. 2000. *Coalitions Across the Class Divide: Lessons from the Labor, Peace and Environmental Movements.* Ithaca and London: Cornell University Press.

Rosen, Gerald. 1974. "The Development of the Chicano Movement in Los Angeles from 1967 to 1969." *Aztlán* 4:1:155–183.

Rosen, Ruth. 2000. *The World Split Open: How the Modern Women's Movement Changed America.* New York: Viking.

Ross, Lorretta J. 1993. "African-American Women and Abortion: 1800–1970." In *Theorizing Black Feminisms: The Visionary Pragmatism of Black Women*, edited by Stanlie M. James and Abena P. A. Busia. London and New York: Routledge.

Rossi, Alice. 1970. "Women – Terms of Liberation." Reprint from article in *Dissent* magazine (November/December):531–541. Women's Liberation Ephemera Files, Special Collections, Northwestern University.

Roth, Benita. 1998. "Feminist Boundaries in the Feminist-Friendly Organization: The Women's Caucus of ACT UP/LA." *Gender & Society* 12:2:129–145.

——— 1999a. "The Vanguard Center: Intra-movement Experience and the Emergence of African-American Feminism." In *Still Lifting, Still Climbing: Contemporary African American Women's Activism*, edited by Kimberly Springer. New York: New York University Press.

——— 1999b. "Race, Class, and the Emergence of Black Feminism in the 1960s and 1970s." *Womanist Theory and Research* 2:1 (Fall).

Rothenberg, Mel. 1968. "One Editor's View of the Women's Caucus." *New University Conference Newsletter* (August):5–6.

Ruiz, Vicki L. 1990. "A Promise Fulfilled: Mexican Cannery Workers in Southern California." In *Unequal Sisters: A Multicultural Reader in U.S. Women's History*, edited by Vicki L. Ruiz and Ellen Carol DuBois. New York and London: Routledge.

Rupp, Leila J., and Verta Taylor. 1987. *Survival in the Doldrums: The American Women's Rights Movement, 1945 to the 1960s*. New York: Oxford University Press.

Ryan, Barbara. 1992. *Feminism and the Women's Movement: Dynamics of Change in Social Movement, Ideology and Activism*. New York and London: Routledge.

Sacks, Karen. 1989. "Toward a Unified Theory of Class, Race and Gender." *American Ethnologist* 16:3.

——— 1994. "How Did Jews Become White Folks?" In *RACE*, edited by Steven Gregory and Roger Sanjek. New Brunswick, NJ: Rutgers University Press.

Saldívar-Hull, Sonia. 1991. "Feminism on the Border: From Gender Politics to Geopolitics." In *Criticism in the Borderlands*, edited by Hector Calderón and José David Saldívar. Durham, NC: Duke University Press.

San Miguel, Guadalupe. 1984. "The Origins, Development, and Consequences of the Educational Segregation of Mexicans in the Southwest." *Chicano Studies: A Multidisciplinary Approach*, edited by Eugene E. García, Francisco A. Lomelí, and Isidro Ortiz. New York and London: Teachers College Press.

Sánchez, Rosaura. 1990. "The History of Chicanas: A Proposal for a Materialist Perspective." In *Between Borders: Essays on Mexicana/Chicana History*, edited by Adelaida R. del Castillo. Encino, CA: Floricante Press.

Sandoval, Chela. 1990. "Feminism and Racism: A Report on the 1981 National Women's Studies Association Conference." In *Making Face, Making Soul/Haciendo Caras: Creative and Critical Perspectives by Women of Color*, edited by Gloria Anzaldúa. San Francisco: An Aunt Lute Foundation Book.

——— 1991. "U.S. Third World Feminism: The Theory and Method of Oppositional Consciousness in the Postmodern World." *Genders* 10 (Spring):1–24.

"SDS on Women's Lib." 1969b. *The Daily Gater*. Unsigned article (December 10):4.

Seattle Radical Women. c. 1971. "Women in the Struggle." Reprint of Third World Women's Alliance "History of the Organization." Women's Liberation Ephemera Files, Special Collections, Northwestern University.

Seattle Women's Liberation. 1969. "Lilith's Manifesto." Unpublished position paper. Women's Liberation Ephemera Files, Special Collections, Northwestern University.

Seese, Linda. 1969. "You've Come a Long Way, Baby – Women in the Movement." *Motive* 29 (March–April):6–7.

Segura, Denise A. 1986. "Chicanas and Triple Oppression in the Labor Force." In *Chicana Voices: Intersections of Class, Race and Gender*, edited by Teresa Córdova et al. Austin: CMAS Publications, University of Texas at Austin.

Smelser, Neil J. 1963. *The Theory of Collective Behavior*. New York: The Free Press.

Smith, Barbara. 1979. "Notes for Yet Another Paper on Black Feminism, or Will the Real Enemy Please Stand Up?" *Conditions 5: The Black Woman's Issue*:123–127.

——— 1983. "Introduction." In *Home Girls: A Black Feminist Anthology*, edited by Barbara Smith. New York: Kitchen Table/Women of Color Press.

Smith, Barbara, and Beverly Smith. 1981. "Across the Kitchen Table: A Sister to Sister Dialogue." In *This Bridge Called My Back: Writings by Radical Women of Color*, edited by Cherríe Moraga and Gloria Anzaldúa. Watertown, MA: Persephone Press.

Smith, Fredi A. 1970. "Meet Women of the Black Panthers." *Daily Defender* (January 24).

Smith Reid, Inez. 1972. *"Together" Black Women*. New York: The Third Press.

Snow, David A., and Robert D. Benford. 1992. "Master Frames and Cycles of Protest." In *Frontiers in Social Movement Theory*, edited by Aldon D. Morris and Carol McClurg Mueller. New Haven and London: Yale University Press.

Sosa Riddell, Adaljiza. 1974. "Chicanas and El Movimiento." *Aztlán* 5:1:155–165.

Sotomayor, Marta. 1971. "Mexican-American Interaction with Social Systems." In *La Causa Chicana: The Movement for Justice*, edited by Margaret M. Mangold. New York: Family Service Association of America.

Spelman, Elizabeth V. 1982. "Theories of Race & Gender/The Erasure of Black Women." *Quest: A Feminist Quarterly* 5:4:36–62.

Springer, Kimberly. 2001. "The Interstitial Politics of Black Feminist Organizations." *Meridians: feminism, race, transnationalism*. 1:2:155–191.

Standley, Anne. 1990. "The Role of Black Women in the Civil Rights Movement." In *Women in the Civil Rights Movement: Trailblazers and Torchbearers 1941–1965*, edited by Vicki L. Crawford, Jacqueline Anne Rouse, and Barbara Woods. Bloomington and Indianapolis: Indiana University Press.

Stone, Betsy. 1970. "Sisterhood Is Powerful." Pamphlet reprinted from *The Militant* (October 23). N.p.: Pathfinder Press.

Stone, Michael. 1970. "Liberation Struggle Generates Tension on Race, Sex Issues." Reprint of an article from *The Christian Century* (June 10). Social Action Files, State Historical Society, Madison, WI.

Stoper, Emily. 1983. "The Student Nonviolent Coordinating Committee: The Growth of Radicalism in a Civil Rights Organization." In *Social Movements of the Sixties and Seventies*, edited by Jo Freeman. New York and London: Longman.

1989. *The Student Nonviolent Coordinating Committee: The Growth of Radicalism in a Civil Rights Organization.* New York: Carlson Publishing.

Students for a Democratic Society (SDS). 1968. "National Resolution on Women." Sophia Smith Collection, Smith College, Northampton, MA.

Students for a Democratic Society (SDS) Women's Liberation Committee. 1970. Letter in *The Phoenix* (May 15). Joan Jordan Papers, State Historical Society, Madison, WI.

Tait, Vanessa. 1999. "'Workers Just Like Anyone Else': Organizing Workfare Unions in New York City." In *Still Lifting, Still Climbing: Contemporary African American Women's Activism*, edited by Kimberly Springer. New York: New York University Press (297–324).

Tanner, Leslie B. 1971. "Venceremos Brigade: An Elitist Authoritarian Organization." *RAT* (March/April).

Tarrow, Sidney. 1988. "Old Movements in New Cycles of Protest: The Career of an Italian Religious Community." *International Social Movement Research.* Vol. 1. Greenwich, CT: JAI Press.

1994. *Power in Movement: Social Movements, Collective Action, and Politics.* Cambridge and New York: Cambridge University Press.

Taylor, Michael. 1988. "Rationality and Revolutionary Collective Action." In *Rationality and Revolution*, edited by Michael Taylor. Cambridge: Cambridge University Press (63–97).

Taylor, Verta. 1989. "Social Movement Continuity: The Women's Movement in Abeyance." *American Sociological Review* 54 (October):761–775.

Taylor, Verta, and Nancy Whittier. 1992. "Collective Identity in Social Movement Communities: Lesbian Feminist Mobilization." In *Frontiers in Social*

Movement Theory, edited by Aldon D. Morris and Carol McClurg Mueller. New Haven and London: Yale University Press.

——. 1998. "Guest Editors' Introduction: Special Issue on Gender and Social Movements: Part 1." *Gender & Society* 12:6 (December):622–625.

Terborg-Penn, Rosalyn. 1978. "Discrimination Against Afro-American Women in the Women's Movement, 1830–1920." In *The Afro-American Woman: Struggles and Images,* edited by Rosalyn Terborg-Penn and Sharon Harley. Port Washington, NY, and London: Kennikat Press.

"Them and Me." 1970. *Notes from the Second Year.* New York: Shulamith Firestone and Anne Koedt (self-published).

Third World Women's Alliance. 1971. "History of the Organization." *Third World Women's Alliance* 1:6 (March).

——. c. 1971. "Third World Women's Alliance (Bay Area Chapter)." Unpublished document. Pam Allen Papers, State Historical Society, Madison, WI.

Thomas, James Eugene. 1964. "The Role of Negro Women in the Battle for Equality." *Negro Digest* (February).

Thompson, Becky. 2001. *A Promise and a Way of Life: White Antiracist Activism.* Minneapolis and London: University of Minnesota Press.

Thorne, Barrie. 1975. "Women in the Draft Resistance Movement: A Case Study of Sex Roles and Social Movements." *Sex Roles* 1:2.

Thorton Dill, Bonnie. 1983. "Race, Class and Gender: Prospects for an All-Inclusive Sisterhood." *Feminist Studies* 9:1 (Spring).

Thursday Night Group (Leslie Hawkins, Sydney Halpern, Anna Kehela, and Randy Rappaport). 1969. "On Autonomy" position paper (August), Berkeley Women's Liberation. Women's Liberation Ephemera Files, Special Collections, Northwestern University.

Tilly, Charles. 1978. *From Mobilization to Revolution.* Reading, MA: Addison Wesley.

Townsend Gilkes, Cheryl. 1980. "'Holding Back the Ocean with a Broom': Black Women and Community Work." In *The Black Woman,* edited by La Frances Rodgers-Rose. Newbury Park, CA: Sage Publications.

——. 1994. "'If It Wasn't for the Women . . .': African American Women, Community Work and Social Change." In *Women of Color in U.S. Society,* edited by Maxine Baca Zinn and Bonnie Thorton Dill. Philadelphia: Temple University Press.

Trujillo, Carla, ed. 1991. *Chicana Lesbians: The Girls Our Mothers Warned Us About.* Berkeley: Third Woman Press.

Turner, Ralph H., and Lewis M. Killian. 1987. *Collective Behavior.* Englewood Cliffs, NJ: Prentice Hall.

Ugarte, Sandra. 1997. "Chicana Regional Conference." In *Chicana Feminist Thought: The Basic Historical Writings,* edited by Alma García. New York and London: Routledge. Originally appeared in *Hijas de Cuauhtémoc* 1:1:1–3 (1971).

Urban Ed., Inc. 1974. *Minority Enrollment and Representation in Institutions of Higher Education: A Report to the Ford Foundation*. New York: The Ford Foundation.

U.S. Bureau of the Census. 1975. *Historical Statistics of the United States: Colonial Times to 1970, Part 1*. Washington, DC: U.S. Government Printing Office.

    1980. *Statistical Abstract of the United States*. 101st ed. Washington, DC: U.S. Government Printing Office.

    1982–1983. *Statistical Abstract of the United States*. 103d ed. Washington, DC: U.S. Government Printing Office.

    1994. *Statistical Abstract of the United States*. 114th ed. Washington, DC: U.S. Government Printing Office.

U.S. Department of Health, Education and Welfare/Office for Civil Rights. 1970. *Racial and Ethnic Enrollment Data from Institutions of Higher Education, Fall 1970*. (OCR-72-8). Washington: U.S. Government Printing Office.

    1976. *Racial, Ethnic and Sex Enrollment Data From Institutions of Higher Education, Fall 1976*. (Published April 1978). Washington: U. S. Government Printing Office.

U.S. Department of Labor 1989. *Handbook of Labor Statistics* (August). Washington, DC: U.S. Government Printing Office.

U.S. Department of Labor, Women's Bureau. 1966. "Fact Sheet on Nonwhite Women Workers" (October). Washington, DC: U.S. Government Printing Office.

    1967. "Fact Sheet on Educational Attainment of Nonwhite Women" (May). Ibid.

    2001 (May). "20 Facts on Women Workers." http://www.dol.gov/dol/wb/public/wb_pubs/20fact00.htm. [Accessed May 3, 2001.]

Van Deburg, William L. 1992. *New Day in Babylon: The Black Power Movement and American Culture, 1965–1975*. Chicago and London: The University of Chicago Press.

Vanauken. 1971. "A Primer for the Last Revolution" (March). Reprinted position paper, originally published in 1968 by the Southern Student Organizing Committee in Nashville. Women's Liberation Ephemera Files, Special Collections, Northwestern University.

Vásquez, Carlos. 1977. "Women in the Chicano Movement." In *Essays on La Mujer*, edited by Rosaura Sánchez. Los Angeles: Chicano Studies Center Publications, University of California, Los Angeles.

Verner, Brenda. 1974. "Brenda Verner Examines 'Liberated' Sisters." *Encore* (April):22–24.

Vidal, Mirta. 1971a. "Women: New Voice of La Raza." In *Chicanas Speak Out/Women New Voice of La Raza*. New York: Pathfinder Press.

    1971b. "600 Attend National Chicana Conference." *The Militant*:10.

    2000. Interview with author.

Von Eschen, Donald, Jerome Kirk, and Maurice Pinard. 1969. "The Disinte-
    gration of the Negro Non-Violent Movement." *Journal of Peace Research*
    3:215–234.
Walker, Alice. 1983. *In Search of Our Mother's Gardens: Womanist Prose*. San
    Diego, New York, and London: Harcourt Brace Jovanovich.
Wallace, Michelle. 1982. "A Black Feminist's Search for Sisterhood." In *All the
    Women Are White, All the Men Are Black, but Some of Us Are Brave: Black
    Women's Studies*, edited by Gloria T. Hull, Patricia Bell Scott, and Barbara
    Smith. Old Westbury, NY: Feminist Press.
    1996. *Black Macho and the Myth of the Superwoman*. London and New York:
    Verso.
Ware, Celestine. 1970. *Woman Power: The Movement for Women's Liberation*.
    New York: Tower Publications.
Washington, Cynthia. 1979. "We Started from Different Ends of the Spec-
    trum." In *Personal Politics: The Roots of Women's Liberation in the Civil
    Rights Movement and the New Left*, edited by Sara Evans. New York: Vintage
    Books.
Weathers, Maryanne. 1968a. "An Argument for Black Women's Liberation as
    a Revolutionary Force." Position paper (October) issued by Third World
    Women's Alliance, Cambridge, MA. Social Action Files, State Historical
    Society, Madison, WI.
    1968b. "Black Women and Abortion." Ibid.
Webb, Marilyn. 1968. "Towards a Radical Women's Movement." Reprinted
    (February) by Chicago–Hyde Park Women's Group. Social Action Files,
    State Historical Society, Madison, WI.
    1969a. "We Are Victims." *Voice of the Women's Liberation Movement*
    (February).
    1969b. "History of Women's Liberation." *The Daily Gater* (December 10).
    1970. "Seize the Press Sisters." *off our backs* (April).
Weinfeld, Marta. 1970. "Women's Liberation Advances the Movement." Un-
    published position paper (December 15) for Wednesday Night New Course
    Group, Berkeley Women's Liberation. Women's Liberation Ephemera
    Files, Special Collections, Northwestern University.
Weisstein, Naomi. 1970. "Sexual Caste System Chicago Illinois." *Spark* 3:3
    (March). Women's Liberation Ephemera Files, Special Collections, North-
    western University.
Wells, Lyn. 1969. "A Movement for Us." *the great speckled bird* (February 28).
West, Chester. 1971. "Are Black Male Artists Prejudiced Toward Women?"
    Amsterdam News (January 30).
West, Guida, and Rhoda Lois Blumberg, eds. 1990. *Women and Social Protest*.
    New York and Oxford: Oxford University Press.
Whalen, Jack, and Richard Flacks. 1987. *Beyond the Barricades: The Sixties Gen-
    eration Grows Up*. Philadelphia: Temple University Press.

White, E. Frances. 1984. "Listening to the Voices of Black Feminism." *Radical America* 18:2–3:7–25.

"Why Liberation?" 1969a. *The Daily Gater*. Unsigned (December 10).

Williams, Maxine. 1970. "Why Women's Liberation Is Important to Black Women." In *Black Women's Liberation*, reprinted 1970, 1971, and 1972. New York: Pathfinder Press.

Willis, Ellen. 1969a. "Declaration of Independence." *Voice of the Women's Liberation Movement* (February).

1969b. "Liberation Forum." Pamphlet. Women's Liberation Ephemera Files, Special Collections, Northwestern University. Originally appeared in the *Guardian* (February 15, 1969).

1970. "Women and the Left." *Notes from the Second Year*. New York: Shulamith Firestone and Anne Koedt (self-published).

Wilson, William Julius. 1978. *The Declining Significance of Race: Blacks and Changing American Institutions*. Chicago and London: University of Chicago Press.

"Women and Anti-war Work: Two Perspectives." 1970. *It Ain't Me Babe* 1:8 (June 11–July 1).

Women's Liberation, Washington, DC. 1968. "Conference Summary." Leni Wildflower Collection, Southern California Library for Social Science and Research.

Wright, Margaret. 1972. "I Want the Right to Be Black and Me." In *Black Women in White America: A Documentary History*, edited by Gerda Lerner. New York: Vintage Books.

Young, Nigel. 1977. *An Infantile Disorder? The Crisis and Decline of the New Left*. London and Henley: Routledge and Kegan Paul.

Zald, Mayer N., and Roberta Ash. 1970. "Social Movement Organizations: Growth, Decay and Change." In *Protest, Reform and Revolution*, edited by Joseph R. Gusfield. New York: John Wiley & Sons, Inc.

Zald, Mayer, and John D. McCarthy. 1979. *The Dynamics of Social Movements*. Cambridge, MA: Winthrop Publishers.

Index